ASPECTS OF
EUROPEAN HISTORY
1494–1789

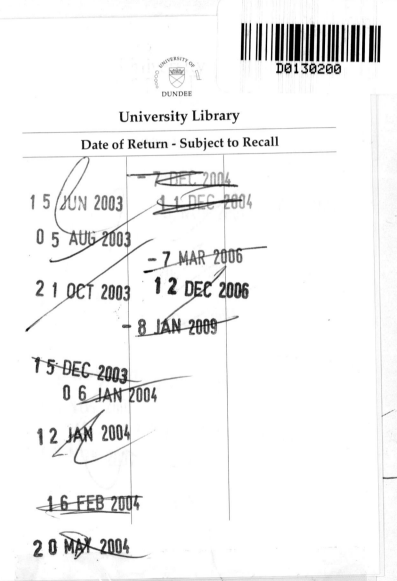

By the same author

Aspects of European History 1789–1980

STEPHEN J. LEE

ASPECTS OF
EUROPEAN HISTORY
1494–1789

Second edition

LONDON AND NEW YORK

For Margaret

First published in 1978 by Methuen & Co. Ltd
Second edition 1984
Reprinted 1986

Reprinted 1990, 1992, 1994, 1996 by Routledge
11 New Fetter Lane
London EC4P 4EE
29 West 35th Street
New York, NY 10001

© 1978 and 1984 Stephen J. Lee

Photoset by Rowland Phototypesetting Ltd
Bury St Edmunds, Suffolk

Printed in England by Clays Ltd, St Ives plc

British Library Cataloguing in Publication Data
Lee, Stephen J.
    Aspects of European history 1494–1789.—2nd ed.
    1. Europe—History—1492–1648
    2. Europe—History—1648–1789
    I. Title
    940.2'2   D208

Library of Congress Cataloguing in Publication Data
Lee, Stephen J.
    Aspects of European history, 1494–1789.

    Bibliography: p.
    Includes index.
    1. Europe—History—1492–1648. 2. Europe History—
1648–1789. I. Title
    D228.L43 1984   940.2   84–600

ISBN 0-415-02784-5

Contents

List of illustrations

Introduction

This book presents an interpretative approach to a wide range of topics in early modern European history. It is designed to be used in addition to, but not instead of, specialist works and standard textbooks. The main intention is to stimulate thought and to assist in the preparation of essays and seminar papers by encouraging the student to develop an angle or argument, whether in agreement with the chapters or in opposition to them.

The chapters also suggest a variety of methods by which a theme or argument may be presented.

(1) Some topics have been given straightforward chronological coverage; Chapters 7, 8 and 12 and examples of this.

(2) Others have an analytical approach; Chapters 1, 2, 3, 6, 10, 11, 13, 18, 19, 20 and 37 concentrate on issues rather than chronology. Chapters 15 and 27 examine different interpretations of the issues and suggest a synthesis.

(3) Some arguments are intended to be persuasive, even dogmatic. They avoid referring to alternative views and are supported by carefully selected factual material. Examples are Chapters 3 and 28.

(4) Some topics are approached from several different angles, with a certain common ground of factual material. An example is Chapter 6.

(5) Chapters 21 and 27 examine the extent to which major statesmen were indebted to past achievements and the impact which their changes made on subsequent events; the emphasis, therefore, is very much on overall historical perspective.

(6) Occasionally, comparisons and contrasts are drawn, as in Chapters 5, 17 and 33. This technique is widely demanded in essay work.

It is assumed throughout that the reader will have a certain amount of preliminary factual knowledge or, alternatively, that he will follow up any terms with which he is unfamiliar. All chapters should be regarded as separate units, although there are overlapping themes. The themes for the chapters are, for the most part,

Aspects of European History 1494–1789

political, but there is also some treatment of economic, social, cultural and religious factors.

Finally, it is hoped that the book will assist examination revision, by providing a series of summaries, by stimulating thought and criticism and by giving some structure to what must sometimes seem an inert mass of facts.

1

Renaissance Humanism

Humanism was a basic source of inspiration for all the cultural changes of the Renaissance, heavily influencing literature, history, painting, sculpture and political ideas.

Humanist scholars devoted themselves to the *studia humanitatis* by examining the texts of antiquity with renewed interest. Although classical works had some influence on medieval thought, they had acquired an extensive superstructure which scholars from the fourteenth century onwards set about dismantling. Increasing emphasis was laid on understanding the classics in their original form, and this was inevitably accompanied by an insistence on grammatical precision and stylistic purity. A particularly import-ant development was the revival of Greek. This language, which had virtually disappeared from the West during the Middle Ages, spread during the fifteenth century not, as is often supposed, with the flight of scholars from the East after the Turkish capture of Constantinople in 1453, but as a result of invitations extended to Byzantine scholars like Manuel Chrysoloras to lecture in Florence and Rome in the 1390s. A widespread search for Roman and Greek manuscripts followed. By the end of the fifteenth century interest had reached dramatic proportions, with 27 principal editions of Greek works published between 1494 and 1515. Meanwhile, various humanist circles had been established, the most important of these being the Platonic Academy in Florence (1439). At times their members were excessively concerned with detail and produced commentaries on the classics rather than works of originality.

Aspects of European History 1494–1789

Leonardo da Vinci, himself excluded from the inner sanctum of humanist study, observed bitterly of the members of the Platonic Academy: 'They go about puffed up and pompous in fine raiment and bejewelled, not from the fruits of their own labours, but from those of others.' But, although the humanists were often, in Leonardo's words, 'trumpeters and reciters of the works of others', they performed a service of inestimable value for the arts either by opening the renaissance world to the influence of little known Greek and Roman writers or by re-examining, in the original, works which had already had an impact on the Middle Ages.

The result was the emergence of humanism as a broader intellectual influence which was more significant than the sum of its humanist parts. Following the maxim of the Greek, Protagoras, that 'man is the measure of all things', it focused attention on the nature, achievements and potential of humanity rather than on the power and mystery of divinity. It was not necessary to be a member of a humanist academy to be influenced by humanism. Painters expressed it when they represented the human figure with greater accuracy and grace, made possible by a more extensive anatomical knowledge. Architects incorporated it into the circular and domed structures so characteristic of Italy in the fifteenth and sixteenth centuries. Writers emphasized it through introspective analysis of the emotional and rational sides of man's nature. Historians reflected it in their conception of the past, which underwent a radical change in the fifteenth century. Medieval scholars had regarded their world as existing on a higher plane than antiquity, suffused with the glow of Christianity and solidly based on political institutions and social structures which were permanent because they had divine authorization. Antiquity, by contrast, had been insecure and unenlightened, certainly until the Christian faith had established itself in the Roman Empire. By the fifteenth century, however, humanist historians had permanently reversed the entire emphasis. The medieval world was now associated with a superstition and barbarism that choked the more positive achievements of antiquity; the Middle Ages had been superseded by a better era. This value judgement was assiduously spread by writers like Conrad Celtis, who congratulated his fellow Germans on 'having cast off your vile barbarity',[1] and Rabelais, who wrote: 'Out of the thick Gothic night our eyes are opened to the glorious torch of the sun.'[2]

Geographically, humanism originated in Italy, spreading

Renaissance Humanism

through the peninsula from its original centre in Florence. During the last decade of the fifteenth century and the beginning of the sixteenth, its influence had permeated much of Europe beyond the Alps. This was the result of the extensive contacts between northern and southern Europe by which new ideas could be readily transmitted. Italian ecclesiastical legates, diplomats, traders and professors travelled to the north, and there was a corresponding flow from France, Germany and England into Italy. Italian humanism gradually combined with autochthonous intellectual developments to produce regional and national variations, the main exponents of which were Lefèvre d'Etaples and Budé in France, Agricola, Celtis, Reuchlin and von Hutten in Germany, Ximenes in Spain, Colet and More in England, and, most significantly of all, Erasmus.

Like most general movements, humanism assumed different shapes, two of which were especially pronounced. The first was Christian humanism, in which the new learning was synthesized with basic Christian belief. Sometimes, although not always, this was officially sanctioned by the Church; several Popes were classical scholars, and Leo X thought that 'nothing more excellent or useful has been given by the Creator to mankind – if we except only the knowledge and true worship of Himself – than these studies'.[3] The second type, particularly strong in Italian politics, was the more obviously secular humanism which exerted a powerful influence on historians.

Christian humanism was undoubtedly the mainstream of renaissance thought, for the rediscovery of man did not necessarily mean the abandonment of God. Humanism had a considerable capacity for idealism and its search for ultimate perfection used human knowledge and skills in a manner which was often religious. This was apparent in the growth of neo-Platonism, the spread of Biblical study and criticism of medieval theology, and the strong leaning towards Christianity in the arts.

Neo-Platonism emerged in fifteenth-century Italy. At first it was a philosophical movement, deriving inspiration from Plato's *Republic* and *Laws*, and contrasting sharply with the medieval form of theology and philosophy known as Scholasticism. The medieval Church had itself used certain classical concepts to construct an impregnable system of doctrine and political thought. Beginning with Aristotle's assumption that 'man is naturally a political and

3

social animal', St Thomas Aquinas (1235–74) had developed a hierarchical structure of authority and of the obligations involved in man's relationship with God and with his ruler. This had been followed by a system of philosophical reasoning which by the fourteenth century had become so elaborate and tortuous that fundamental questions were often submerged by trivia. Neo-Platonism was an attempt to bypass the entire edifice of Scholasticism and to return to the ideas of Plato in their pure form. Since the hold of Christianity was so powerful, however, neo-Platonism rapidly assumed a religious tone, although it was not usually sanctioned by the Church. As developed by Pico and Ficino, neo-Platonism encouraged man to see and understand more clearly the different aspects of Creation, human and inanimate, in their idealized as well as actual form. This required successive degrees of contemplation and the full use of all the faculties, the driving force being, in Pico's words, 'the intellectual desire for ideal beauty'.[4] The emphasis was on man's striving to see God, the source of perfection, by developing the gifts which he had been given. Pico believed that 'God the Father endowed man, from birth, with the seeds of every possibility and every life.' This was something of a departure from the traditional view of man, vitiated by original sin as a result of the Fall.

Christian humanism also developed in northern Europe, taking the form of biblical research and sustained attacks on Scholasticism. Italian scholars had established a precedent in their accurate and detailed study of a wide variety of classical texts. By the beginning of the sixteenth century the same attention was being given to the scriptures, particularly by Colet, Lefèvre d'Etaples and Erasmus. They believed that classical learning, applied to biblical study, could provide a greater harmony between faith and intellect, reinforcing the effects of neo-Platonism by a solid return to scriptural directives. The northern humanists let forth a blast of satirical invective against the Scholastics. Erasmus complained in his *Praise of Folly*: 'Then there are the theologians, a remarkably supercilious and touchy lot. . . . They are fortified . . . with an army of schoolmen's [Scholastic] definitions, conclusions and corollaries, and propositions both explicit and implicit.'[5] Ulrich von Hutten's *Letters to Obscure Men* contained requests to eminent (and fictitious) theologians for advice on a whole series of 'fiddle faddles', a reference to the intricacies of Scholastic thought.

The artists of the Renaissance benefited from the humanist in-

4

Renaissance Humanism

fluence which greatly enhanced accuracy and realism. Their aims were not, however, purely representational. Leonardo da Vinci wrote, in his *Treatise on Painting*: 'The good painter has two principal things to paint: that is, man and the intention of his mind.'[6] Artists used the religious theme as the most popular vehicle for their idealism. Typical subjects included the Crucifixion, the Resurrection, the Ascension and, above all, the Madonna and Child. The last featured in the work of Lorenzo Costa, Signorelli, Francesco Cossa, Masaccio, Leonardo, Raphael, Correggio, Giorgione, Titian, Veronese, Bellini and Carlo Crivelli. Old Testament themes were also popular, the best examples being in the paintings and sculptures of Michelangelo, intricate in their workmanship, accurate in their observation and idealized in their conception. The religious synthesis with humanism is apparent in the Creation of Adam on the roof of the Sistine Chapel, where Adam is created in God's image, but God is an idealized version of man.

Architecture also displayed for all to see the revised connection between God and man. Two views of the proportions of the Renaissance church illustrate the emphasis on the human and the divine. Nikolaus Pevsner explains that in the elongated medieval cathedral 'the prime function . . . had been to lead the faithful to the altar'. In the renaissance church, however, with its new circular shape, this was no longer possible, for 'the building has its full effect only when it is looked at from one focal point', the central altar. Thus man enjoys 'the beauty that surrounds him and the glorious sensation of being the centre of this beauty'.[7] The circle, indeed, had a mystic significance. The renaissance architect, Andrea Palladio, put forward another explanation for its use. The church would be 'enclosed by one circumference only, in which is to be found neither beginning nor end, and the one is indistinguishable from the other; its parts correspond to each other and all of them participate in the shape of the whole; and moreover every part being equally distant from the centre, such a building demonstrates extremely well the unity, the infinite essence, the uniformity and the justice of God'.[4] To a Christian humanist, especially a neo-Platonist, would not these two views be entirely reconcilable?

A more distinctively secular type of humanism developed in Italy during the fifteenth and early sixteenth centuries.

One of the forms which it took has been described as 'civic' humanism, or the replacement of asceticism by active involvement in civic affairs as the most worthwhile of human endeavours. Many humanists were appointed as leading officials in town governments and chanceries, a situation openly applauded by Palmieri (1406–75) in his *De vita civile*. Others became extensively involved in business transactions, accumulating considerable wealth and property. Such activities, it was argued, enhanced the human potential for achievement, whereas poverty, traditionally regarded as a Christian virtue, stunted the complete development of the personality.

Civic humanism, in turn, contributed to a fundamental revision of the approach to historical study. No longer was history regarded merely as an illustrative adjunct to theology; the efforts of Leonardo Bruni and Flavio Biondo in the fifteenth century, together with those of Machiavelli and Guicciardini in the early sixteenth, enabled it to emerge as a discipline within its own right. The emphasis was switched from exemplifying divine direction of human affairs to providing narrative accounts of human political developments, devoid of divine planning or intervention. The study of the past, particularly the classical past, could also be used to make deductions about the feasibility of present political actions. Machiavelli, for example, observed that 'for intellectual training the prince should read history, studying the actions of eminent men to see how they conducted themselves during war and to discover the reasons for their victories or their defeats, so that he can avoid the latter and imitate the former. Above all, he should read history so that he can do what eminent men have done before him.'[8]

The influences of humanism which showed particularly strongly in Machiavelli's works were the considerable debt to classical writers like Livy, a belief in the importance of public life, and an uncompromisingly secular approach to history and statecraft. He brought all his knowledge to bear on examining the political chaos in the Italy of his day, although some of the conclusions he reached were considered too extreme by most contemporary humanist scholars. He sought, in his *Discourses* and *The Prince*, to examine, by historical references, the forms of political and military action which were most likely to ensure a ruler's political survival. Openly abandoning any religious connection, he emphasized the importance of *virtù* (courage and vigour) in taking advantage of the opportunities and overcoming the obstacles presented by *fortuna* (the unpredictable form of change). The activity urged by

Renaissance Humanism

Machiavelli was generally incompatible with Christianity, although not with the beliefs of the ancients. He accepted that there was 'a difference between our religion and the religion of those days. For our religion ... leads us to ascribe less esteem to worldly honour.' Consequently, the ancients 'displayed in their actions more ferocity than we do'.[9] In his rejection of Christian ethics as the basis of political action, Machiavelli provided reasoned justification for pragmatism. He believed, in the words for which he is most famous: 'It is a sound maxim that reprehensible actions may be justified by their effects.'[10]

The practical application of these principles was described in *The Prince*. This work, dedicated to Lorenzo de' Medici, was expressed with simplicity and clarity, for although Machiavelli was himself a member of the Florentine Platonic School, he avoided abstruse ideas and 'any other charm or superfluous decoration of the kind which many are in the habit of using to describe or adorn what they have produced'.[11] After categorizing the different types of state, Machiavelli examined the various methods of achieving power, before proceeding to offer advice on the maintenance of effective rule. The prince must, in effect, be ruthless, disposing of all opponents and establishing a powerful army. Indeed, he should excel in the art of war, for this 'is all that is expected of a ruler'.[8] In diplomacy and in his relations with his subjects he must be versatile, acting 'as a fox' and breaking his word when necessary. He should cultivate the people's support by projecting virtues and qualities which he need not necessarily possess, and, in the true spirit of the Renaissance, showing 'his esteem for talent, actively encouraging able men, and paying honour to eminent craftsmen'.[12] In his final chapter Machiavelli departed from clinical analysis and launched an impassioned appeal to Lorenzo de' Medici to liberate Italy from 'foreign inundations' and 'barbarous tyranny' which 'stinks in everyone's nostrils'.[13] This pointed to his higher aim, the end of political anarchy within Italy and a return to the spirit of ancient Rome.

Is it possible to assess the impact of humanism on sixteenth-century Europe? In its synthesis with Christianity the mainstream of humanism led, indirectly, from the Renaissance to the Reformation. Christianity, for so long assimilated into an elaborate doctrinal and intellectual structure, now became the focus of reinterpretation and argument. Neo-Platonism offered a more individual approach to religious belief than had Scholasticism. Classical research, at the same time, brought a new approach to the scriptures, calling into question many previously accepted assumptions about their precise meaning. A considerable hole was therefore knocked in the established thought of the Church, coinciding, as the next chapter will show, with serious institutional weakness. This provided the opportunity for a new generation of religious reformers to re-examine the basis of Catholic dogma and to give renewed emphasis to the concepts of grace, faith and predestination. Humanism, therefore, made possible the rise of a more fervent and extreme form of dissent and criticism. The result, in a metaphor common to the period, was that Erasmus's egg, when hatched by Luther, produced a different breed of bird. Humanism also had some contact with the eventual revival of the Church and the beginning of the Catholic Reformation. Throughout the period of crisis the Spanish Church was strengthened by the reforms and humanist studies of Cardinal Ximenes. When it was invigorated by the fervour of mysticism and of religious orders the Spanish Church became the vanguard of the assault on Protestantism although, in the process, it lost sight of the principles of toleration and the capacity of self-criticism which were essential features of humanism.

The precise influences of humanism in its purely secular form are more difficult to establish. It is true that the Italian states experienced considerable diplomatic intrigue in the fifteenth century which was devoid of religious influences and which, many humanists believed, bore some resemblance to the problems and crises of antiquity. On the other hand, Renaissance studies in history and statecraft did not themselves secularize Italian politics; rather, they described and rationalized a process which had been occurring for centuries. Similarly, Machiavelli did not invent expediency in diplomacy, but he did examine it more scientifically than ever before, drawing attention to the full range of opportunities which it offered to the adventurous statesman. It is certain that *The Prince* was read by some of the leading figures of the period: W. Durant cites Charles V, Henry III and Henry IV of France, Richelieu and William of Orange, who kept a copy under his pillow. Officially, however, Machiavelli's methods were not regarded as legitimate until the eventual emergence of *Realpolitik*. Before the period of Cavour and Bismarck, Machiavelli was often imitated secretly, but

Renaissance Humanism

always denounced openly; as Frederick the Great showed in the mid-eighteenth century, the more successful the imitation the louder the denunciation.

2
The Background to the Reformation

The Reformation can be defined as the open expression of dissatisfaction with the abuses within the Church, with the role of the priesthood and with the ecclesiastical hierarchy itself. At the same time, it adapted to particular regions and was connected with the process of secularization; this was mainly because papal authority was challenged by state rulers and anti-Italian feeling reached a climax in the early sixteenth century, especially in Germany. The close liaison between Protestant reformers and the political authorities resulted in the development of national churches and the appropriation of Church property, including, of course, the dissolution of monasteries. Popular support was sought through the translation of the scriptures into the vernacular, the new versions generally being sanctioned and enforced by the law of the land.

As has been pointed out by many historians of this period, radical movements and the expression of dissent were not unique to the sixteenth century; the Church had a long record of corruption and there had been attempts at reform long before Luther. On the political side, the Church had frequently come into conflict with state rulers, especially with the Holy Roman Emperors. Yet conditions in the Middle Ages were unfavourable to revolutionary change. Hus and Wycliffe were no less impressive as religious leaders than Luther, but they appeared in the wrong parts of Europe at the wrong time; Hus was burned as a heretic, while Luther prospered as a reformer. The Reformation took place in the sixteenth century rather than the fifteenth or fourteenth because of

The Background to the Reformation

the combination of three things in the right proportion. First, the papacy reached the lowest depths of unpopularity at the end of the fifteenth century and the beginning of the sixteenth. Second, this was precisely the time when the Renaissance was producing more potent weapons of criticism, while the introduction of the printing press provided a vital means of communication. Third, the Church could no longer depend upon a general political acceptance of its concept of universalism and now had to hold its own against the growth of nation states and nationalism. Each of these problems will now be examined separately.

The basic problem confronting the Church was a crisis of leadership. In 1302 Pope Boniface VIII had asserted, in the Bull *Unam Sanctam*, the papal claim to supreme spiritual and temporal authority in Europe. This, however, was not made effective over the next hundred years, largely because of the Avignon captivity between 1305 and 1376 and the Great Schism (1378–1417), which produced two and, in one instance, three, rival popes. During the first half of the fifteenth century the Church made a great effort to reform its organization and to compensate for the lack of an effective authority. The Conciliar Movement (examples of which were the Councils of Pisa, 1409, Constance 1414–17, and Basle, 1431–49) attempted to persuade the papacy to delegate authority, and writers like Nicholas of Cusa argued that papal absolutism was no more justifiable than secular tyranny. The failure of the Conciliar Movement was due mainly to the intransigence of the Popes themselves, and it had dire consequences. The papacy degenerated further and by the end of the fifteenth century there was a sense of bitter frustration among the faithful, bred by the knowledge that institutional reform led from above was impossible.

The outward manifestations of papal decline were perhaps exaggerated, but there was probably more cause for complaint in the fifteenth and early sixteenth centuries than at any other time in history. In 1514 Erasmus launched a bitter attack on Pope Julius II in his satire *Iulius Exclusus*, in which St Peter was depicted turning the Pope away from the gates of Heaven and concluding: 'O wretched man! O miserable Church! . . . I am not surprised that so few now apply here for admission, when the Church has such rulers. Yet there must be good in the world, too, when such a sink of iniquity can be honoured merely because he bears the name of Pope.'[1] The sensationalism of *Iulius Exclusus* did Erasmus little credit, but it was widely accepted as being a true description of a corrupt institution. After the first twenty years of the Reformation the need for radical reform came to be accepted even in Rome, and a special commission of Cardinals, appointed by Paul III to consider the basic priorities, pointed an accusing finger in the same direction as had Erasmus. The report, published under the title *Consilium dilectorum cardinalium de emendanda ecclesia* (1538) attacked the papacy as the source 'from which, as from the Trojan Horse, every abuse broke forth into the Church'.[2] Much as the Catholic world distrusted Erasmus there appeared to be basic agreement on this one point.

It is possible to find examples of Popes who were quite unsuited for their position (for example, between 1492 and 1503 Alexander VI is known to have given priority to furthering the careers of his illegitimate children), but the more serious problem was what has been described as the 'secularization of the papacy' over a long period of time, a process in which morally upright Popes were also involved. With its declining reputation the papacy forfeited its image as a power above national considerations, and the depredation of Italy by European monarchs forced it to compete directly with the political forces of the day in a struggle for temporal survival. A whole series of Popes became involved in the Italian Wars; these included Alexander VI (1492–1503), Julius II (1503–13), Leo X (1513–21), Adrian VI (1522–3) and Clement VII (1523–34). The measure of disregard for the papacy can be seen by the way in which the national powers, especially France, were prepared to align themselves with or against Rome as and when it suited them. The ultimate catastrophe was the destruction of Rome in 1527 by the supposedly Catholic armies of the Emperor Charles V; this evoked from a contemporary the words: 'What Goths, what Vandals, what Turks were ever like this army of the Emperor in the sacrilege they have committed?'

Political entanglements inevitably created heavy financial demands, and it was the methods used to meet these which created the most bitter hostility and provided the immediate background to the Reformation in Germany in 1517. The papacy, being a temporal state as well as the supreme spiritual power, had gradually built up an extensive fiscal system. In order to defray the expenses of the Italian Wars, to finance a proposed crusade against the Turks and to pay for the rebuilding of St Peter's basilica in Rome, traditional

The Background to the Reformation

forms of extracting revenue were now used in exaggerated and intensified form. Mainly affected were the Tenths, First Fruits, Annates, Tithes, Dispensations for uncanonical marriages and, most notorious of all, Indulgences. Somehow the papacy needed to augment its average total revenue of 450,000 ducats (compared with that of 600,000 for Naples[3] – a state with far fewer obligations). It therefore resorted to selling Cardinalates; in 1500 Alexander VI sold twelve for a total of 120,000 ducats. Another method was to farm out the sale of Indulgences to the Fuggers (the Augsburg bankers), and this spurred Luther into action. In his *Ninety-Five Theses* (1517) he denounced the whole principle of Indulgences. These were being hawked near Wittenberg by the Dominican Tetzel on behalf of the Archbishop of Mainz, who intended to clear himself of a debt to the Fuggers by undertaking the distribution of Indulgences in his part of Germany. The Fuggers themselves were extensively involved in the sale of Indulgences and sometimes retained 50 per cent of the total proceeds. Luther was, therefore, also attacking a vast and complex financial network which demonstrated as much as anything how secular the papacy had become.

Lack of effective papal leadership inevitably meant the proliferation of abuses among the lower clergy. In the late fifteenth century, for example, 36 of the 83 incumbents of Paris were non-resident.[3] This situation was pointed out by the 1537 Commission of Cardinals, which maintained that 'almost all the shepherds have deserted their flocks and entrusted them to hirelings'.[2] The Church as a whole underwent a general decline which affected the entire continent, although areas like Spain and Ireland were less susceptible than Italy and Germany. Particularly distressing was the impact on the soul of the Church – monasticism. Many monasteries were renowned for their corruption and their domination by non-clerical owners and interests. Erasmus and Luther saw monasticism at its worst, and had no hesitation in attacking it openly, while many state rulers welcomed the opportunity provided by the Reformation to close down religious houses and appropriate their lands. This was entirely in keeping with the growing cynicism and pragmatism which dominated the attitudes of most European rulers towards the papacy and its possessions.

It was unfortunate for the papacy that the period of its greatest weakness should have coincided with an era of increased intellectual activity and more extensive and articulate criticism. The problems of the Church had been publicly discussed at several points in the Middle Ages; for example, both Wycliffe and Hus had criticized the sale of Indulgences and emphasized the supremacy of the scriptures long before Luther. But the intellectual environment of their time was hostile and they could never stimulate the interest of the universities and the political authorities. By the beginning of the sixteenth century reformers who attacked the Church had more extensive support, engendered by the force of the Renaissance. The works of Erasmus of Rotterdam and of a series of German humanists led to a basic re-examination of medieval theology and of the power of the papacy. The main writers were Rudolf Agricola (1444-85), Conrad Celtis (1459-1508), Johannes Reuchlin (1455-1522) and Ulrich von Hutten (1488-1523). German humanism appeared to develop into two identifiable but overlapping planes. The first was progress towards religious change, even revolution, and the second was the development of a powerful nationalist opposition to Italian influences in Germany. The former provided extensive support for Luther's proposed reforms, while the latter convinced the rulers of northern Germany that they had ideological justification in severing their ties with the papacy.

It would be misleading to emphasize too strongly the links between the Renaissance and Lutheranism; many aspects of Luther's theology were, after all, early medieval, bearing a close resemblance to the doctrines of Augustine. Nevertheless, he was greatly assisted by the preliminary spread of humanism. This had been accompanied by the foundation of new universities, including, in 1502, the University of Wittenberg, which became the intellectual headquarters of Lutheranism. Luther lived in an age when criticism of established institutions was an accepted part of the intellectual life of the new Academies and he did not, therefore, have to break new ground to get his views heard. The response to his *Ninety-Five Theses* was immediate and beyond his expectations. The Catholic Church attempted to counter the growing dissent in a series of debates with Luther, the disputation between Luther and Eck at Leipzig in 1519 being the most important. It soon became obvious, however, that Catholic arguments based on rigid Scholasticism made no impression on humanist university environments, and the experiment was discontinued.

Luther's initial impact, therefore, was made possible by the New

The Background to the Reformation

Learning. The spread of his ideas beyond Saxony was made physically possible by the invention of the printing press. This originated in Germany, with the efforts of John Gutenberg of Mainz. The technology spread to Italy, Paris, London, Stockholm and Madrid, gaining a firm foothold in most of Europe by 1500. By this time, it has been estimated, there were approximately nine million printed books in circulation. Luther benefited as much from this as anyone. For example, he was able to circulate copies of the *Ninety-Five Theses* throughout Germany. This was followed, at the time of his excommunication by the Pope in 1520, by the widespread distribution of three new works: *To the Christian Nobility of the German Nation*, *The Babylonish Captivity of the Church* and *The Liberty of a Christian Man*. As the Reformation gathered momentum the printing press remained the vital instrument with which the reformers cut into the fabric of the Church. It would have been surprising indeed if such an immense technical advance in the dissemination of ideas had not had a major impact on contemporary thought and institutions.

The third necessary component for revolutionary change within the Church was political support and sanction, without which reformers would have remained heretics, excommunicated by the Church and 'relaxed to the secular arm' for punishment. In the face of open political defiance, however, the papacy was usually helpless. Again, this conflict was not entirely new to Europe. The Middle Ages had seen disputes between Church and state on three main grounds. The first was legal: the papacy had asserted the judicial autonomy of the clergy from the state, and this had precipitated constitutional arguments with rulers like Henry II of England. The second was political: most monarchs had pointed out that papal representatives, usually legates, exercised too much influence in state affairs. The third was economic: Pope Boniface VIII (1294–1303) had claimed that no form of taxation should be levied on ecclesiastical property by the state, and most monarchs ignored or defied this. Serious as these issues had been, however, they had not produced a situation where rulers were actually prepared to break with the Church and make use of new theological trends to establish regional or national alternatives (which is, of course, what happened in the sixteenth century).

What really made the crucial difference was the development of more centralized states, like England and Sweden, in which the Church came to be regarded as part of the internal constitutional structure and not as an external unit based on Rome. The methods varied considerably; Anglicanism was originally intended to substitute royal for papal authority with minimal doctrinal change, whereas the Swedish Lutheran Church introduced doctrinal changes at the beginning. But the fear of the Pope, which had once cowed medieval monarchs and caused the Emperor Henry IV to kneel in the snow of Canossa as a penitent before Pope Gregory VII in 1077, had now entirely disappeared. Even those monarchs who remained Catholic adopted an increasingly territorial approach and maintained a tight control over the Church, an example of which was the development of Gallicanism in France.

Another factor preparing the ground for the Reformation, this time in Germany, was the growth of nationalism or, at least, a strong national consciousness which antedated the growth of a national frontier. There is considerable evidence of a powerful anti-Italian and anti-Roman feeling in Germany, based on the belief that Germany was being exploited by the papacy. In 1457, for example, Martin Mair, Chancellor to the Archbishop of Mainz, wrote: 'As a result of these abuses, our proud nation, once renowned for the ability and courage with which it gained the Roman Imperium and became lord and master over the world, has been reduced to beggary, subjected to humiliating exactions, and left to cower in the dust, bemoaning its misery.'[4] The sale of indulgences, as we have seen, stirred up strong anti-Italian propaganda. Luther's *Ninety-Five Theses* expressed the thoughts of a large part of northern Germany in attacking the use of Germany's money for the reconstruction of St Peter's. 'The revenues of all Christendom are being sucked into this insatiable basilica. The Germans laugh at calling this the common treasure of Christendom. Before long all the churches, palaces, walls and bridges of Rome will be built out of our money. . . . We Germans cannot attend St Peter's. Better that it should never be built than that our parochial churches should be despoiled.'[5]

At the beginning of the sixteenth century Germany was, paradoxically, becoming increasingly disunited and decentralized at the very time that German national pride and resentment were expressing themselves most forcefully. The reason for this was that the traditional form of imperial unity was based on medieval institu-

The Background to the Reformation

tions sanctioned by the Church and the Pope; nationalism, on the other hand, became anti-imperial and anti-papal and often manifested itself in the struggle of state rulers for independence from central control. The association between the state rulers and Lutheranism was therefore a natural alliance of political and religious dissent, the results of which will be examined in the next chapter.

3
Political Factors in the Spread of Lutheranism in Germany Between 1517 and 1555

The political situation in Central Europe was of crucial importance for the survival and spread of Lutheranism during the first half of the sixteenth century. It is very doubtful whether the religious beliefs and fervour of Luther and his followers could have made the permanent impression they did without the assistance of three factors. The first was the surprisingly muted reaction of the Pope and the Emperor Maximilian I to Luther's initial outbursts between 1517 and 1519, attributable to their preoccupation with German issues and the problem of the imperial succession. The second was the adoption of Lutheranism as the official state religion by a large number of German princes and Free Cities during the 1520s and 1530s, the motive for which was sometimes strongly secular. The third was the inability of the forces of orthodoxy to crush Lutheranism and its political protectors, largely because of the enormous range of internal and external problems confronting the Emperor Charles V between 1519 and 1556.

Luther posted his *Ninety-Five Theses* on the church door in Wittenberg in December 1517. For the next two years very little action was taken, and neither the Pope nor the Emperor immediately attempted to eradicate the new dissent. Indeed, Luther was not excommunicated until 1520, nor outlawed until 1521.

Pope Leo X did, it is true, set in motion the usual procedure for dealing with heresy by summoning Luther to Rome in July 1518. But instant complications saved Lutheranism at its inception. For

German Lutheranism 1517–1555

reasons which will be explained in the next section, Luther was afforded full protection by the Elector Frederick of Saxony, who openly objected to papal attempts to extradite and try one of his most illustrious subjects. Leo had to tread warily to avoid needlessly antagonizing Frederick and stirring up the latent hostility of the German political authorities, for he had higher objectives in 1518 than the cross-examination of Luther. He hoped to persuade the German princes to agree to an extra tax, on secular and ecclesiastical property, to finance a crusade against the Turks in an effort to win back the eastern Mediterranean to Christendom. Compared with this magnificent design, the silencing of one dissident academic must have appeared a relatively trivial matter, and there is no reason why Leo should have suspected, in Luther, a new threat to the Catholic Church at least as dangerous as Islam.

Meanwhile, the Emperor Maximilian I had, since 1517, been preoccupied with his own objective: to ensure the succession of his grandson Charles to the imperial throne. Although he had no sympathy with religious dissent of any kind, Maximilian did not intend to create difficulties for himself by putting pressure on one of the key Electors to surrender Luther for examination in Rome; Frederick might well retaliate by withholding crucial support for Charles's candidature. Indeed, Maximilian did what he could to avert any confrontation over Luther, advising the Pope to act with leniency and great caution. As a result, Leo withdrew his summons and agreed to allow Luther to appear instead before Cardinal Cajetan at Augsburg. When Luther refused to recant at this meeting, Leo dispatched a special envoy, Miltitz, to persuade the Elector of Saxony to put a little more pressure on his protégé to moderate his views. The Pope was eminently tactful, going so far as to confer on Frederick the Golden Rose, a signal papal favour. Luther, therefore, had little to fear, especially as events in 1519 pushed him even further into the background.

Maximilian's death in January 1519 was followed by an intensive campaign to elect a successor. The most prestigious title in Europe was contested by Charles (King of Spain, Archduke of Austria and Duke of Burgundy), Francis I of France and Henry VIII of England. The attitude of the papacy to these candidates was of vital importance and accounts for the continued leniency shown towards Luther. Leo X wanted to prevent the election of Charles, for he feared that the combination of Charles's enormous inheritance and the imperial

19

Aspects of European History 1494-1789

title would create a formidable political power in Europe and thereby revive the old conflict between Emperors and Popes which had been a common theme in the Middle Ages. He therefore backed Francis I, but then swiftly changed his mind in favour of a candidate who would be politically weaker and more susceptible to papal influence in the future. Thus the Pope tried to persuade Frederick of Saxony to stand, knowing that Frederick had a reasonable chance of securing the support of some of the other Electors and thereby depriving Charles of their vote. Naturally, Leo had to suspend any proceedings against Luther in deference to Frederick's views. The result was that Luther's ideas spread with impunity through Saxony during the course of 1519, receiving considerable publicity between 27 June and 8 July in the disputation with Eck at Leipzig. Eventually papal diplomacy collapsed; Frederick wisely refused to stand for the title and Charles was elected Emperor on 28 June. Although this was a thoroughly unsatisfactory outcome as far as Leo was concerned, it did mean that he was no longer so dependent on Frederick's good will, and that he could now re-examine the problem posed by the professor at Wittenberg. Unfortunately for Leo, Luther's reputation had grown rapidly during the two year respite – so much so that several political authorities were prepared to throw in their lot with Lutheranism and to risk the censure and counter-measures which would inevitably follow.

Frederick of Saxony, the first of Luther's supporters was a leading sponsor of German humanism and the founder of Wittenberg University in 1502. He had no intention of allowing any external interference in the academic or religious life of Saxony and, although he did not agree with all of Luther's opinions, he firmly upheld his right to express them. Between 1517 and 1519 Frederick's task was simplified by the predicament in which the Emperor and the Pope found themselves. But even when Leo X assumed a tougher policy in 1520, Frederick continued to support Luther, despite the latter's excommunication. More important still was Frederick's decisive intervention immediately after the Diet of Worms in 1521; by arranging to have Luther secretly taken to Wartburg Castle he saved him from being hunted down as an outlaw, and enabled him to concentrate for the next few years on his writing. During the decade after the Diet of Worms Lutheranism gained extensive support beyond the borders of Saxony. It was adopted as the state religion by Philip of Hesse, the rulers of Brunswick, Württemberg, Mecklenburg, Brandenburg and Pomerania, and the Imperial Cities of Strasbourg, Ulm, Augsburg, Nuremberg, Hamburg, Bremen and Lübeck. Many of these authorities were not merely toying with the new religion. They were prepared to commit themselves to alliances like the Leagues of Torgau (1525 and 1551) and the Schmalkaldic League (1531). Although these were intended primarily to exert diplomatic pressure on Charles V to accept Lutheranism, the princes were prepared to resort to active military resistance against heavy odds, as they showed in the Schmalkaldic War.

In addition to having a genuine religious commitment to Lutheranism, the princes were heavily influenced by political considerations. They seized upon the new religion as an ideological justification for separatism and for their defiance of imperial authority; they could always argue that the Emperor had no legitimate claim of sovereignty as long as he remained a Catholic. At the same time, Luther showed that he was firmly behind the political authority of the individual princes, and that his demands for religious reform would not degenerate into a socio-political movement aimed at overthrowing rulers. During the Peasants' War (1524–5) he condemned the use of rebellion as a means of settling grievances, and told the rebels, in his *Friendly Admonition to Peace Concerning the Twelve Articles of the Swabian Peasants*: '. . . no matter how right you are, it is not for a Christian to appeal to law, or to fight, but rather to suffer wrong and endure evil'.[1] This was an argument which the authorities naturally found very attractive. Also, in many cases, the conversion of rulers to Lutheranism was followed by a scramble to secularize Church property, and Melancthon complained: 'Under cover of the Gospel, the princess were only intent on the plunder of the Churches.'[2] There certainly seems to have been a strong element of opportunism in the attacks made on the Church for its wealth, and much of the proceeds went into the state coffers. Philip of Hesse, for example, allocated 59 per cent of the confiscated property and revenues to charity and education, but kept 41 per cent for himself.[3]

What was Luther's reaction to the political connections developed by his movement? At first he expressed himself very cautiously on the subject of political authority. In an ideal world, composed entirely of devout Christians, 'no prince, King, lord, sword or law would be needed'. Unfortunately: 'This you will never accomplish: for the world and masses are and always will be unchristian.'[4] On the whole the Christian was, in Luther's view, obliged to submit to the sovereign power, and was not entitled to rebel. During the 1520s Luther experienced a crisis of conscience. He clearly did not wish to become the focal point of a wide-scale rebellion against the Emperor's authority; this is why he refused to be associated in any way with the Knights' War in 1522. He avoided using the powers which he realized he possessed, observing of the 1521 Diet: 'Had I desired to foment trouble, I could have brought great bloodshed upon Germany. Yea, I could have started such a little game at Worms that the Emperor would not have been safe.'[4] Nor did he entirely approve of those Princes who were beginning to question imperial authority. In his opinion, some of them were self-seeking and unscrupulous, apparently justifying his maxim that 'He who wants to be a ruler must have the Devil for his godfather.'[4] Yet, by 1530, Luther had responded to the support of the princes and had come to realize that a conflict with the Emperor was inevitable: 'Thus one of two things must happen, war or revolt; maybe both together.'[5] Before long he had lost his remaining misgivings and at last gave his open approval of princely separatism.

Three reasons can be advanced for this gradual change in attitude. First, Lutheranism never possessed an inherent capacity for organization, and it came to depend upon the state rulers to provide a workable structure and to exercise control in the form of the Visitation, or inspection. It therefore became more and more involved in the power struggles within the Empire, being aligned with the aspirations of the princes. Second, Luther could not appeal for the support of the masses, and cut through this dependence on aristocratic patronage, because he had alienated huge sections of the peasantry by his advice to the authorities in 1525: 'Therefore strike, throttle, stab, secretly or openly, whoever can, and remember that there is nothing more poisonous, more hurtful, more devilish than a rebellious man.'[6] Indeed, many peasants returned to Catholicism or joined more extreme movements like Anabaptism. Finally, of course, Luther continued to depend on the princes for his protection. When Charles V rejected Luther's Augsburg Confession in 1530, Luther realized that the prospects for future compromise were so remote that he could no longer express unqualified opposi-

German Lutheranism 1517–1555

tion to rebellion without also depriving himself of the means of survival.

At the Diet of Worms Charles V declared his policy towards Luther. 'I am', he said, 'descended from a long line of Catholic emperors of this noble German nation, of the Catholic kings of Spain, the archdukes of Austria, and the dukes of Burgundy. They were all faithful to the death to the Church of Rome, and they defended the Catholic faith and the honour of God. I have resolved to follow in their steps. A single friar who goes counter to all Christianity for a thousand years must be wrong. Therefore I am resolved to stake my lands, my friends, my body, my blood, my life and my soul . . .'[2] The Edict of Worms, which declared Luther an outlaw, followed the Papal Bull of Excommunication (1520) in reversing the previous cautious measures. The future of Lutheranism looked bleak, for Charles V had access to more resources than any of his predecessors. Yet the nature of his dominions and the problems associated with them absorbed much of his attention, preventing him from keeping his counter-attack at full strength.

As ruler of the largest Christian empire in Europe since that of Charlemagne, Charles was inevitably confronted by extensive administrative and economic problems. He had no overall capital, no central executive, and no common budget or treasury. He had to make separate arrangements for each of his dominions, and spent much time visiting them individually as the need arose. Internal dissent was a constant threat and a major source of distraction; Castile, for example, revolted in 1520, Ghent in the late 1530s, and many of the German princes and cities systematically undermined imperial authority throughout the period. Charles was even forced to deal with a bitter family dispute over the succession to the Habsburg dominions, involving his brother, Ferdinand, and his son, Philip.

External difficulties were even more serious. The Habsburg dominions were threatened from the west by France and from the east by the Ottoman Empire; these peripheral powers, in fact, formed the most significant alliance of the century. Charles V was obliged, on many occasions, to abandon his schemes to eradicate Lutheranism and turn, instead, to face the latest invasion. While Charles was thus preoccupied, Lutheranism was able to consolidate its position or to recover from a previous reverse. Three examples illustrate this. During the 1520s the Habsburgs were continually at war, Charles V with France (1521–9), and Ferdinand with the Turks. As a result, Charles V could not attend the crucial Diet of Speyer in 1526, at which it was conceded that each German prince should decide his own policy towards Lutheranism. This encouraged more rulers to take the plunge and adopt Lutheranism as their state religion. Then, during the 1530s, Charles had to deal with a concerted Franco-Turkish offensive in the western Mediterranean, which kept Habsburg resources fully stretched. Finally, Lutheranism was threatened with extinction after the Battle of Mühlberg in 1547, only to be reprieved by the French invasion of the Empire in 1552.

Even the Emperor's relations with the Pope were strained. The papal fear of Charles's power, so evident in the imperial election campaign of 1519, re-emerged at times, to prevent a united Catholic offensive against Luther. Pope Clement VII, for example, drew up a treaty with France in 1524 and joined the League of Cognac against Charles V in 1526, only to see Rome captured and sacked by the Emperor's troops in 1527. Pope Paul IV, as a Neapolitan, opposed the Habsburg domination of southern Italy and therefore formed an alliance with France against Charles in 1556. The Counter Reformation might have been expected to effect a reconciliation between Emperor and Pope, but unfortunately there were disagreements between Charles V and Paul III over the precise purpose of the General Council of the Church. By the time that the Catholic Church was sufficiently revived to take active measures against Protestantism, Charles V had abdicated and Lutheranism had been given legal status within the Empire by the Religious Peace of Augsburg.

4
The Spread and Significance of Calvinism

Lutheranism had been most successful in northern Germany and Scandinavia because it had suited the rulers of these areas to tolerate or sponsor it for political and economic reasons. Calvinism, by contrast, spread itself more widely and thinly across Europe, particularly in the regions outside the Lutheran-dominated Baltic coast and the purely Catholic Italian and Iberian Peninsulas. It might take root in states which provided government support, or become a vigorous opposition to the existing political and religious establishment.

From its original centre in Geneva Calvinism became the official religion of the northern Netherlands and the German states of the Palatinate, Nassau, Hesse and Anhalt. The Heidelberg Catechism, an adaptation of Calvin's ideas, was the main source of doctrinal orthodoxy, and the Rhenish area became the most radical and consistent opponent of the Catholic Church, Spain and the Emperor (for example, the northern Netherlands rebelled against Philip II of Spain and the Palatinate supported the revolt of Bohemia against the Habsburgs and the Empire). The position of Calvinism in France and Scotland was altogether different; both countries possessed Catholic monarchies which were vigorously attacked, in France by the Huguenots and in Scotland by the Presbyterians, under inspiration from Languet, Knox and Buchanan. Both countries experienced political violence, which in France spread into civil war. On the whole, however, conditions proved more favourable in Scotland; Calvinism gradually took over from Catholicism as the major re-

ligion, whereas it never achieved more than minority status in
France. In England Calvinism attracted less numerical support but
it had a powerful political impact on Parliament and successfully
attacked the Stuart 'despotism' of the first half of the seventeenth
century. It failed, however, to reform the Anglican Church, which it
sometimes regarded with almost as much suspicion as Catholicism.
Finally, there were three areas in Europe where Calvinism became
associated with anti-German as well as anti-Catholic movements:
Poland, Bohemia and Hungary. Poland remained largely Catholic,
but some members of the nobility adopted Calvinism as a more
desirable form of dissent than Lutheranism, since the latter was
associated with the expanding frontier of Brandenburg. Bohemia
and Hungary possessed a wider variety of religions than any other
part of Europe. In Bohemia, Calvinism competed with Catholics,
Lutherans and the Bohemian sects, while it shared Hungary with
Catholicism, Lutheranism and Islam. In each case, however,
Calvinism became a catalyst for the growing resentment of the
strongly pro-German policies of the Holy Roman Emperors.

The basic factor contributing to the spread and survival of Calvinism was its resilience. Lutheranism grew in the rich soil of political
protection; Calvinism usually flourished in the stony ground of
opposition and persecution. The twin pillars of Calvinism were its
effective organization and its clearly defined doctrine of predestination. Its system of Church government could operate effectively
either in conjunction with the secular authority or as a self-
contained unit. As an illustration of the latter, Calvinism in France
was organized into local assemblies, and Provincial and National
Synods, all of which operated in defiance of the French monarchy
and the Catholic Church. (This contrasted with Lutheran organization, which was based on the Visitation, normally under the control
of the state ruler.) Calvinist doctrine reinforced the structure of
Church government and provided a considerable capacity to resist
persecution. The concept of predestination was not initiated by
Calvin – it can be traced back to St Augustine and beyond. Nevertheless, the Catholic Church had always treated it with great
caution and it was Calvin who gave it renewed emphasis. Briefly,
Calvin's version of predestination was based on the premise that 'all
are not created in equal condition; rather, eternal life is fore-
ordained for some, eternal damnation for others'. This occurs 'without any respect of human merit', and salvation is a gift bestowed by

The Spread of Calvinism

the Grace of the Creator, who has 'the right to distribute this treasure to whom He pleases'.[1] The 'Elect' (for most Calvinists being among the 'Elect' was an inner conviction) were to combine asceticism and rigid self-discipline with involvement in the world around them. Thus armed, Calvinists became formidable competitors in politics and finance wherever they operated.

The nature and extent of this political and economic influence has been the subject of considerable speculation and is worth a brief survey. The doctrines of Calvin placed little direct emphasis on the concept of the individual, on parliamentarianism or on political liberty. Nor was Geneva in any sense an example of a liberal society. Initially this Calvinist dominated government was authoritarian rather than libertarian, imposing doctrinal orthodoxy and morality as rigidly as any state in Europe. By a curious sequence of events and ideas, however, Calvinism gradually assumed a more progressive and sometimes revolutionary attitude to politics, although the precise nature and effect of this radicalism varied from country to country and involved extensive reinterpretation of Calvin's original ideas. England and France in the sixteenth and seventeenth centuries can be used as examples.

✗ In England Calvinism developed as an important influence in a minority movement, Puritanism. The main target of its criticism, the Anglican Church, possessed something of a dual nature. It embraced both advanced Protestant doctrinal concepts (during the reign of Edward VI), and a substantial degree of neo-Catholicism which could be thoroughly hostile to Protestantism; this reached its peak during the reign of Charles I. Nevertheless, the one consistent factor was the accomplishment of all doctrinal changes and Church administrative reorganization by statute at the behest of the monarch, and this influenced the method by which Calvinism took root. Since Anglicanism was directly linked to the English constitution by, for example, the Acts of Supremacy and Uniformity (1559), any fundamental religious change would have to be accomplished by political means. During the reign of Elizabeth (1558–1603) Puritans attacked the Crown and the Anglican Church for their lack of Protestant ardour at home and abroad, and mounted a campaign in the most influential quarter open to them – Parliament. This opposition intensified during the reign of James I (1603–25) and was reinforced by theoretical denunciations of absolutism.

Aspects of European History 1494–1789

The climax occurred when Charles I (1625–49) defined Parliament and attempted to assert the right of the Crown as supreme in Church and State. The Parliament which, for constitutional and economic reasons, resisted the monarchy to the point of civil war and beyond, was dominated increasingly by Puritanism, in terms not of numerical superiority but of clarity of aim, leadership and discipline. Cromwell's Commonwealth and Protectorate abolished some of the instruments of despotism, for example the Star Chamber and the Court of High Commission, and introduced a considerable quantity of Puritan social legislation. But the political supremacy of Puritanism was shortlived. With the accession of Charles II in 1660 it was again subject to restrictive legislation, along with other forms of dissent. Once more, however, it emerged in Parliament and contributed to the development of the Whig Party, which became increasingly hostile to the extensive use of the royal prerogative. By the end of the seventeenth century the Whigs had adopted a largely non-religious platform and were inspired mainly by the writings of John Locke. The connection between the Revolution Settlement of 1689 and the ideas of Calvin must therefore appear very remote. Nevertheless, it is possible to say that Calvinism in its English form, though hardly Calvin himself, contributed much to the concept of parliamentary sovereignty.

In France the spread of Calvinism was more extensive and rapidly resulted in civil war. During the Wars of Religion the Huguenot side had definite political motives and powerful support. Some of these motives were opportunist; for example the Bourbon princes, who dominated the southern and western areas of France, supported the Huguenots because of their own intense rivalry with the Catholic Ducs de Guise. Other motives were ideological, and assumed a more revolutionary emphasis than any Puritan ideas of the sixteenth century. Languet provided justification for the Huguenot rebellion in his *Defence of Liberty against Tyrants* (1579), arguing that royal authority was acceptable only so long as it observed certain constraints and that in extreme cases tyrannicide could be justified. Since France not only experienced civil war but also developed arguments for disposing of despotism before England, it might be assumed that France would be a better breeding ground for radicalism than England. But this was not so; while the Puritans were becoming increasingly aggressive in England, the Huguenots were being reconciled with Catholicism. The main reason for this was the

The Spread of Calvinism

conversion of their leader, Henry of Navarre, to Catholicism in 1593 (a decision based on expediency rather than on religious conviction). As Henry IV, he pursued a deliberate policy of healing the religious rift by issuing the Edict of Nantes in 1598. Until the last two decades of the seventeenth century the Huguenots remained relatively quiet, although there were occasional revolts. The next period of ideological opposition to the administration began in 1685 when Louis XIV revoked the Edict of Nantes and initiated another era of persecution. The Huguenots were by that time politically helpless. Unlike the Puritans in the first half of the seventeenth century, they had no institutional means of opposing the arbitrary policies of absolutism; the Paris Parlement could in no way be compared with the English Parliament, and the Estates General never met between 1614 and 1789. The French monarchy during the seventeenth century raised itself to new heights of power which, for a time, were beyond the reach of any opposition, religious or secular. The pen was all that was left for the Huguenots, but this was used to some effect to renew the attacks on tyranny. The most famous of the dissident writers was Jurieu, whose *Soupirs de la France esclave qui aspire après la liberté* (1689) drew contrasts between French absolutism and the development of limited monarchy in England. This and other expressions of discontent naturally had little impact on the regime, but they did publicize arguments for representative institutions and helped to make the French bourgeoisie more receptive to the completely secular political theories of eighteenth-century writers like Montesquieu. The convulsion which eventually destroyed the French monarchy and created a new type of radicalism was due to the frustration of all previous opposition and demands for reform, but by no stretch of the imagination could the nature of this revolution be associated with either Calvinism or Calvin.

More controversial is the relationship between Calvinism and European economic development; there are two main sides in the debate between historians as to whether Calvinism was associated with emergent capitalism. It is possible here to give only a brief and composite outline of each.

M. Weber (*The Protestant Ethic and the Spirit of Capitalism*) and E. Troeltsch (*The Social Teaching of the Christian Churches*) argued that there was a definite relationship. Ascetic Protestantism, with its emphasis on 'calling', self-discipline and hard work for its own

29

sake, fostered a 'spirit of modern capitalism'. Money-making was no longer regarded with opprobrium, as it had been in the Middle Ages, but was seen by Calvinists as a method of fulfilling the 'work ethic' and carrying out a sacred trust, at the same time caring for and increasing wealth, not for self-indulgence but as an act of 'stewardship' for God, all profits being used for the relief of the poor and other social works. The spread of capitalism was most rapid in those countries which adopted Calvinism, or in which Calvinism flourished as a minority religion, and it affected primarily the bourgeoisie. R. H. Tawney (*Religion and the Rise of Capitalism*), although not convinced about the existence of a 'spirit of capitalism' and doubtful whether Calvin would ever have wished to associate his teachings in any way with capitalism, asserted, nevertheless, that Puritanism in the seventeenth century stimulated capitalism and encouraged writers like Baxter to provide support and rules for capitalist activities.

The connection has been criticized on various grounds. W. Sombart (*The Quintessence of Capitalism*) maintained that Calvinism, far from fostering capitalism, was a better enemy and that, wherever they were established, the Calvinist Churches were hostile to capitalist activities; Catholicism, on the other hand, was more conducive to it, and 'the Papacy did much to foster the spread of capitalism through its financial policies'.[2] Several historians have claimed that the rise of capitalism had nothing to do with religion at all and that it existed throughout the Middle Ages in Byzantium and Italy. An example of a purely secular interpretation is P. Gordon Walker's belief that the acceleration of capitalism was due to the Price Rise which 'hastened the arrival of the Industrial Revolution'.[3]

Both sides can be supported by factual examples and by contemporary texts. Whichever view is adopted, however, there appear to be two main methods by which Calvinism can undoubtedly be said to have influenced directly the development of finance, industry and commerce. First, Calvinists, as a minority group, frequently found themselves discriminated against by the law of the land or by social attitudes. As a result, they were sometimes prevented from entering the professions and were therefore forced into private enterprise, a position comparable to that of the Jews throughout European history. The most successful form of private enterprise was commerce and there may well have been an interplay between this and the

The Spread of Calvinism

further dissemination of Calvinism; trade routes have always been the most effective form of communication before the age of the mass media. Second, minority Calvinist groups were sometimes actively persecuted and therefore took their skills elsewhere, thus spreading the net of their activities. The major example of this was the Revocation of the Edict of Nantes in 1685. Huguenot refugees were welcomed into Brandenburg-Prussia and greatly enhanced that country's economic growth. They also fled to the Netherlands and England and contributed to the development of frontier societies abroad, especially in South Africa. Again, a parallel can be drawn with the Jews. In 1492 Ferdinand and Isabella forced large numbers of Spanish Jews to emigrate, mainly to Eastern Europe, one of many examples of the persecutions and purges which are a feature of many civilizations.

5
Calvinism and the Jesuits

Many general histories of Europe or of the Reformation have included comments about the similarities and differences between the Calvinists and the Society of Jesus. This is hardly surprising, since the rise to prominence of these movements was concurrent and the stimulus which they gave to flagging Protestantism and assailed Catholicism precipitated another round of religious conflict in the second half of the sixteenth century. The purpose of this chapter is to emphasize the comparisons and contrasts between the organizations, taking as points of reference, their origins, doctrines, structure and impact on Europe and the rest of the world.

John Calvin (1509–64) and Ignatius Loyola (1491–1556) were of very different backgrounds. Calvin was a typical member of the French bourgeoisie and spent his youth in thorough and systematic study: theology at Paris and law at Orleans. Loyola, on the other hand, was born into the Spanish nobility in the province of Guipuzcoa and showed an early interest in military matters rather than education.

These backgrounds determined the roads to their religious commitment. Calvin developed his spiritual awareness through his education; his writings show the influence of his training in law in the presentation of his ideas, while the radical content of his beliefs was stimulated initially by his growing interest in the works of Erasmus and Luther. The whole process was gradual and predictable. With Loyola the reverse was true. His commitment was the

32

result of conversion, which took place while he was suffering from a leg wound sustained while assisting in the defence of Pamplona, Navarre, against French attacks in 1521. He lived in great austerity until 1523, and education had little to do with his early devotion; he came to realize the importance of study after the failure of his mission to Palestine in 1523, and he attended the Universities of Alcalá (1526), Salamanca (1527) and Paris. Loyola, therefore, experienced a radical change, which Calvin did not.

Both became closely involved in the process of reform and regeneration. To some extent, however, the actual achievement of their status and influence was due to the current political situation; in the formative years both of their careers took unexpected turns. Calvin was expelled from the University of Paris in 1533 and fled to Basle with no obvious future. His opportunity came as a result of the situation in Geneva, which was in revolt against the Duchy of Savoy and had expelled the Catholic bishop. Calvin was invited to take up residence in Geneva to fill the gap left by the destruction of the Church hierarchy. His reforms were not universally popular and he spent a period in exile between 1538 and 1541 before his regime became really effective. Loyola's opportunities were somewhat different. Like Calvin, he incurred the displeasure of the authorities, his trouble with the Spanish Inquisition being one of the main reasons for the continuation of his studies in France rather than in Spain. By 1537 he had conceived a plan to pursue a holy life in Palestine (despite the failure of his attempt to convert the Muslims there between 1523 and 1524) and he formed the *Compaña de Jesú* for this purpose. This, however, was thwarted by a war between Venice and the Turks, which affected normal sea routes to the Middle East. Loyola took the momentous decision to devote his order to the service of the Pope and this was given recognition in the bull *Regimini militantis ecclesiae* in 1540. Rome was the headquarters of the society and, like Geneva, soon became the centre of a process of religious conversion and widespread political influence.

The main part of Calvin's doctrinal teachings is contained in his *Institutes of the Christian Religion* (1536) and in his *Reply to Sadoleto* (1540); Loyola's ideas are set forth in his *Spiritual Exercises*, compiled during the 1520s. The contrast between them is considerable.

The most obvious is their attitude to the Catholic Church. According to Calvin, the hierarchy of the Church was based on 'usurped instruments of tyranny and ambition'[1] and authority should be restored to the 'magistrates' or civil government. Calvin was far more uncompromising than Luther in his rejection of the claims of the Church to provide the only true interpretation of the scriptures and to act as an essential intermediary between man and God. By contrast, Loyola insisted on total obedience to all doctrine as interpreted by the Church. The first of the Rules for Thinking with the Church contained in the *Spiritual Exercises* stated: 'Laying aside all private judgement, we ought to hold our minds prepared and prompt to obey in all things the true Spouse of Christ our Lord, which is our Holy Mother, the hierarchical Church.'[2] Furthermore, according to the Thirteenth Rule: 'To arrive at the truth in all things, we ought always to be ready to believe that what seems to us white is black, if the hierarchical Church so defines it.' What Calvin attempted to destroy, therefore, Loyola sought to uphold and preserve.

As a result of his radical views Calvin became a doctrinal innovator. His main departure from Catholic ideas was his emphasis on predestination, although he claimed that the concepts of grace and predestination were evident in the early teachings of the Church and that therefore 'our agreement with antiquity is far closer than yours'.[1] The Church had 'nefariously effaced' predestination from the memory of man, and 'those who shut the gates that no-one may dare to seek a taste of this doctrine wrong man no less than God'.[3] Loyola showed the innate caution of the Catholic Church in dealing with the issue. He did not deny the validity of predestination but observed in the Fourteenth Rule: 'Although it is very true that no-one can be saved unless he is predestined, and has faith and grace, we must be very careful in our manner of speaking and treating of these subjects.'[2] Indeed, according to the Fifteenth Rule: 'We ought not habitually to speak much of predestination.' Loyola was convinced that overemphasis on predestination would result in the paralysis of man's own striving for salvation and that the role of 'good works' would be considerably undermined. He also feared that this 'poisonous teaching' would destroy the whole basis of 'free will', a vital part of man's relationship with God. On the whole he avoided any detailed interpretation of the concepts of grace, faith and predestination and relied on the official pronouncements of the Church. The Jesuit contribution to the debate came later, when Louis Molina in his *De liberi arbitrii cum gratia donis concordia*

Calvinism and the Jesuits

(1588) tried to provide a synthesis between predestination and free will.

Calvin's attack on the Church included a revision of the sacraments which was again based on the assumption that Catholicism had departed from early practices. 'In the sacraments, all we have attempted is to restore the native purity from which they had degenerated, and so enable them to resume their dignity.'[1] In the process, he roundly condemned 'your gross doctrine of transubstantiation'. Loyola upheld the sacraments in their entirety and devoted the Second, Third, Fourth and Fifth Rules for Thinking with the Church to the importance of regular and complete observance. The rejection of Calvin's revision by the Jesuits was followed by the strengthening of the role of the sacraments in the Catholic Church by the Council of Trent (1545–63). The Jesuits were therefore the spearhead of orthodoxy in upholding traditional institutions.

Calvinists and Jesuits differed totally in their attitude to ceremony and the use of the senses. Calvin was uncompromisingly hostile to 'the accursed worship of images'[1] and referred to Church ceremonies as 'childish in their import, and vitiated by innumerable forms of superstition'. Loyola, however, firmly believed in the importance of sensuousness in private devotion and in public worship; the Eighth Rule therefore called Catholics 'to praise the building and adornment of churches, and also images, and to venerate them according to what they represent'. He also upheld 'pilgrimages, indulgences, jubilees, crusades and candles lighted in churches' (Sixth Rule). Again, the Council of Trent affirmed the importance of ritual, refusing to come to terms with any form of Protestantism. In 1530 Luther had attempted to initiate a measure of doctrinal compromise between Protestantism and Catholicism. Such a prospect, however, became increasingly unlikely as Calvinism exerted more radical influences in one direction and the Society of Jesus restored the concept of the Church militant in the other.

The institutions set up by Calvin and Loyola were intended to be self-contained and capable of close co-operation with political authority or, if necessary, of survival in the face of political opposition and persecution. There was, however, a fundamental difference in purpose. Calvinist organization, as laid down in the *Ecclesiastical Ordinances* (1541), was designed to replace the previous hierarchy

35

of the Catholic Church in Geneva and to establish close co-operation between secular authorities and the Calvinist ministry in defining and regulating all doctrine and morality. Calvinism, therefore, affected the lives of the entire population. The Jesuits, on the other hand, were in essence a minority movement operating within the framework of the Church. The basis of the Order was Loyola's *Constitutions* (1550) and its purpose, as defined in the papal bull of 1540, was to educate, to propagate Christianity and to hear confessions. The Society of Jesus was so successful as a pressure group with an almost military structure and as the guardian of the interests of the larger institution which it served that later non-religious bodies imitated aspects of its organization.

Both Calvinism and the Society of Jesus stressed the importance of obedience, discipline and morality, and the details of their institutions were directed towards these. These details, however, were so different that they are difficult to compare directly. Calvinism in Geneva was based upon four main types of official: pastors, who were responsible for religious activities and for the care of souls, teachers or doctors, who interpreted the scriptures, elders, who regulated moral discipline and deacons, who dispensed funds and cared for the poor. Doctrine and morality were enforced by the Consistory, which comprised six pastors and twelve lay elders. With the full co-operation of the City Council they imposed punishments for a variety of offences ranging from drinking and swearing to heresy and witchcraft. The death sentence was frequently applied in Geneva, and victims included the writers Gruet (1547) and Servetus (1553). The Jesuits, by contrast, made no claims to state assistance in the enforcement of morality or orthodoxy: more serious cases were seen to be within the scope of the Spanish Inquisition, while censorship was directed by the Vatican in the form of the *Index librorum prohibitorum*, established by Pope Paul IV in 1559. The organization and rule of the Jesuits proved to be more complex than those of Calvinism even though they affected only a few, those who voluntarily entered the Order. Membership included novices, who trained for a probationary period of two years, lay brothers and scholastics of the second class, 'coadjutors' of the third class, and the 'professed' of the fourth class, usually about one tenth of the entire organization.[4] The overall leader was the General of the Order, under the personal authority of the Pope, and the central institution was the General Congregation. The Society of Jesus was, therefore, a compromise; it

Calvinism and the Jesuits

reaffirmed the importance of the role of the religious order, which both Luther and Calvin had rejected, but it substituted worldly contact and semi-military discipline for the more extreme asceticism of monasticism.

What was the impact of Calvinism and the Society of Jesus? Loyola died in 1556 and Calvin in 1564, by which time their influence was already deeply rooted. The second half of the sixteenth century saw a struggle between Calvinism and reformed Catholicism, spearheaded by the Jesuits, in most of Europe. Calvinism established itself firmly in the northern Netherlands, Scotland and several German states, including the Palatinate; other areas, including France, Bohemia, England, Poland and Hungary, saw Calvinism emerging as a militant minority movement. Geographically it is more difficult to assess precisely the spread of Jesuit influence, since it was part of the more general offensive of the Counter Reformation. Usually, however, the Jesuits were most successful in those areas which had become partially Lutheran, such as Austria, Bavaria and Hungary, or in combating the new threat of Calvinism, especially in the southern Netherlands and Poland.

Of primary importance to the success of Calvinism was its ability to harmonize with the political authority (as in the Netherlands) or to establish a cohesive opposition unit (as in France and Scotland). The latter involved adapting some of Calvin's ideas and superimposing concepts of resistance and natural law – Languet and Buchanan provided approval, in certain cases, for rebellion. The Jesuits, too, operated on a political plane, although they were rarely directly associated with political institutions. They overcame the traditional Catholic abhorrence for regicide which was so pronounced in the writings of St Thomas Aquinas, and developed an acceptance of regicide in those instances where Catholic interests were threatened. This explains Jesuit involvement in various plots to overthrow Elizabeth (whom the Pope had excommunicated as a 'Calvinist'). The Jesuits increased their influence over those in high places. They established themselves as confessors to most of the leading Catholic monarchs of Europe by the end of the sixteenth century and, as such, were able to exert political pressure through advice after consultation. The Emperors Rudolf II, Matthias, Ferdinand II and Ferdinand III all had Jesuit confessors who had some influence on the events before and during the Thirty Years' War. It was not until the eighteenth century that the Jesuits came to be universally regarded as a source of political danger, and that the Catholic countries vied with each other in expelling them.

Education was regarded by both Calvinists and Jesuits as a crucial element in the process of conversion, although that provided by the Jesuits was more systematic, thorough and permanent. Calvin's emphasis on scriptural knowledge necessitated a widely literate population and it was to this that the main priority was given. Nevertheless, there was sometimes little attempt to go beyond basic requirements and any science subject was regarded with some suspicion. The Jesuits made a conscious decision to aim at the higher reaches of the educative process in Europe, concentrating on secondary and university education, often leaving the gap of primary education to be filled by other Orders. They provided the most systematic structure for secondary education until the state eventually assumed responsibility over three hundred years later. The courses provided by the Jesuits included not only doctrinal training as defined by the Council of Trent but also teaching in the sciences.

The vitality and irrepressible nature of Calvinism and the Society of Jesus resulted inevitably in the spread of their activities outside Europe. Again, the reasons and results were different. Calvinism was not exported as a deliberate policy but as part of a series of refugee movements from persecution in Europe. The two main examples were the origins of the North American colonies in the early seventeenth century and the development of the Cape Colony in the late seventeenth and early eighteenth centuries. Puritans and Huguenots carried with them the basic ethos of Calvinism, including the doctrine of predestination which was adapted to the rigours of frontier societies and assumed a greater degree of harshness as a result. Calvinist settlers set themselves apart from, struggled with, and overcame the indigenous populations whom they encountered. The Jesuits spread their influence with greater calculation and planning, the scope of their activity extending from China and India, through much of Africa to most of the South American continent. They made careful study of the areas which they intended to convert and frequently tried to harmonize their activities, practices and doctrine with indigenous customs. Their willingness to experiment, which produced among other things the

Calvinism and the Jesuits

famous Paraguay settlement, sometimes brought them into conflict with the colonial administrations of Spain and Portugal but this rarely acted as a deterrent. Increasingly, the Jesuits gave a spiritual purpose to Spanish and Portuguese imperialism; at the same time Calvinism was contributing much to the initial impetus of colonial activity for the countries of Western Europe.

6

The Counter Reformation

During the Middle Ages the Catholic Church had frequently been confronted by heresy and the threat of schism. Yet it had survived intact, only to be taken completely by surprise by the Reformation. Initially, reformers like Luther were regarded as no more serious a threat than the Waldensians and the Albigensians in the twelfth and thirteenth centuries or the Hussites in the fifteenth. The papacy, which had reached its lowest ebb by the turn of the fifteenth century, largely because of the process of secularization explained in Chapter 2, was probably quite unaware that the Protestant Reformation was potentially more dangerous than a medieval heresy with minority appeal.

The Church became much more conscious of the grave threat of disintegration during the 1520s and 1530s, took action during the 1540s and 1550s and seemed to have placed itself firmly on the offensive by the 1560s. It adjusted to this change by coming to terms with two basic questions. First, how could the Catholic Church, which Wycliffe had once described as 'the Synagogue of Satan',[1] resist the growth of further offshoots from its trunk? And second, how could the Lutherans, Calvinists and Anabaptists be prevented from making too many converts at the expense of Catholicism? The first was dealt with by a carefully structured movement of internal reform to eliminate those abuses which had precipitated the emergence of Protestantism. This is generally covered by the description 'Catholic Reformation' (some historians, in fact, see this process as being more typical of a reformation than the achievements of

The Counter Reformation

Protestantism, which they regard as revolutionary). The second provoked a more militant response, best described as a 'Counter Reformation'; the Church identified its enemies more accurately and developed a series of instruments with which to eradicate them. Although internal reform (by the 'Catholic Reformation') and external action (by the 'Counter Reformation') were part of the same process of Catholic regeneration in the sixteenth century, it is worth separating them for the purpose of analysis.

The Catholic Reformation took the form of spiritual revival, movement towards institutional improvement, and attempts to heal the schism by trying to come to some form of agreement with Protestants on the basis of shared beliefs.

During the Middle Ages the Church had been assisted in times of crisis by an apparently spontaneous growth of several new religious orders which had purified it spiritually and, for a while, strengthened its institutions. The eleventh century produced the Order at Cluny, sanctioned by Gregory VII, while the thirteenth century saw the recognition of the Dominicans and Franciscans. This process of revival through inner regeneration was resumed in the sixteenth century; it was no coincidence that the period in which the Church faced its greatest danger also saw the most intensive activity of religious orders and of individuals who were inspired by mystical fervour. Spain led the way, with St Ignatius Loyola (1491–1556), who established the Society of Jesus, St Teresa (1515–82) and St John of the Cross (1542–91). Italy, meanwhile, produced the Cappuchines (1529), the Barnabites (1530), the Ursulines (1535) and a series of Oratories and Brotherhoods, the most famous of which was the Oratory of Divine Love in Rome (1517). The general effect was to emphasize the need for institutional reform, particularly in the Papal Curia, and to bridge some of the gap between clergy and laity which had given Protestantism so many prospects for recruitment.

This need for reform was not an awareness suddenly reached in the late 1520s and 1530s. It had been realized by a series of Cardinals and Popes, including Adrian VI (1522–3), but little had been accomplished. The turning point came in 1527 with the sack of Rome by the troops of the Emperor Charles V. This had a profound psychological impact on the Church. It occurred, according to an Italian bishop, 'because all flesh has become corrupt; we are citizens not of the holy city of Rome, but of Babylon, the city of corruption'.[2]

Aspects of European History 1494–1789

Thus reform became more urgent because its delay seemed to have incurred a terrible divine reminder. The first major step was the appointment of a Reform Commission of Cardinals by Pope Paul III which reported in the *Consilium directorum cardinalium de emendanda ecclesia* (1537) that the major problem was the secularization of the papacy itself and that major change could be accomplished only from above. 'You have taken the name of Paul. We hope that you will imitate his charity . . . you, we hope . . . have been chosen . . . to heal our sickness, to unite Christ's sheep again in one fold, and to avert from our heads the wrath and already threatening vengeance of God.'[2]

How could this be accomplished? The Papal Curia resisted the measures taken by Paul III in 1538 to end absenteeism and nepotism, and it became apparent that a major institutional development would be needed. Again, the Church produced a medieval idea as a solution, the convocation of a Church Council, although one designed to be more productive than the brief sessions of 1512 and 1536. The Council of Constance (1417) had expressed the possibility of conciliarism as an instrument of reform in its Decree *Frequens*: 'A frequent celebration of general councils is an especial means for cultivating the field of the Lord and effecting the destruction of briers, thorns and thistles, to wit, heresies, errors and schism.'[3] The Council of Constance had, in 1415, considered itself appropriately constituted and sufficiently representative to undertake a 'general reformation of the Church'.[4] The Council of Trent, which convened in the years 1545–7, 1551–2 and 1562–3, saw the partial and successful application of these principles and the accomplishment of a series of reforms by conciliar recommendation, largely under pressure from the Spanish delegation. These included a ban on the use of monetary Indulgences, new attention to the education of the clergy by means of theological seminaries, and a close examination of the duties and responsibilities of bishops. The reforming spirit seems, therefore, to have arisen from the grass roots of the religious orders and to have become institutionalized as a result of a closer co-operation between the papacy and the Church Councils. There was, however, no radical innovation. The revival of Councils was not based on any weakening of papal authority or the establishment of any real democratic process. The sixteenth-century Church came to terms with its problems within a thoroughly traditional and hierarchical framework.

42

The Counter Reformation

The Catholic Reformation attempted to win Lutheran converts back to the Church by argument and doctrinal compromise, at least until 1541. From the beginning of the threatened secession, Catholic theologians like Eck and Cajetan engaged in disputations with Luther. During the 1520s the Papal Curia included moderating groups who believed that the Lutheran emphasis on justification by faith could be accommodated within the body of the Church's teachings. This, it was argued, was due to the nature of the medieval Church, which had not undertaken any really rigid definition of doctrine and had allowed, for example, the development of Augustinian and Thomist interpretations. Protestantism was, in effect, a further exploration of the Augustinian approach, while late medieval Scholasticism had been based more on the methods of St Thomas Aquinas. The majority of the papal party still branded Lutheranism as heresy and stated categorically that re-assimilation could not take place without fundamental doctrinal changes. For a while, however, moderation had a say, and some sort of doctrinal synthesis was sought at Ratisbon in 1541. Only when this failed did the Church finally give up hope of winning back Protestants by compromise and begin to concentrate all its resources on the use of coercion.

This was the main characteristic of the Counter Reformation. It would be a mistake to see 1541 as a dividing line between the Catholic Reformation and the Counter Reformation, as each operated throughout the century. But the emphasis of the earlier period was mainly on internal reform, while the later period saw a much more militant approach to the problem of separatism.

Effective treatment of the enemy required easy preliminary identification. This was one of the basic purposes of the doctrinal decrees emanating from the Council of Trent. The majority of the delegates, who were staunchly behind the Pope, believed that dogma should be tightened so as to remove the area of ambiguity within which the moderates of both Catholicism and Protestantism had worked to effect a compromise. Between 1545 and 1547 the Council of Trent emphatically denounced the Protestant emphasis on justification by faith, reaffirming the role of the sacraments and the power of the Church to act as an intermediary between man and God. It also declared that the traditions of the Church were of equal importance to the scriptures, thus warning that any individual interpretation ran the risk of lapsing into heresy. In 1562 the Council restored in full the credibility of purgatory, invocation of the saints and the absolute supremacy of the Pope. The uncompromising nature of the decrees is evident in the frequently repeated phrase applying to anyone of a different view: 'Let him be anathema.' Not: 'Let him be persuaded.'

One of the major obstacles to reconciliation between Protestants and the Church had been that of papal supremacy. The Catholic Reformation accepted it but, within the prevailing atmosphere of papal corruption, with understandable reservations. Some of the more democratic sentiments of Nicholas of Cusa still exerted a slight influence, as did the declaration of the Council of Constance (1415) that 'this Synod, legally assembled, is a general council, and represents the Catholic church militant and has the authority to speak directly from Christ; and everybody, of whatever rank or dignity, including also the Pope, is bound to obey this council'.[4] The Counter Reformation, however, based its attack on Protestantism on a total reaffirmation of papal power. Pius II had anticipated this in his 1459 bull *Execrabilis*, in which he described any process undermining the authority of 'the vicar of Jesus Christ' as 'pestiferous poison'.[5] The Council of Trent saw open, if not unanimous, approval of papal autocracy, agreeing that no Conciliar recommendations could be applied without papal sanction. In return, the papacy was expected to provide the vanguard of the counter offensive against Protestantism, which it did with the assistance of militant orders, like the Jesuits, and specially adapted instruments, like the Inquisition and the Index.

The Spanish Inquisition, set up during the reign of Ferdinand and Isabella for the suppression of religious minorities, was imported into Rome in 1542 as the Holy Office. The date, significantly, is one year later than the failure of doctrinal discussions with the Protestants at Ratisbon; the use of the Inquisition exemplifies the abandonment of conciliation in any form. The Regulations of the Holy Office contained what could have been the battle cry of the Counter Reformation: 'No man must debase himself by showing toleration toward heretics of any kind.'[6] Pope Paul IV (1555–9) who, as Cardinal Caraffa, had been instrumental in getting the Inquisition established in Italy, put this view even more forcefully: 'Even if my father were a heretic, I would gather wood to burn him.'[6] A medieval approach, certainly, but the result, in practical terms, was

The Counter Reformation

remarkably successful. Italy was virtually purged of Lutheranism, just as Spain had been of heresy. An effort was also made to control the output of religious and secular literature from the printing presses. Pope Alexander VI had first pointed out the dual nature of printing in his bull of 1501: 'The art of printing is very useful in so far as it furthers the circulation of useful and tested books; but it can be very harmful if it is permitted to widen the influence of pernicious works.'[7] Paul IV formally established the *Index auctorum et librorum prohibitorum* (Index of Prohibited Authors and Books) in 1559, which rapidly became the main means of issuing papal approval or condemnation of any publication. The Counter Reformation also spread its influence to painting and music in an effort to integrate culture more closely with the aspirations of the Church and to establish visual and other types of sensuous assistance for Catholic doctrine.

The two areas most closely connected with the Catholic Reformation and the Counter Reformation were Spain and Rome. Spain provided the influence for both reform and counter offensive, while Rome provided leadership and institutions.

During her struggle with the Moors in the *Reconquista* Spain had developed a crusading spirit which made her the most militant of Catholic states and certainly the most accustomed to fighting religious dissent. But she also had the greatest capacity for internal ecclesiastical reform, as the activities of Cardinal Ximenes proved, and for religious devotion (hence the considerable number of mystics and orders originating in Spain). Without the Spanish example it is doubtful whether Catholic regeneration could ever have got under way. Rome, after all, was the centre of corruption, and needed a powerful shove from outside.

The existing hierarchical nature of the Church could be retained only if change was led by the papacy. Hence the Spanish initiative in the Catholic and Counter Reformations had to pass to Rome. The process was a gradual one; Spanish religious fervour influenced the growth of Italian orders and oratories which, in turn, prevailed upon the Popes to sponsor reform. The most obvious link between Spain and Rome was the official recognition by Pope Paul III in 1540 of the Society of Jesus. With a leader of Spanish origin, this dedicated itself to the full restoration of Roman authority. The Jesuits were among the papal party's most influential spokesmen at the Council of Trent. The papacy was not, however, inclined to extend its acceptance of Spanish religious influences to being politically subservient to Spain. The Neapolitan Pope Paul IV (1555–9) engaged in constant diplomacy against Philip II for the ejection of Spanish political power from southern Italy.

Other areas made their own adaptations to the Catholic and Counter Reformations. The Italian states, which had been the most secular area in Europe at the time of the Renaissance, had been battered into submission by a series of invasions by Catholic powers in the Italian Wars. They all accepted the Inquisition, although Venice was less heavily influenced than the others. Spain continued in the fervour which had started the process of regeneration, now reactivating it in a sporadic but unsuccessful attack on northern Protestantism. Austria and the southern German states also adopted a political and military solution to the religious divisions within the Holy Roman Empire, their conflict with Calvinism and other Protestant sects eventually leading to the Thirty Years' War. France experienced a more immediate purge in the form of civil war. All of these were examples of the final emergence of the papacy and its hierarchy from corruption, and the renewal of the concept of the Church Militant.

7

The Political Development
of Spain 1474–1598

The Iberian Peninsula experienced more intense political upheaval
before the sixteenth century than almost any other part of Europe.
Until the fifth century AD the region was the province of Hispania
within the Roman Empire; it was then conquered by invading
Germanic tribes and became the independent Visigothic kingdom
between 466 and 711. The last King of the Visigoths, Roderic, was
defeated by the Moors, who, inspired by the new and militant faith of
Islam, had crossed over from North Africa with the intention of
conquering Western Europe. By the eighth century the Moors were
actually advancing across the Pyrenees, but their progress was
arrested and reversed by their defeat at the hands of the Franks at
the Battle of Tours (732). The Moors retreated into Spain and, for the
next seven centuries, struggled to hold their conquests. Gradually,
however, a series of Christian states emerged, initially in the north
and then spreading their influence into central Spain. The main
ambition of rulers like Ferdinand the Great (1035–65) of Castile
and Alfonso the Warrior (1102–34) of Aragon, and of military
commanders like Rodrigo Diaz (*El Cid*), was to drive the Moors out
of the entire Peninsula.

Although the process of the *Reconquista* continued slowly and
successfully, the Christian Kingdoms of Aragon, Castile, Navarre
and Portugal frequently came into conflict with each other. The
turning point came in 1469 with the marriage between Isabella
(who became Queen of Castile on the death of Enrique IV in 1474)
and Ferdinand (who succeeded Juan II as King of Aragon in 1479).

Aspects of European History 1494-1789

Although Castile and Aragon were brought under one crown, however, they were not forced together constitutionally as a unitary state. Each retained its own possessions abroad (which meant that the foreign policies of Aragon and Castile were based on very different interests) and its own identity and character. Nevertheless, Ferdinand and Isabella ruled the Kingdoms with a common overall policy and on the basis of a shared heritage, culture and religion.

The main achievement of the new reign was the extension of royal authority. This was accomplished by more frequent use of royal councils in central government, more effective control over the nobility, the appointment of royal officials in local government, and a reduction of the powers of the legislatures of both Aragon and Castile. The whole process, however, was gradual and did not involve a revolution from above.

A widespread institution in the Middle Ages had been the *Curia Regis*, a Great Council possessed by many European monarchies. Composed of the leading members of the nobility, this had advised the Crown and had been an integral part of the feudal hierarchy. As the medieval period drew to a close, the *Curia Regis* of several countries contracted into a more specialized council, in which the King was served by a limited number of professional advisers and ministers. An example of this was the emergence of the *Conseil des Affaires* in France, and much the same happened in Spain. The great medieval Councils of Castile and Aragon were extensively reorganized in 1480 and 1494 respectively. Previously the highest members of the nobility had predominated, but after the reforms they lost their advisory capacity and their right to vote, both of which were assumed by *letrados*, royal servants who had received a legal training. The two Royal Councils, which maintained separate territorial jurisdiction, were responsible for the supervision of all internal affairs and justice. They also set a precedent for the establishment of the complex conciliar system which governed sixteenth-century Spain. Further contributions by Ferdinand and Isabella were the Council of the Inquisition (1483), the Council of Military Orders (1495) and the Council of *Cruzada* (1509).

The extension of royal power was accomplished, as in other countries, partly at the expense of the nobility. At first the Castilian nobles posed a potential threat. Over the centuries they had

48

amassed considerable powers, and the constant warfare with the Moors had enabled them to set up a series of military orders capable of fighting as independent units. When the crusades against the Moors ended, the continuation of these orders presented a challenge to royal supremacy. Any attempt to disband them could well have precipitated major revolts, and the solution had to be more subtle. The Pope was persuaded to agree to a new procedure whereby Ferdinand acquired the power to fill the Grand Mastership of each of the orders (which had, of course, dedicated themselves to the papacy) as it became vacant. Overmighty subjects also faced the prospect of prosecution by special judicial commissioners, or of having their estates and financial assets confiscated by the Crown under Acts of Resumption. On the whole, the monarchy aimed at curbing the power of the great feudal lords by elevating the lower nobility and even members of the bourgeoisie as a reward for loyal service.

The aristocracy was not the only separatist element in Spain. Many of the walled cities of Castile had a long history of semi-independence and had been granted charters of liberties during the Middle Ages. Most possessed their own assembly and officials, or *Regidores*. Royal policy was based on a carefully considered compromise. Municipal privileges were not withdrawn, but new real officials, known as *Corregidores*, were appointed to assume joint responsibility with the *Regidores* for judicial and administrative duties. The Crown made a similar decision to retain but regulate traditional institutions in suppressing violence, especially in the areas of Galicia and Andalusia. Brigandage, a by-product of the violent era of the *Reconquista*, was dealt with by the revival of the *Santa Hermandad* (Holy Brotherhood), which was given powers of arrest, detention and summary justice. The majority of lawbreakers in rural areas passed through *Hermandad* courts and the incidence of banditry was greatly reduced by the end of the fifteenth century.

The major institutional casualty caused by the extension of royal authority was the legislature which, in all Spanish Kingdoms, had been accustomed to considerable power. The Cortes of Aragon, for example, insisted on a curious formula as an oath of loyalty to the King: 'We, who are as good as you, swear to you, who are no better than we, to accept you as our King and sovereign lord, provided you observe all our liberties and laws; but if not, not.'[1] Isabella complained frequently about this attitude and once asserted that 'it would be better to reduce the Aragonese by arms than to tolerate the arrogance of their Cortes'.[2] But such an extreme measure was never seriously considered. Instead, the Crown gradually reduced its dependence on the Cortes by building up a financial reserve through the resumption of previously alienated lands and property and through a more intensive application of the tax known as the *alcabala*. The Cortes of both Aragon and Castile remained in existence but their role was increasingly to confirm royal policy. Wherever possible, the Crown avoided confrontation and reduced the scope and frequency of the sessions. The first two estates of the Cortes of Castile were rarely summoned, and there were only 36 representatives of the third estate from a total of 18 cities.[3] Between 1475 and 1503 the Cortes of Castile met a total of nine times and was not convened at all between 1482 and 1498.[4]

Ferdinand and Isabella presided over a relatively uncomplicated transition from a series of semi-feudal kingdoms into a federal state based upon a powerful monarchy which was served by an effective bureaucracy. In 1516 Spain was politically stable. The bureaucracy grew during the rest of the sixteenth century, but administration was not necessarily more efficient.

The first three years of Charles I's reign as King of Spain (from 1516) were relatively uneventful, but his decision to contest the Imperial Crown in 1519 brought many problems to Spain. When he became Emperor his priorities inevitably changed: his political ambitions increased and he came to regard himself as the secular leader of Christendom whose role was to establish a universal empire and overcome heresy. His territorial responsibilities were enormous and he found it impossible to create an overall system of government to administer Spain, the Empire, Austria, Burgundy and the Italian possessions. The result was that each of his dominions had to develop its own constitutional arrangements, the guiding principle of which was usually to maintain an administration which could function in Charles's absence.

Between 1516 and his abdication in 1556, Charles spent a total of 16 years in Spain (1517–20, 1522–9, 1533–5, 1536–9 and 1541–3).[5] Yet, after the initial problem of the revolt of the *communeros* of Castile in 1520, Spain continued to develop a basically stable constitution. The conciliar system, used by Ferdinand and Isabella to increase the power of the Crown, was the key. This was greatly augmented but also modified so that the power of the Crown need not necessarily be equated with the personal authority of the King. To the advisory and departmental councils were added the Council of War in 1517, the Council of State (for general policy) in 1522 and the Council of Finance in 1523. The gradual acquisition of an overseas empire by Castile led to an additional territorial council. In 1524 the Council of the Indies was set up to supervise the administration of Spain's colonies in America, and was partially modelled on the Council of Castile. The Council of the Indies was responsible for the activities of colonial officials, like the Viceroys of New Spain and Peru, and of advisory councils like the *Audiencias*. The conciliar system thus became increasingly complex, but generally worked well because of the exceptional ability of some of the administrators to whom Charles delegated his authority during his absences; the most famous of these was Francisco de los Cobos, who held the conciliar system together in the 1530s and 1540s.

The political development of Spain during the reign of Charles V was stable but it could not be described as healthy. Bureaucracy grew very rapidly to compensate for an absentee King; the legislature continued to decline, thus reducing the scope for opposition to royal policy; finally, all Spain's institutions were subordinated to one overriding principle: that Spain should provide the resources for an ambitious foreign policy which affected most of Europe. Political development, therefore, was accompanied by rash diplomacy and severe economic problems.

With Philip II (1556–98) the Spanish monarchy came home. When Charles abdicated in 1556 he divided his dominions between his brother, Ferdinand (who became Holy Roman Emperor) and his son, Philip (who was King of Spain and Duke of Burgundy). Philip was therefore relieved of the necessity of touring one dominion after another and was able to adopt a fixed government. His main contributions to Spanish constitutional development were the establishment of a permanent capital, the increase of the personal involvement of the Crown in government, and the further extension of the range of the bureaucracy.

Being a Spaniard by birth and upbringing, Philip was determined to avoid the peripatetic habits of his father and he selected Madrid as his capital, using the Palace of the Escorial, built to his specifications some twenty miles away, as his administrative headquarters. This reduced the delay in communication between King and royal officials but it did not eliminate it altogether. Many argued that a seaport rather than the geographical centre of Spain should have been chosen as the seat of government. This assertion seems particularly appropriate to the period after 1580, when Spain acquired Portugal and a second overseas empire; Philip's foreign policy might have assumed a great maritime emphasis and been more successful against England and the Netherlands if he had moved his capital from Madrid to Seville or even Lisbon. As it was, Madrid and the Escorial became symbolic of Spain's ties to a Continental policy similar in scope to that of Charles V.

Philip II believed in close personal involvement in the process of administration and that his duties were primarily to ensure the impartial dispensation of justice, to protect the Church and Inquisition and to uproot heresy. He had a considerable capacity for hard work, a quality essential for administration. Unfortunately, he was unable to delegate responsibility; too often he concentrated on the details of administration rather than the formulation of policy, with the result that the presence of the King actually slowed the whole process down.

The conciliar system continued to expand. One example was the evolution of the *Cámara de Castilla*, originally a core of advisers within the Royal Council of Castile, into a council within its own right in 1588. The main emphasis, however, was on councils covering an ever wider area territorially. This was strictly in line with Philip's decision to reside permanently in Spain: institutions and officials were necessary to administer Spanish territory and commitments elsewhere in Europe. Shortly before his abdication Charles V had introduced the Council of Italy (assuming the role of the Council of Aragon); this was maintained and extended by Philip II. The Council of Portugal was established in 1582 (two years after the union between Spain and Portugal) and the Council of Flanders in 1588. In addition to these Councils, the administration of Spanish possessions in Europe also involved Viceroys, who were responsible to the relevant Council and corresponded with the King and his secretaries. The Councils of Italy and Portugal were relatively successful, but the Council of Flanders was introduced far too late to stem the revolt of the Netherlands against Spanish rule. The Spanish conciliar structure is shown in Fig. 1.

Philip II's personal contributions to Spanish constitutional

Spanish Political Development 1474–1598

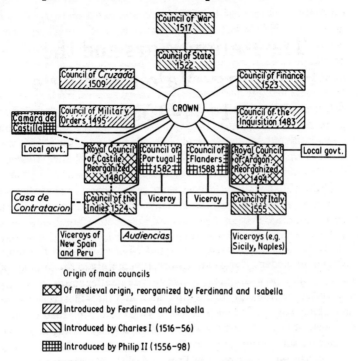

Origin of main councils

▓ Of medieval origin, reorganized by Ferdinand and Isabella

▨ Introduced by Ferdinand and Isabella

▧ Introduced by Charles I (1516–56)

▦ Introduced by Philip II (1556–98)

Fig. 1   Spanish Councils in the sixteenth century

growth were generally negative. The administration was hampered by the decreased efficiency of a bureaucracy which had adapted itself to the need to act on behalf of an absentee King but now found itself supervised by one who made his presence constantly felt and who was too meticulous over detail. He also showed a new intensity of intolerance to opposition and to minorities, stating that he would rather resign his throne than rule heretics. His use of the Inquisition to enforce orthodoxy resulted in the rebellion of the Moriscos (1568–70) and the Dutch revolt, while the excessively Castilian nature of his regime precipitated strong resentment in Aragon between 1591 and 1592. As a ruler, Philip II was never universally popular among his subjects, and Protestant Europe regarded him as the personification of tyranny. Perhaps he could more accurately be described as a dedicated royal bureaucrat whose lack of an overall sense of perspective stretched Spain's resources to breaking point.

8

The Italian Wars and the Habsburg–Valois Struggle 1494–1559

The series of wars between 1494 and 1559 are among the most complex in modern European history, due mainly to the number of participants, the willingness of many of the smaller states to change sides after a round of intricate diplomacy and the widespread use of mercenary troops. The wars can be divided into two broad phases. Between 1494 and 1516 they were confined largely to Italy and were concerned with the acquisition of territory. Between 1522 and 1559 they spread into other parts of Europe and the Mediterranean and became a life and death struggle between the Valois Kings of France and the Habsburg ruler of Austria and Spain. The expanding scope of the wars was due to the fruition of Maximilian I's marriage alliances which, by conferring enormous areas of territory on Charles V, intensified French fears of encirclement.

Every century has seen a part of Europe which is wealthy enough to be a great temptation to its neighbours because of its internal political disunity and weakness. Poland was exploited in the eighteenth century, Germany in the seventeenth and Italy at the beginning of the sixteenth. A contemporary Italian historian described Italy's attractions in 1490: 'not only did Italy abound in inhabitants, merchandise and riches, but she was also highly renowned for the magnificence of many princes, for the splendour of so many most noble and beautiful cities, as the seat of majesty and religion'.[1] On the other hand, the lack of effective centralized leadership caused Italy to be the scene of warfare and destruction. Machiavelli considered that she was 'more enslaved than the Hebrews, more widely scattered than the Athenians; leaderless, lawless, crushed, despoiled, torn, overrun'.[2]

What were the attractions of Italy for other European states? The main consideration was undoubtedly Italy's strategic and geographical importance as the cockpit of Europe. Later, when the balance of power shifted northwards, the Netherlands, Germany and Poland would come to occupy this unfortunate position. But, at the end of the fifteenth century and during the first few decades of the sixteenth, Italy seemed the most attractive area for the future expansion of the major powers. French expansion was directed south-east into Savoy and Milan, and then into central and southern Italy. The Emperor Maximilian I, in his capacity as guardian of the Empire, claimed the northern territories of Italy which, with the exception of Venice, were still legally within the frontiers of the Holy Roman Empire. As head of the Austrian Habsburgs, Maximilian intended to acquire territory along a southern and south-western axis, thus coming into direct conflict with French claims in northern Italy; France and the Empire were on opposite sides for most of the Italian Wars, with the notable exception of the League of Cambrai (1508). Ferdinand of Aragon acquired a major interest in southern Italy. In 1494 he already possessed Sicily and Sardinia and proposed to expand Aragon's territorial control into Naples and central Italy in order to make Aragon a major Mediterranean power and to complement the growing maritime and colonial activity of Castile. The result was a clash between Aragon and France, with a more or less permanent alliance between Aragon and the Emperor. Turkish interest in Italy was, at first, cursory and was confined to coastal raids and reconnaissance. There can be little doubt, however, that the Sultans aimed at including parts of Italy in a vast Eastern Mediterranean Empire. Turkish involvement in Italy eventually became a serious factor after the Franco-Turkish Alliance of 1536.

This rivalry of major powers was drawn into Italy by the political anarchy which existed there. Italian states, in their constant wars and intrigues with each other, frequently brought in foreign assistance. For example, in 1494 Ludovico Sforza of Milan, fearing a secret alliance against him between Florence and Naples, invited Charles VIII of France to enforce a rather dubious French dynastic claim to Naples. In 1508 Pope Julius II started a war against Venice in the hope of capturing mainland Venetian territory for the papacy. He formed the League of Cambrai which was joined for a while by Aragon, the Empire and France. 1515 saw a struggle by Venice, supported by France and England, against Milan, Florence and the papacy, supported by Aragon and the Empire. There were other examples of major powers exploiting, and even creating, civil war in Italy and of a cynical attitude to diplomacy used by both Italian and foreign leaders. Despite all this, it should be emphasized that Machiavelli's exhortation for a united Italy was ahead of its time and that the renaissance princes of Italy regarded themselves and their states as autonomous political and diplomatic entities.

Another attraction for the major powers was the cultural reputation and wealth of Italy. Florence was seen as the cultural centre of Europe before the turn of the century, while Venice possessed a revenue which was almost equivalent to that of Spain. Foreign armies had a greater prospect of immediate reward and plunder, as the badly disciplined troops of Charles V later discovered in 1527 when they sacked Rome. Even as late as 1796 the myth of enormous Italian wealth survived, and Bonaparte told his troops on the eve of his first Italian campaign: 'I am about to lead you into the most fruitful plains in the world. Rich provinces, great cities will be in your power.'

The first phase of the Italian wars lasted from 1494 until 1516, the outcome being indecisive. By the Treaty of Noyon, concluded in 1516, France was in control of Milan, while Aragon had gained a permanent hold on Naples. The aspirations of the French, however, were unsatisfied and the individual Italian states remained open to influence and pressure from the major powers in the future, whether from France or from the Habsburgs.

The Habsburg–Valois struggles between 1522 and 1559 were a continuation of the Italian Wars with two new elements: the reduction of the number of combatants from three major powers to two (plus, at various stages, the Italian states and the Turks) and the spread of the conflict into other parts of Europe. The character of the struggle became more intense and bitter. The main reasons for this were Charles V's desire to protect his extensive dominions and Francis I's fear of being overwhelmed by the powerful Habsburg combination of Austria and Spain. By 1519 Charles was Holy Roman Emperor; King of Spain and her Italian possessions;

The Habsburg–Valois Struggle

Archduke of Austria; and Duke of Burgundy. His military commitments in defence of such a far-flung empire were greater than those of any ruler since Charlemagne.

Italy continued to be a major area of warfare. As Holy Roman Emperor from 1519 and King of Spain from 1516, Charles inherited the claims in Italy of both the Emperor Maximilian I and Ferdinand of Aragon. Aragon and the Emperor had usually fought on the same side during the previous phases of the Italian Wars; for example, as members of the League of Venice of 1495, their common enemy was France. Yet they usually fought independently of each other, the Emperor being interested mainly in northern Italy, while Aragon concentrated on Naples. They had often acted separately in diplomacy; for example, Aragon switched from the League of Cambrai to the Holy League before the Emperor; and Charles I negotiated the Treaty of Noyon with France in 1516 independently of the Empire. When, however, Charles I acquired the imperial crown in 1519 and became the Emperor Charles V as well as King of Spain, imperial and Spanish interests were united and the number of major participants in the wars in Italy was reduced from three to two: the Habsburg-Imperial bloc and France. The conflict in Italy initially went against France. Francis I was defeated at the Battle of Pavia (1525) and humiliated by the Treaty of Madrid (1526). His repudiation of the Treaty in the same year was followed by his participation in the League of Cognac against Charles, but the Treaty of Cambrai (1529) represented the lowest ebb of French influence and the apparent victory of the Habsburgs in Italy: Charles was crowned King of Italy by the Pope in 1530. The period of conflict between 1536 and 1538 was indecisive, for France had by now recovered from her early defeats, and had formed an alliance with the Turks in 1536. This period was ended by a compromise in the Truce of Nice in 1538. In the final phase, between 1552 and 1559, Italy was part of a general European conflict, the climax of the Habsburg–Valois struggle, which resulted in the abdication of Charles V in 1556 and the Treaty of Cateau Cambrésis in 1559.

As Duke of Burgundy, Charles V continued the traditional fifteenth-century rivalry between Burgundy and France. In 1477 Charles of Burgundy had been killed at the Battle of Nancy, and Maximilian (later Emperor Maximilian I) married Mary of Burgundy in the same year to protect what was left of Burgundy – the Netherlands, Luxemburg and Franche Comté. When these came

57

under the rule of Charles V they were yet another area for him to defend and they came to be regarded by France as increasingly vital. Francis I was obsessed with the Habsburg peril; for France was almost surrounded on the land side by Habsburg territories. Of these, however, the Burgundian lands were probably the weakest and they offered France future access into the Holy Roman Empire if she could conquer them. Hence Burgundy featured prominently in the Habsburg–Valois struggles. By the Treaty of Madrid (1526) France surrendered those parts of Flanders which she had previously conquered, and in 1529 she gave up all further claims to that area by the Treaty of Cambrai. Between 1542 and 1544 Henry II launched a French invasion of Luxemburg which, however, he restored to Habsburg rule by the Treaty of Crépy (1544), following a brief but threatening invasion of France by Charles V's armies. Eventually the Treaty of Cateau Cambrésis confirmed Habsburg rule over the Burgundian areas which Charles V had taken over in 1519. The real gains made by France in this direction were to be in the seventeenth century, under Mazarin and Louis XIV.

As Holy Roman Emperor, Charles V inherited the problem of defending the western frontier of the Empire, as well as the Burgundian territories, against French encroachments. The most vulnerable area was Lorraine, which extended from Luxemburg to Franche Comté. Francis I regarded this as another weak spot in the Habsburg defences and he intended to establish a French bridgehead for future operations deep into the Empire. Lorraine became particularly important after the accession of Henry II, who invaded the region in 1552, ostensibly to assist the Lutheran states in their struggle for survival against Charles V. The more tangible gains made by France during this campaign were the bishoprics of Metz, Toul and Verdun, French possession of which was confirmed in 1559.

The Habsburg forces of Austria and Spain, together with imperial resources, therefore came into increasing conflict with France across an ever widening front in the south and west. There was also a major threat in the east, this time from the Turks. In 1519 Charles succeeded Maximilian as Archduke of Austria, although he handed this title over to his brother Ferdinand in 1521. In 1526 Ferdinand added Bohemia and part of Hungary to the Habsburg dominions, territories which he acquired through his wife Anne, sister of King Lewis of Hungary and Bohemia. Lewis had attempted to stem the

The Habsburg–Valois Struggle

advance of the Turks under Suleiman the Magnificent and had been killed at the Battle of Mohacs in 1526. Hungary ceased to exist as an independent state, most of it being absorbed into the Ottoman Empire, the rest going to Austria. Austria was therefore deprived of a vital buffer state between Central Europe and the Turks; and the city of Vienna was now vulnerable to Turkish attack. This conflict was brought within the scope of the Habsburg–Valois struggles by the diplomacy of Francis I. In his efforts to find a way out of his humiliations at Madrid in 1526 and Cambrai in 1529, Francis sought to use the Turkish peril as a means of weakening the Habsburgs by constant attacks from the rear. He therefore urged Suleiman to take Vienna in 1529 and, although the siege failed, Francis formed an open alliance with the Turks in 1536. Francis also succeeded in extending the theatre of war to the Mediterranean. The Sultan agreed to attack Naples; the Turkish admiral, Barbarossa, raided the Italian coastline; and an attempt by Charles V to capture Algiers in 1541 failed. By 1543 the French and Turks virtually controlled the Mediterranean and were sufficiently confident to launch an attack on Nice. The Franco-Turkish Alliance was undoubtedly the main reason for the rapid French recovery after the humiliations of the 1520s and for the increasing success of the anti-Habsburg bloc.

The Treaty of Cateau Cambrésis (1559) was an acknowledgement of the stalemate reached in the Habsburg–Valois struggles and the terms reflect the relative advantages gained by the combatants at the time. France was to retain Metz, Toul and Verdun but to restore Luxemburg, Savoy and Piedmont; Spain's possessions in Italy were confirmed; Philip II and Henry II agreed to suppress heresy in their dominions; and Philip II was betrothed to Elizabeth, Henry II's daughter.

Who gained most from this Treaty? During the 1520s it had appeared that France was in the process of being crushed by a greatly superior power. Yet, by 1559, a treaty had been drawn up between powers acknowledged to be equal in status. The Habsburgs had, therefore, suffered losses since the 1520s. France had begun to make inroads into the Holy Roman Empire, much of Hungary had fallen to the Turks, the Empire had divided itself along religious lines, Charles V had been forced to abdicate and the Habsburg dominions had been divided between Philip II and Ferdinand I.

Aspects of European History 1494–1789

Heavy demands had been made on the wealth and resources of Spain and a dependence on treasure shipments from the New World would shortly amount to addiction, followed by bankruptcy for Spain and economic collapse. Charles V's concept of universal empire was shattered, although Philip II, to his cost, attempted to revive it. France, on the other hand, had gained enormously in power and prestige. Yet she was unable to hammer home the advantages she had earned. The decision to uproot heresy in France precipitated a period of civil war in France which removed any further French threat from the Habsburg territories for the rest of the sixteenth century.

The Treaty could not provide a permanent settlement between France and the Habsburgs. It did not dispel France's fear of the Habsburg combination; Richelieu later revived the anti-Habsburg emphasis of French foreign policy, and made use of French gains at Cateau Cambrésis as a means of extending France's frontiers further towards the Rhine. Once Richelieu had destroyed the spectre of Austro-Spanish power by successfully involving France in the Thirty Years' War, it was left to Mazarin and Louis XIV to complete the destruction of Spanish territory in the Rhine area in a series of wars between France and Spain in the second half of the seventeenth century. The settlement in Italy lasted rather longer; but even so, the Spanish possessions confirmed at Cateau Cambrésis eventually passed to Austria by the Treaty of Utrecht (1713) and then to France after Bonaparte's invasion of Italy in 1796.

9

The Foreign Policy of Philip II

Philip II has been the subject of more extreme views than almost any other ruler in modern European history. Until recently northern Europe produced a traditionally hostile reaction. Some contemporaries regarded Philip as so fanatical a supporter of the Counter Reformation as to be, in William the Silent's words: 'estranged from every sentiment of honour and humanity'.[1] To his own subjects, however, he was known as Philip the Prudent, under whom Spain reached the peak of her power and influence, guided by policies which were embarked upon only after careful consideration and with certainty of success.

The overall picture presented is of a statesman who was strongly inclined to uphold Catholicism and yet who could remain pragmatic in his relations with Islam and Protestantism if it suited him to do so, who weighed the advantages and defects of some policies and yet was susceptible to impulsive and impetuous decisions in others, and who could be alternately flexible or rigid. He tended to exercise less caution in the second half of his reign, particularly in the 1580s and 1590s, although he retained the ability to learn from some of his mistakes, even if, while rectifying them, he committed others. He was certainly one of the most paradoxical figures of his age, and exceptionally inconsistent. The reasons are not difficult to find. The nature of his inheritance from Charles V was in itself a curious mixture of strength and weakness, of great wealth and military potential, but territorially vulnerable to several major enemies. The problems posed by his inheritance therefore required a variety of responses and solutions. Moreover, the difficulty of making these responses weighed heavily on Philip personally, and his reactions varied considerably, according to the nature of the crisis. On some occasions he showed marked caution, sometimes in the face of considerable diplomatic pressure. On others he alarmed subordinates like Alexander Farnese by pushing through a policy which they regarded as precipitate. Normally, however, Philip sought advice from all quarters before committing himself. Although admirable in theory, this sometimes resulted in excessive delays, particularly since he became over-involved in detailed paperwork.

Between 1556 and 1598 Philip's attention was concentrated on the Mediterranean, where he encountered considerable success; the Netherlands, which constituted his greatest and most persistent problem; England, where he met with mixed success and failure; and France, which showed him at his worst.

Philip II's Mediterranean policy was a direct response to the threat posed to the very existence of Spain by Islam. Charles V, in concentrating on a land struggle against France, the Ottoman Empire and Lutheranism, had neglected the naval security of Spain in the western Mediterranean. Consequently, when Philip II came to the throne in 1556, the navies of the Sultan, completely secure in the Levant, were threatening to establish their supremacy west of Sicily as well. The peril was compounded by the operation of the Barbary corsairs from the Islamic coast of North Africa (particularly Tunis and Algiers) against merchant shipping in the western Mediterranean. There was frequent, if sporadic, co-operation between these pirates and the Turkish admirals. Finally, Spain possessed a substantial population of dissidents who identified with the external forces of Islam. The Moriscos (Moors who had been forced to become partial Christians) would have welcomed a Turkish invasion to put an end to their exploitation and sufferings. One of Philip's officials summarized the prevailing government view: 'We must count all the Moriscos avowed enemies.'[2]

To Charles V these problems had been important but peripheral. They concerned the southern flank of his dominions and he had concentrated his resources on maintaining his position in Central Europe. To Philip II the crisis in the south was paramount because the focal point of his dominions was the Iberian Peninsula and

The Foreign Policy of Philip II

southern Italy, and thus encompassed the whole western Mediterranean. Central Europe was now the concern of Ferdinand I and beyond Philip's control. Philip was therefore able to give priority to the struggle against the Ottoman Empire as Charles V could not have done. Although his policy was initially a continuation of that of Charles V, he altered it rapidly to meet the new circumstances.

In 1560 Philip's expedition to capture Tripoli, a Barbary stronghold, was soundly defeated by a Turkish fleet at Djerba. Like the sporadic and half hearted thrusts made by Charles V against hostile bases in North Africa (for example, Algiers), it had been badly prepared. Thereafter, Philip adopted a more careful strategy. The Turk was to be confined to the eastern Mediterranean and priority was to be given to increasing Spain's naval strength in the western Mediterranean, cutting the links between the Barbary strongholds and the Turkish fleets, and maintaining key strategic islands in the central Mediterranean. Of these one was Malta, besieged by the Turks in 1565. Philip took nearly a year to come to Malta's assistance, but this was because he was building up Spain's naval resources. When he struck in 1566 there was no repetition of the Djerba fiasco and the Turks were driven back. The Morisco Revolt in Spain (1568–70) prevented Philip from consolidating his position in the western Mediterranean, as he had to divert resources to suppress it. Nevertheless, the beginning of the 1570s saw Spain and her Italian possessions more secure than they had ever been under Charles V.

Philip II's policy was now one of restraint and consolidation. He encountered considerable pressure to move from defence to attack and destroy Ottoman power in the eastern Mediterranean; the papacy and Venice both urged direct confrontation with the Turks. But when Philip joined the Holy League in 1571 he did so partly for defensive purposes. He had no intention of saving Venetian possessions like Cyprus from the Turks, nor of landing a crusading army to destroy Islam. For this reason, the defeat of the Turkish navy at the Battle of Lepanto (1571) produced different expectations among the victors. Venice and the papacy expected a further offensive, while Philip realized that this would be counter-productive. This assessment was certainly correct; no European power in the sixteenth century had the resources for a frontal attack on the Ottoman Empire. Philip therefore regarded the Battle of Lepanto as a defensive victory, intended to confine Ottoman naval power to the area east of Italy. Although Ottoman naval strength was by no means eliminated and Spain suffered several subsequent reverses, the Turkish peril had been diverted by a broadly successful defensive strategy. The one thing which Philip must have regretted was that the pressure of problems elsewhere prevented him from mopping up the various pockets of resistance in North Africa.

The worst of these other problems was the Netherlands. Geographically they were the most difficult of all Spain's European possessions to defend, and doubt has frequently been cast on Charles V's wisdom in bequeathing them to Philip at all. These remnants of the Burgundian lands had nothing in common with Spain, and only the personal interest of Charles V had overcome temporarily their strong feeling of separatism. Possibly the Emperor Ferdinand would have had less difficulty in integrating the Netherlands with the Austrian branch of the Habsburgs. As it was, Philip's reactions showed that he was thoroughly bemused. He confessed that he was caught in the Netherlands 'not only up to my neck but over my head'.[3] Only one issue remained clear. Of all his dominions the Netherlands were the most likely to show political and religious dissent. Therefore Philip felt that he had to do everything within his power to overcome rebellion and eradicate heresy. He had an innate horror of the latter, observing: 'Before suffering the slightest damage to religion and the service of God, I would lose all my estates, and a hundred lives if I had them, because I do not propose, nor do I desire, to be the ruler of heretics.'[4] It is doubtful that Philip used the suppression of dissent in the Netherlands as the basis of a general crusade against northern Protestantism, as is often asserted, but he did regard Spanish strength and the credibility of the Counter Reformation as being on trial.

Philip lost control over the Netherlands because he approached a virtually impossible task with policies that were inconsistent and ill-timed. This was due largely to his own ignorance of the situation. Immersed in his Escorial he failed to foster the personal relationship which Charles V had maintained with the dominion by means of his more mobile government. Philip's initial approach was tactless and ultimately disastrous. Against the advice of the Regent, Margaret of Parma, he ordered the intensification of the Inquisition and, in his desire to extract subsidies swiftly, seriously antagonized the Estates. These early measures showed a lack of sensitivity rather

The Foreign Policy of Philip II

than open despotism, and total dependence on the advice of Granvelle and Father Lorenzo de Villa Vincencio. By 1567 discontent was openly expressed and Philip made another mistake. Instead of travelling to the Netherlands himself to assess the situation, he sent the Duke of Alva with orders to deal with dissension and maintain the flow of subsidies. By the time that Alva's administration was ended in 1573 the damage was already done. The Northern Provinces had seceded and the Sea Beggars were by now active in Holland and Zeeland. Yet this was precisely the time that Philip became aware of the failure of his hard line. He said, in 1572: 'I see that things have arrived at such an extreme that we shall be obliged to adopt other measures.' Although the administration of Requesens (1573–6) made a definite attempt at moderation and conciliation, it came too late. The next decision was a serious blunder. Following the disturbances of 1576, in which the Estates took temporary control, Philip sought a military solution, but with the minimum of diplomatic finesse. His decision to send Don John was unfortunate because the victor over the Moriscos in 1570 and the Turks in 1571 had no understanding of the more complex issues of the Netherlands. Philip seemed to become aware of this, for he replaced Don John in 1578 with Alexander Farnese, Duke of Parma. Undoubtedly the best appointment ever made by Philip, Parma succeeded in restoring the southern Netherlands to Spanish rule. But even here Philip erred. Instead of leaving Parma to complete his task, he interfered at critical times and, ignoring Parma's protests, forced him to become involved in the Armada campaign of 1588 and the Spanish intervention in France in the 1590s.

Spain's enemies sensed Philip's uncertainty over the Netherlands and seized the opportunity to aid the rebels. England, for example, formed a treaty with the northern Netherlands in 1585 and sent troops under Leicester. The Huguenots also regarded the revolt as a means of uniting northern Protestantism against Spain. For Philip the Netherlands became a constant drain on Spanish resources and a target for the intrigues of his opponents. He now began to regret his lack of naval supremacy in the north and turned his attention to England.

If Philip's policies over the Netherlands showed fluctuation and indecision, his attitude to England underwent a more profound and definite change. He began with caution, using various forms of

Aspects of European History 1494–1789

diplomacy and intrigue, and ended with inflexibility, tending to ignore loose ends and subsidiary problems.

There is no doubt that Philip hoped to maintain close relations between Spain and England, even after the death of his wife, Mary Tudor, and the accession of Elizabeth in 1558. There is no evidence in these early years of a crusading spirit against Anglicanism; indeed his attitude was far more moderate than that of the papacy. Philip restrained Pius IV from excommunicating Elizabeth in 1561 and later gave his reason that such a bull would 'embitter feelings in England and drive the Queen and her friends to oppress and persecute the few good Catholics who still remain there'.[5] His main reason for supporting Elizabeth, however, was political. He feared that the accession of Elizabeth's rival, Mary Queen of Scots, would place England under the influence of the Guises and result in a powerful Anglo-French combination against Spain. Hence he was prepared to tolerate almost too much from Elizabeth. She seized ships carrying pay for Spanish troops in the Netherlands in 1568 and encouraged the activities of the Sea Beggars in the Netherlands and English privateers in the Caribbean. Philip's response was invariably cautious and was usually confined to reluctant involvement in plots against Elizabeth – the Ridolfi Plot (1571), the Throckmorton Plot (1583) and the Babington Plot (1586).

Philip made two errors in his diplomacy in the 1570s and 1580s. He remained patient and inactive too long in the face of provocation, and then passed too rapidly to a policy of open aggression. The St Bartholomew Day Massacre (1572) greatly reduced the possibility of conflict between France and Spain, as the Guises became increasingly dependent on the support of a fellow Catholic in their struggle against the Huguenots. But Philip failed to take full advantage of this turn of events and it was only the threat of large-scale English involvement in the Netherlands from 1585 which stirred him to action. After this he appeared to cast off all restraint and to reject some of the sounder advice offered to him. The struggle against England now took on the nature of a crusade, and Philip increasingly placed his trust in divine assistance to deal with two major problems. The first of these was that the execution of Mary Queen of Scots in 1587 removed the Catholic candidate for the English throne and therefore dissipated the chances of internal Catholic support for Philip's attack on England. The second was the incomplete nature of the invasion plan; Philip refused to go into the details of co-ordination between naval and land forces in 1588. The launching of the Armada, therefore, saw Philip at his most inflexible.

The underlying difficulty with which Philip had to deal was the vulnerability of the Spanish navy in the Atlantic. He had an inadequate understanding of the role of seapower beyond the Mediterranean and seemed to apply a policy similar to that which had succeeded against the Turks. Though careful to defend the sphere of influence around Spain and the Spanish colonies, he had been wary about encroaching on the territorial waters of his opponents. This was entirely the wrong strategy to use against England, for he had gradually lost control of the sea routes to northern Europe and had allowed the English Channel and the North Sea to become dangerous waters. This was particularly crucial in the struggle for the Netherlands and eventually resulted in a huge commitment of resources in the 1588 Armada to clear the obstacles which had been allowed to accumulate for three decades. This stroke was intended to solve all of Philip's remaining problems simultaneously. It would destroy England's seapower and stop her attacks on Spanish colonies and shipping. It would end the liaison between English and Dutch, and make possible the Spanish reconquest of the northern Netherlands. However, Philip had fallen behind English commanders in his understanding of strategy and tactics. He was unable to combine effectively the plans of Santa Cruz and Parma, one concentrating on a seaborne attack on England, the other on an invasion of the English coast by Spanish troops from the Netherlands. No precise provision was made for the collection of Parma's troops by the Armada since the Flanders coastline lacked a deep water port to serve as an anchorage. Although this was pointed out by Parma on several occasions, Philip still allowed the Armada to sail without a definite solution to the problem. Moreover, Philip had no clear proposals to deal with the line ahead manoeuvres of the English fleet. His instructions to Medina Sidonia were thoroughly vague, showing an awareness of English tactics but suggesting no specific response. 'You should take special note, however, that the enemy's aim will be to fight from a distance, since he has the advantage of superior artillery . . . while we must come to grips at close quarters.'[6] Philip soon came to realize that he had committed a number of serious mistakes in the execution of his 'Enterprise of England', and changed his tactics somewhat from 1589 onwards. He devoted more resources to his naval struggle with England, fitting out further Armadas for the protection of his treasure shipments from the Americas and greatly strengthening the defences of his colonies. If anything, Spain was in a stronger position at sea after 1588 than she had ever been before. But this rapid programme of reconstruction crippled the Spanish economy, and Philip's involvement in France prevented him from conducting anything more than a holding action against English attacks. Once again, he was on the defensive.

Philip's dealings with France showed a transition from moderation to aggression which was similar to his policy towards England. It could be argued that the change was forced upon him in the case of England, but his pursuit of aims which were openly imperialistic in France in the 1590s deserves less justification.

On his accession in 1556 Philip inherited a long-standing conflict with France which he managed to conclude with reasonable success. The Spanish victory at St Quentin (1557) was not followed by an attempt to conquer France (Philip had, at this stage, too healthy a respect for the French capacity for rapid military recovery), but it did put pressure on France to negotiate a settlement. Philip's caution was maintained after the Treaty of Cateau Cambrésis and the death of Henry II. He had no desire to precipitate a conflict with France which might divert his attention from the Turks or lead to the renewal of the Franco-Turkish alliance. The situation was more difficult between 1571 and 1572, when the French Regency came under the influence of Coligny, who advocated the renewal of war against Spain. But Philip's luck changed in 1572 with the St Bartholomew Day Massacre, which brought about civil war in France and made a Spanish alliance necessary for the Guise faction. The possible accession of a Huguenot to the French throne did, it is true, pose a threat to Spain's position in the Netherlands. For a while, calculated diplomacy and selective support for the Guises seemed to provide the answer but the assassination of the Catholic, Henry III, in 1589, and the accession of the Huguenot, Henry IV, seemed to revive the problem.

This also presented an irresistible temptation to Philip to push his own claim to the French throne. He therefore abandoned diplomacy and concentrated on achieving a dynastic union between France and Spain. He became obsessed with the grandeur of his vision and

The Foreign Policy of Philip II

failed to see that Spain did not possess the resources to open another front in France while, at the same time, maintaining the struggles against England and the Netherlands. Inevitably, Philip was obliged to draw upon his forces elsewhere in order to sustain his ambitions in France. Parma was ordered, protesting, into France from the Netherlands in 1592, the immediate result of which was the paralysis of Spanish control in Brussels. Philip's design collapsed altogether in 1593 when the Catholic and Huguenot factions united behind Henry IV to resist Spanish encroachments. By 1596 Philip was fighting a Triple Alliance: France, the Netherlands and England. He eventually realized that his priorities had become confused and he therefore concluded the Peace of Vervins with France in 1598. But nothing had been achieved and substantial resources had been diverted from his struggle with longer-standing enemies.

It had been argued that Philip scored a major success in keeping France a Catholic country at a time when her monarchy was confronted by a powerful Calvinist threat. Yet, ironically, Catholic France was to be a greater menace to the future integrity of Spain than any Protestant state. Ultimately the strength and status of Spain were eroded primarily by a series of struggles with Richelieu, Mazarin and Louis XIV, and only secondarily by England and the Netherlands.

10
The Development of the
Ottoman Empire to 1566

In 476 AD the Roman Empire in the West finally collapsed with the deposition of Romulus Augustulus. This was the climax of a prolonged period of internal weakness, and intolerable pressure by the German tribes forced into Roman territory by the westward expansion of the Huns. While Western and Central Europe lived through the Dark Ages, the Roman imperium passed to Constantinople, the capital of the Eastern Roman Empire (which became known as Byzantium). From the eleventh century onwards, however, Byzantium experienced the same problems as had the Western Roman Empire: political disintegration and constant attacks from outside. These attacks were conducted mainly by various branches of the Turkish people, who originated from Central Asia and migrated westwards. In 1453 the last bastion of Byzantium, Constantinople itself, was captured by the Ottoman Turks, who were already by this stage the new masters of the eastern Mediterranean.

The origins, survival and growth of the Ottoman Empire encompassed a particularly complex period of Near Eastern history. The purpose of the next two sections will be to examine the use made by the Ottoman Turks of external factors and to explain the internal strength and formidable military capacity of the early Sultanate.

The Ottoman Turks were one of several peoples competing for supremacy in the Near East in the late Middle Ages. But they alone managed to control events and to take advantage of the three major elements which interacted with each other in this area. These were the Asiatic intrusions into Anatolia, the political vacuum across the

70

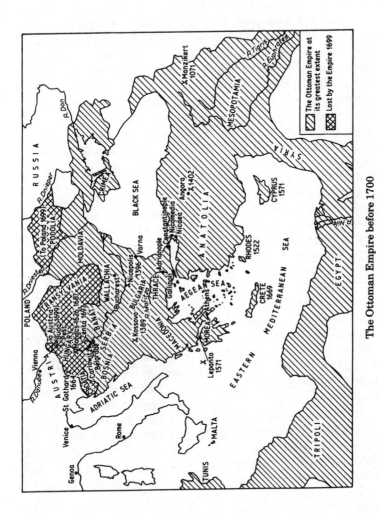

The Ottoman Empire before 1700

Straits in the Balkans, and the negative response of the Christian powers of Europe to the growing Turkish peril.

The Asiatic intrusions totally altered the balance of power in Anatolia, making possible the emergence of a new state. The first invaders were the Seljuk Turks. Driven westward by the pressure of other nomadic tribes in Central Asia, particularly the Mongols, they destroyed most of the Asiatic part of the Byzantine Empire after their victory over the Byzantine army at Manzikert in 1071, one of the really significant battles in world history. The eastern and central parts of Anatolia were now detached from Byzantium and became part of the Seljuk Sultanate. In many ways, however, this state was weaker than the unit which it had replaced, and the Seljuks were unable to provide an administration capable of bonding together the many different Turkish factions in Anatolia. It needed only one major catastrophe to release the strongest of these factions in a bid for supremacy. This happened in 1243, when the Mongols themselves poured into the area with an enormously efficient and destructive military capacity first forged by Genghiz Khan (1167–1227). They smashed the Seljuks at the Battle of Kozadagh (1243) and the Sultan was forced to pay homage to the Khan. But instead of remaining to rule the region which they had conquered, the Mongols lost interest and diverted their attention to Russia and Eastern Europe. They left behind them a series of semi-autonomous Turkish principalities who now completed the destruction of Seljuk authority. From the chaos emerged the Ottomans. They had not been strong enough to challenge the power of Byzantium, the Seljuks or the Mongols, but were now capable of welding together the shattered pieces and forming a new state. Mainly responsible for this was Osman, who expanded his principality of Sogut into a large part of western Anatolia, becoming the first Ottoman Sultan (1290–1326). His son, Orkhan I (1326–61) added further conquests, the most important being Nicaea (1331) and Nicomedia (1337), both from Byzantium. For the rest of the fourteenth century the Ottomans concentrated on gaining a foothold in Europe. Then, in 1402, the Asiatic element intruded again. The distant rumblings of the Mongols reached another crescendo as they launched a second great invasion on Anatolia, led by Tamerlane. The Ottomans managed no better than the Seljuks against Mongol cavalry and they were defeated at the Battle of Angora (1402). But, unlike the Seljuk Sultanate, the Ottoman Sultanate did not col-

The Ottoman Empire to 1566

lapse. Again the Mongols withdrew; and the Ottomans recovered because of their more effective administration and the lack of any substantial tribal group to challenge their authority as they had challenged the Seljuks. Indeed, the Mongol attack actually benefited the Ottomans. Although it precipitated the worst defeat in early Ottoman history, it did force subsequent Sultans like Mehemet I (1413–21) and Murad II (1421–51) to reconstitute Ottoman power in a more important and advantageous area, South-Eastern Europe.

The Balkans were not a difficult prey for the Ottomans because the entire area was experiencing serious internal political problems. Byzantium declined steadily until the end of the twelfth century, the process being greatly accelerated after 1204. But emergent states like Serbia and Bulgaria, which sought to replace Byzantine hegemony with their own, were unable to achieve any kind of unity or effective alliance. The various parties to the squabbles of the fourteenth century attracted the attention of the Ottomans, although the latter first arrived in Europe by invitation. In 1345 the Byzantine Emperor, John Cantacuzene, requested Ottoman military assistance in an internal succession crisis, and again, in 1352, to deal with the Serbs. Serbia, under King Stephen 'Dushan' (1331–55), appeared a far greater threat to John Cantacuzene than the Turkish mercenaries hired for Byzantium. This soon proved to be a disastrous miscalculation. The troops of Sultan Orkhan I (1326–61) refused to leave Thrace. Too late, the Emperor realized his blunder, and appealed to Serbia and Bulgaria to assist him to expel his 'guests'. Their refusal to do so was later paid for by their total extinction as more Ottoman armies poured across the Straits and into the Balkans. Gradually the Balkan rulers came to recognize the enormity of the Turkish threat. Over the next hundred years Sultans Murad I (1361–89), Bayazid I (1389–1402) and Murad II (1421–51) had to deal with a total of four coalitions assembled against the Turks. In the end, however, these confederacies all failed, being defeated by the Ottomans at Chernomen on the Maritza River (1371), Kossovo (1389), Nicopolis (1396) and Varna (1444). The Ottomans were militarily superior to the Serbs and Bulgarians and had been allowed to establish themselves in strength in Thrace during those vital early years. The only real chances of success which the Balkan Christians had were through co-operation with the Asiatic enemies of the Turks and assistance from the rest of Europe. Neither materialized. The Mongols did invade Anatolia in 1402, but this was six years after the Ottomans had crushed the third of the Balkan coalitions and there was therefore no possibility of planning a pincer movement.

The other alternative, assistance from Catholic Europe, had always been illusory. The reaction of the major Christian powers to the plight of the Balkan states was at best inappropriate and at worst destructive. As early as the eleventh century Byzantium had requested western assistance against the Seljuks. The Crusades, which were the West's reply, went badly wrong. The first three Crusades concentrated on the recapture of Palestine from the Seljuks, and had no bearing on the military problems of Byzantium in Anatolia. Gradually the crusading spirit degenerated and acquired strong economic and commercial motives. The infamous Fourth Crusade was a prime example of this. Venice, a long-standing competitor with Byzantium for commercial supremacy in the eastern Mediterranean, deliberately made use of a Byzantine succession crisis to persuade the Crusaders to attack and sack Constantinople in 1204, a blow from which Byzantium never fully recovered. The fall of Constantinople in 1453 to Mohammed II (1451–81) should have brought home to the Western world the reality of Turkish military power and prepared it psychologically for the need to act to prevent any further contraction of Christian Europe.

Yet even now Christian Europe pursued a dual policy, which was skilfully exploited by Suleiman the Magnificent (1520–66). Charles V and Ferdinand I found themselves committed to a defensive struggle in Hungary and Central Europe following the great Turkish victory at Mohacs in 1526. The Habsburgs also tried to contain Turkish expansion in the Mediterranean, without much success. On the other hand, France departed from any concept of a united Christendom defying the power of Turkey, and gave priority to dynastic interests in her own struggle with the Habsburgs. After his defeat at Pavia by Charles V in 1525 and the humiliating Treaty of Madrid (1526), Francis I urged Suleiman to divert Habsburg pressure on France by launching a Turkish attack on Vienna. Although this was attempted without success in 1529, a precedent had been established. The Ottoman Empire, an alien religious entity, had now become an inseparable part of the European diplomatic scene. France openly defied any religious motives for alliances by drawing up a formal treaty with Suleiman in 1536. This was accompanied by joint Franco-Turkish action in the Mediterranean in an at-

The Ottoman Empire to 1566

tempt to weaken the vulnerable southern flank of Habsburg power. By the time of Suleiman's death in 1566 the Turkish threat to Central Europe had finally been contained. But, on balance, the first ten Sultans had been enormously successful in spreading Islam into what had once been a wholly Christian continent. True, the Ottomans had failed to capture the city of Vienna, but then no Christian army had come within three hundred miles of Constantinople.

Sustained conquest and active diplomacy presupposed the existence of two inherent advantages: a stable situation internally and readily available military strength.

Internal stability is essential to prevent the possibility of revolt and civil war at the very time that military resources are fully stretched. The Sultans pursued a policy towards their conquered subjects which was generally more tolerant than that of western monarchs. This showed in the more heterogeneous nature of Turkish society and in the use of the Millet system. By this the subject races were given permission to pursue their own religion. The recognition of the relevant religious leaders by the Sultan was an essential part of this policy; one of the first official acts of Mohammed I after the capture of Constantinople in 1453 was to organize the election of a new Patriarch of the Greek Orthodox Church (the office eventually going to Gennadios II). Also confirmed were the structure of Judaism, with the appointment of Chief Rabbis, and the minority Armenian Patriarchate. Generally, subject peoples like the Greeks and Jews realized that they were much better off under Ottoman rule than they would be in Spain or Austria – when the Jews were expelled from Spain by Ferdinand and Isabella, many thousands of them fled to the Ottoman Empire, taking with them their skills in commerce and craftsmanship and thus benefiting the Turkish economy. On the whole, the Sultans were content to allow a considerable degree of internal autonomy, sometimes maintaining the original rulers in the areas which submitted to Ottoman rule. This, admittedly, nurtured national consciousness of the type which cut across a uniform Turkish nationalism, but it kept the subject races relatively quiet while the Empire was expanding. The danger came when the Empire fell into decline and these groups began to assert their separatism more aggressively. This, in turn, provoked a more savage form of repression from the authorities, particularly in the late nineteenth century.

Aspects of European History 1494–1789

Without the backing of a formidable military capacity the Sultans would have been unable to gain the respect of the European powers. At first they depended on the *horde*, light cavalry of the type used by the Mongols. This was gradually replaced by the *sipahis*, a feudal levy of horsemen based on the *timar* fief system. The early Sultans managed to maintain a tight control over the distribution of fiefs, refusing to allow them to become hereditary automatically, as already applied to the estates of tenants in chief in most parts of Europe. But undoubtedly the most important military factor in the growth of the Ottoman Empire was the use of janissaries, introduced by Orkhan in 1326 and fully developed by Murad I. Regular levies were used to extract recruits from among the Christian subjects and the boys selected were given a rigid training which was designed to produce the highest levels of courage and obedience. The majority of parents considered the selection of a son to serve the Sultan an honour or, at least, an advantage. Consequently, there was little resentment and no basis for revolt. The janissaries provided the backbone of the infantry and were particularly effective against the less disciplined troops of Serbia and Hungary – for example, at Kossovo in 1389 and Mohacs in 1526. Under Suleiman the janissaries reached a total of 20,000, the largest really dependable corps possessed by any state in Europe. Until Spain set a new standard for disciplined infantry, the armies of the western countries tended to disintegrate at times into destructive rabbles, the most notorious example being the sack of Rome by the imperial troops of Charles V in 1527. Had the Turks succeeded in capturing Vienna it is doubtful whether the same would have happened there. What made the janissaries particularly effective, apart from their training, was that they were usually armed with the most up-to-date weapons, especially field artillery and firearms. This was of crucial importance in the capture of Constantinople in 1453.

The rise of the Ottoman Empire was remarkably rapid and radically altered the political and economic structure of Eastern Europe and the eastern Mediterranean. Yet, in a sense, the Ottoman state was geared to conquest rather than retrenchment and this meant excessive dependence on the leadership of the Sultans themselves. By the time of the death of the Empire's greatest ruler, Suleiman the Magnificent, crises were already occurring and it was clear, even to contemporaries, that the tide was beginning to turn.

11
The Beginnings of Ottoman Decline 1566–1699

The Ottoman Empire reached the most prominent position which it was ever to occupy in European and Asiatic history during the reign of Suleiman the Magnificent. The end of the reign (1566) is usually seen as the beginning of the process of decline, which assumed a more rapid momentum in the seventeenth century. Although this decline cannot be regarded as continuous and entirely uninterrupted (there were several brief periods of revival), it would be true to say that the power of the Empire by the time of the Treaty of Carlowitz in 1699 was a mere shadow of that which intimidated East and West alike in 1566.

There were three main factors involved in the decay of Ottoman hegemony, each of which will be examined separately. First, there was a crisis of leadership, the Sultans after Suleiman the Magnificent being almost uniformly incompetent and corrupt. The result was a rapidly deteriorating administration. Second, the Empire experienced a host of military problems, and suffered a series of major defeats as the European powers increased in strength. Third, the economic base of the Empire was gravely distorted by the cost of maintaining unsuccessful armies, by the shifting patterns of world trade, and by the gradual disintegration of law and order.

1566 was a turning point in the institution of the Sultanate. It was almost as if history had deliberately arranged that the first ten Sultans (with one exception) should have been the best of all the

Empire's rulers and the next thirteen (with two exceptions) the worst. The statistics are, of their kind, unique. No other country in Europe or the Near East seems to have had such a run of degeneracy or, at best, mediocrity. The first ten Sultans from Osman I to Suleiman the Magnificent covered a span of 276 years (1290–1566); the average length of their rule was therefore 27·6 years. The next thirteen reigns, from Selim II to Mustapha II, lasted for 137 years (1566–1703), with an average of 10·5 years each. Among these only two Sultans were at all politically capable: Murad IV (1623–40) and Mustapha II (1695–1703). Several were drunkards, including Murad IV, who died as a result of a heavy bout of drinking, and Selim II (1566–74) who earned the nickname 'Sot'. Two were mentally deficient: Mustapha I (1617–18 and 1622–3) and Ibrahim I (1640–8). Three were deposed, including Mohammed IV (1648–87); Ibrahim I was assassinated. Most preferred the pleasures of the harem to the duties of administration, the best example being Murad III (1574–95), who fathered 103 children; (when his eldest son came to the throne as Mohammed III in 1595 no fewer than nineteen of Mohammed's brothers were strangled in case they should attempt to usurp the throne). The most gifted of all the Sultans during the whole bleak period was Ahmed II (1691–5) but his talents were in the realms of music and poetry, and he was too unworldly to be politically effective.

The Ottoman Empire was particularly vulnerable to incompetent leadership because it was based upon a more complete form of despotism than any other regime in Europe. The Sultan was the head of the Religious Institution and the Ruling Institution, exerting a direct personal influence at all levels. The Ruling Institution was subdivided into three main sections: the judiciary, staffed mainly by personnel from the Religious Institution, the army, with its core of janissaries and the bureaucracy under the *diwan* (cabinet). The activities of these branches were co-ordinated by the Grand Vizier (whose title, appropriately, meant 'bearer of burdens'), the major official below the Sultan himself. The power of the Sultan can be gauged from the fact that all members of the Ruling Institution, the Grand Vizier included, were virtually slaves and could be dealt with summarily on the Sultan's orders. The first ten Sultans had personally created and maintained a stable administration based on the exercise of total autocracy. The next thirteen, however, proved that the system was gravely deficient in that it could not

The Ottoman Decline 1566–1699

operate without them. After 1566 the Sultans tended to withdraw from active supervision of state affairs for reasons which ranged from insanity to sustained interest in the royal harem. This was to prove disastrous in a system based on the concept of slavery rather than professional service, and the result was a power vacuum into which contending parties and interests began to pour, assisted by the rapid growth of bribery and corruption.

A traditional Turkish proverb claims that 'the fish begins to stink at the head'.[1] The rest soon followed. The major offices of state were put up for purchase, a practice initiated by Suleiman the Magnificent and greatly accelerated under Selim II. Promotion was supposedly still the prerogative of the Sultan, but it tended to be dispensed by influential women of the harem to favourites. In order to progress to a position of high responsibility it was necessary for the aspirant to have considerable capital behind him; this was often provided by Turkish or foreign bankers. Some attempts were made to uproot the worst elements of corruption, the lead generally being taken by the Grand Viziers. For example, Mohammed Kiuprili (Grand Vizier 1656–61) conducted extensive purges in the administration, but the problems returned after his death, despite further reforms by Mustapha Kiuprili between 1689 and 1691. The extent of corruption by the end of the seventeenth century was surprising, even in a period which was generally tolerant towards financial laxity. In the eighteenth century, Sari Mehmed Pasha wrote a book for the guidance of officials (*Council for Viziers and Governors*) in which he expressed his concern about the depths to which the regime had sunk and added: 'Bribery is the beginning and root of all illegality and tyranny, the source and fountain of every sort of disturbance and sedition, the most vast of evils and the greatest of calamities. It is the mire of corruption than which there is nothing whatever more calamitous to the people of Islam or more destructive to the foundation of religion and government. Than this there is no more powerful engine of injustice and cruelty, for bribery destroys both faith and state.'[2]

One of the more serious results of corruption was the growth of violence, as conditions generally became more favourable to anarchy. The janissaries, who under Suleiman the Magnificent and his predecessors had been the core of the army and the vanguard of conquest and stability, under Selim II became the agents of disorder. By the seventeenth century they had lost most of their personal restraints; they were permitted to marry, enter into commercial transactions and to recruit their sons into service, the Christian levy being ended in 1638. These concessions, although far from unreasonable in themselves, were extracted by threats of revolt and greatly reduced the efficiency of the janissaries as the core of the infantry. At the same time, their participation in politics increased to an unprecedented extent. Murad III (1574–95) was forced to bow to their pressure and have several leading ministers executed. Osman II (1618–22) was deposed and murdered by the janissaries, who also put pressure on his successor, Mustapha I, to abdicate in 1623. Murad IV (1623–40) and Grand Vizier Mohammed Kiuprili (1656–61) both intimidated the janissaries into temporary obedience by extensive exemplary executions. Nevertheless, it was a sad reflection on the Ottoman regime that the once formidable élite of the army should now be feared more in Constantinople than on the battlefield.

To the outside world the most obvious manifestation of Ottoman decline was military. In 1566 the Turks controlled the entire eastern Mediterranean area, ruled most of Hungary, and had a long-standing military and diplomatic connection with one of Europe's emergent powers, France. In 1699 the Turks were forced to sign the humiliating Treaty of Carlowitz, acknowledging the loss of most of Hungary; the French alliance had long since disappeared and France had replaced the Ottoman Empire as the major military power in Europe.

Again, the process of decline was not continuous. There were periods of revival which took the rest of Europe by surprise. For example, Mohammed III defeated the imperial army at Keresztes in 1596; Crete was captured from the Venetians in 1669 after the 21-year siege of Candia; and the Turks appeared before the walls of Vienna in 1683, to be repulsed only by the intervention of John Sobieski, King of Poland. At times, too, western victories over the Turks were inadequately followed up, and this allowed brief periods of Turkish revival; the defeat of the Ottoman fleet at Lepanto in 1571 by the Holy League (consisting of Spain, Venice, Genoa, the papacy and the lesser Italian states) stopped well short of destroying Turkish naval supremacy in the eastern Mediterranean. There were occasions when the West was too preoccupied with its own internecine tendencies to take advantage of Ottoman weakness; it

The Ottoman Decline 1566–1699

was fortunate for the Sultans that the worst period of their misrule happened to coincide with the Thirty Years' War.

Yet, allowing for exceptions, the overall picture was one of deteriorating Ottoman power and the regeneration of that of its opponents. Until 1566 Ottoman victories were the norm and defeats exceptional, but after this date the Turks suffered humiliations even at the hands of the Persians between 1602 and 1617. In Europe attempts to revive the aggressive foreign policy of Suleiman and his predecessors were met by a series of disasters. In 1664 the Austrian general, with the aid of French reinforcements, defeated the Turks at the Battle of St Gothard on the River Raab. John Sobieski of Poland won a notable victory against an Ottoman army at Khoczim in 1673, and again at Lemberg in 1675. In 1676 the Turks lost a war with the Russians and, in 1683, encountered Sobieski for a third time, at Vienna, where their army of 200,000 men was beaten by 40,000 Poles. In 1687 imperial troops under Charles of Lorraine erased the humiliation of 1526 by defeating the Turks at Mohacs. This was followed by the conquest of most of Ottoman-ruled Hungary and its incorporation into Austria. When Mustapha II attempted to resist this, the Turks received their worst battering to date, at Zenta in 1697, at the hands of the imperial troops under Prince Eugène of Savoy. The Treaty of Carlowitz (1699) set the seal to Ottoman defeat; Austria received Transylvania, Slavonica, Croatia and all the other provinces of Hungary except the Banat of Temesvar.

The military reverses suffered by the Ottomans were due partly to the growth of more competent and professional armies in Europe, backed up by more complex bureaucracies and greater financial resources, and partly to the internal crisis of the Empire itself. The tendency of the janissaries to involve themselves in politics removed the advantage which they had once possessed as specialized infantry. Increasingly in the seventeenth century they were outmatched by French, imperial and Polish troops. The rest of the army had also fallen into decay. Some of the conquering forces of the early Sultans had been composed of the *sipahis*, who had been granted fiefs in return for military duty. The largest estates were held by commanders; during the seventeenth century many substantial military fiefs were allocated to the highest bidders rather than to the most able officers, the result being a catastrophic decline in the quality of command. Many *sipahis*, moreover, shirked their military obligations and found excuses for not participating in campaigns. Most of the Ottoman armies encountered by the European states after 1650 were, therefore, below full strength and riddled with dissent and corruption. Without effective leadership from the Sultans anything other than the most temporary revival was impossible.

Another factor which made the Ottoman Empire particularly vulnerable to military defeat was the nature of its frontier. While the Empire was expanding in all directions and incorporating new peoples it experienced a form of stability derived from the momentum of conquest. When the moving frontiers finally halted, however, this stability was destroyed by emboldened minority groups now prepared to risk revolts, and by the weakening of military feudal ties. Gibbon's thesis in *The Decline and Fall of the Roman Empire*, that the expansion of Imperial Rome had implanted within it the seeds of eventual destruction, seems to apply also to the Ottoman Empire. Certainly the Turks had extensive and increasingly vulnerable frontier regions to defend, especially against the revived military power of Persia under Shah Abbas the Great at the beginning of the seventeenth century, and of Austria at the end of it. It could be argued, therefore, that Ottoman frontiers could not remain fixed, and that the end of the process of expansion was not consolidation but contraction and decline.

Political crises and military disasters coincided with economic problems as the regime faced the prospect of rapidly diminishing resources. There appear to have been three main reasons for this.

The expansion of the Empire's frontiers had meant that each campaign had to be fought over larger distances and thus became progressively more expensive. Military success meant that much of the cost could be recovered from the newly conquered areas; the importance of booty remained a constant influence in the creation of the Ottoman war machine. When the victories turned to defeat the machine could no longer sustain itself and had to be financed by other means. The Ottoman Sultans never produced a systematic revenue system and were obliged to resort to hand-to-mouth measures. This partially explains why the administration became a prey to bribery and corruption.

Meanwhile, the position of the Ottoman Empire in the world trading network had altered substantially. In the fifteenth century the Turks controlled the main overland routes to the Far East and

The Ottoman Decline 1566–1699

were able to increase the tolls on produce from India and China on its way to Venice and Genoa for redistribution to the rest of Europe. The conquest of Egypt by Selim I in 1517 ensured Ottoman control over the Red Sea route to the Indian Ocean as well. This stranglehold on the major trade routes with the East was regarded as intolerable by the maritime powers of Europe and did much to accelerate the voyages of discovery in the search for direct sea links with the Orient. Although the major voyages took place at the end of the fifteenth century and the beginning of the sixteenth, the full implications of this reconnaissance did not become apparent until the mid-sixteenth century. By this time both Spain and Portugal had established seaborne empires, and both England and France were becoming increasingly interested in maritime trade. The importance of Ottoman control over the overland routes to the East therefore declined rapidly towards the end of the century, and the decreased volume of commerce caused an irreplaceable loss of revenue.

Even the internal economic balance of the Empire experienced serious disruption. This balance depended on the maintenance of commercial contacts between the four major economic entities:[3] the nomads, who provided the means of transport and some of the primary products; the merchants, who acted as redistributors; and the peasantry and artisans, who were both producers and consumers. The main priority was internal stability – the protection of the caravan routes, the preservation of open access to all urban and rural market centres and the guarantee of effective defence from robbers and private armies. As the military hold of the Sultans on the conquered peoples of the Balkans and Anatolia began to weaken, the expression of political separatism was often accompanied by an increase in violence and anarchy which reduced the extent of the trade routes within the Empire. This was a problem which had been faced by many European countries in the Middle Ages, but a series of efficient monarchs like Henry VII of England, Ferdinand and Isabella of Spain, Louis XI of France and Ivan III of Russia, had managed to subdue separatist elements by policies of centralization. Again, the Ottoman Empire missed a vital period of consolidation and retrenchment such as other powers enjoyed.

Before 1566 the major problem emerging from the East to confront Europe was the prospect of military conquest by Islam. The Moors, after all, had once reached the Pyrenees, and it had taken nearly eight hundred years to expel them from Spain. Could the Turks reach the Alps, and would they be equally difficult to dislodge? As events showed, the menace had dissipated itself by 1699, and a problem of a very different kind faced Europe. What role could a weakened and corrupt regime play in the rivalries between the major powers? What was to become of Turkey's remaining European territories, and what principles should be observed in their partition? The Turkish peril was transformed into the Eastern Question, as historians like to assert, and the problem had become diplomatic rather than military.

12
European Population Growth
1500–1800

The population of Europe grew slowly, but steadily, from ancient times until the middle of the fourteenth century. Then, between 1347 and 1351, the entire continent was ravaged by the Black Death. Recovery took, on average, between 100 and 150 years, which meant that the previous rate of population growth was resumed by the end of the fifteenth century. The period between 1500 and 1600 saw a steady increase in the population of most countries, which was then held back, in the seventeenth century, by an unusually harsh combination of plague, war and famine. During the eighteenth century there was another upward swing in the growth rate, and Europe's population almost doubled between 1700 and 1800; in this can be seen the very beginning of the population explosion of modern times. This chapter will outline some of the reasons which have been suggested for these fluctuations, although it should be emphasized that most are still tentative and open to modification in the light of future research. The final section will consider some of the effects of these changes on European economic and political developments.

The Black Death swept through a continent which was totally unprepared for its coming. The last references made by sources in Christian countries to bubonic plague had been in AD 767.[1] For about six hundred years, therefore, Europe had been free from plague; this offers one explanation for the steady increase of population through most of the Middle Ages. Then, during the 1340s, the

Aspects of European History 1494–1789

Black Death was brought from the Far East along the Mongol caravan routes, moving through the Mediterranean countries into Northern Europe, and eventually returning to Asia. It was transmitted in Europe by the black rat (*rattus rattus*), which acted as host to the plague bacillus (*pasteurella pestis*). The ground had already been well prepared by the spread of this rodent from the Mediterranean world, where it had long been established, to the northern territories, largely as a result of increased commercial contacts from the late thirteenth century onwards. Between them, the three types of plague, bubonic, pneumonic and septicaemic, reduced Europe's population by between 30 and 50 per cent. England, for example, possessed 2·1 m. inhabitants in 1400, only half the figure of 1348.[2]

Pandemics on this scale never occurred again, and so a gradual return to the previous pattern of population growth was inevitable. On the whole, most of Europe had made good the population losses by the early decades of the sixteenth century, and was able to sustain a slow but steady growth for the next hundred years. England, for example, had 4·1 m. inhabitants in 1570 and 4·8 m. in 1600.[3] Switzerland grew from 0·8 m. in 1500 to 1·0 m. in 1600; France from 16·4 m. in 1500 to 18·5 m. in 1600; and Germany, in the same period, from 12·0 m. to 15·0 m. The European total, 81·8 m. in 1500, had reached 104·7 m. by 1600.[4] The most obvious changes occurred in the population of the cities. In 1500 only five urban centres had 100,000 or more inhabitants: Constantinople, Naples, Venice, Milan and Paris. By 1600 the number probably stood at thirteen, while Milan now had 180,000 inhabitants and Paris 200,000.[5]

Yet the population increase was not, at this stage, spectacular, for serious problems remained. Although the plague never again affected the whole continent at once, it frequently revisited individual countries and cities; Venice, for example, lost 30 per cent of her inhabitants between 1575 and 1577,[1] despite the existence since 1485 of a 40-day (quarantine) regulation on all ships entering her harbour. Moreover, several new diseases appeared during the sixteenth century, including syphilis from America and typhus from the East. It is true that bad harvests were less common than they had been in the fifteenth and fourteenth centuries. There were still, however, many years of severe shortage which caused extensive malnutrition and loosened resistance to all infectious diseases. On the whole, Europeans were still vulnerable to sudden catastrophe.

European Population Growth 1500–1800

This became particularly apparent between 1600 and 1700. The more fortunate countries like England, France and the Netherlands, sustained a continued increase, but others, including Spain and the German states, suffered considerable losses. The seventeenth century experienced, in more intensive form than the sixteenth, the three major checks on population growth: plague, war and famine.

Bubonic plague now struck Europe more savagely than at any time since the Black Death. Italy suffered severely in 1630–1, when about 30 per cent of the urban population of Piedmont, Lombardy and Venetia died, and in 1656–7, when central and southern Italy were similarly affected.[7] London's plague epidemics of 1603, 1625, 1636, 1637, the 1640s, and 1665, produced a total of 170,000 deaths, while Spain suffered major outbreaks between 1596–1602, 1648–52 and 1677–85,[1] which did more than anything else to drag her population down by 25 per cent in the seventeenth century.[6] The incidence of plague was irregular and unpredictable. It has been suggested that a large and permanent population of burrowing rodents had become infected by the late Middle Ages, in the Russian steppes,[1] providing a constant source of carriers. Increased seaborne commerce and extensive military campaigns in Central Europe did the rest.

Warfare by itself rarely acts as a decisive check on population growth. But, as an agent for spreading disease and bringing famine, it can have deadly regional effects. The Thirty Years' War (1618–48) reduced the population of Germany from an estimated 21 m. to 13·5 m., and Bohemia's from 3 m. to 0·8 m.[7] The main factors were the spread of plague, typhus, dysentery and other diseases by the many rampaging armies, and the neglect of agriculture which caused a considerable decline in harvest yields. Poland experienced similar problems when she became the battlefield for the armies of Brandenburg, Sweden, Russia and the Ottoman Empire. Between 1578 and 1662, for example, her population slumped from 3·2 m. to 2·25m.[6]

Famine re-established itself as a major threat in the seventeenth century, and its impact on areas devastated by war or ravaged by plague can well be imagined. Even the most powerful state of Europe was adversely affected. During the second half of the century, France experienced severe hunger in 1646–52, 1660–2, 1674–5, 1679 and 1693–4,[6] while bad harvests after 1700 produced starvation on an unprecedented scale, resulting in a decline in population from 21 m. in 1700 to 18 m. in 1715.[8] It was fortunate, indeed, for France that the famine and wars of the last years of Louis XIV's reign were not accompanied by plague.

During the first half of the eighteenth century Europe reverted to the pattern of the sixteenth century. A slow increase was made possible by a slight improvement in ecological conditions. The most beneficial change was undoubtedly the gradual disappearance of the plague in Western Europe, although it continued as an unwelcome visitor in Poland and Russia. Several reasons have been advanced for the decline of this menace. One is that the black rat was gradually replaced after 1600 by the brown rat. Although the newcomer was no less vulnerable to plague fleas, it harboured a flea which was less deadly as a plague vector than that of the black rat.[9] The human contribution to the elimination of plague was the use of brick and tiles, rather than wood and thatch, in the construction of houses, which kept rats away from people to a greater extent. It is no coincidence, therefore, that after the Great fire of 1666 and the subsequent rebuilding programme, London never experienced another plague epidemic. The plague did not disappear at once from Western Europe, for there were recurrences in the Mediterranean area, as for example in Marseilles in 1720. Its decrease was, however, sufficiently rapid to enable the transfer of attention and concern to the other complaints like smallpox and typhus.

From the mid-eighteenth century the population growth accelerated in most countries. Spain increased from 8·0 m. in 1756 to 10·4 m. in 1787, and England from 6·5 m. in 1750 to 9·6 m. in 1800.[8] Europe as a whole progressed from 118 m. in 1700 to 140 m. in 1750 and 187 m. in 1800.[10] Again, the pattern varied, with England assuming a much faster rate than France, whose annual increase had passed its peak. There is little doubt, however, that most countries now experienced the beginning of their population explosion. The main reason was probably an increase in fertility (the number of births), and a less savage rate of mortality, for which the following explanation is usually given. In times of plague and famine, marriages had been less frequent than in normal years. Once the crisis had passed, marriages, and consequently births, rapidly increased, although subsequent disasters would cull the population and cancel the sudden growth. As catastrophes become less common in the first half of the eighteenth century than they had been in the seventeenth, marriages were less likely to be deferred and the birth rate climbed steadily by mid-century. This time, the culling process was much less severe than it had been in the past, and the new adult population was substantially larger. This greatly increased the fertility rate for the next twenty years, and the process was repeated. The one exception to this rapid increase seems to have been France, where primitive forms of birth control were now being practised.

The new population was sustained by an increase in food supplies, for which three reasons have been advanced. The first was another slight change in the climate. This became less harsh after the terrible winter of 1708–9, and fewer harvests were ruined as a result. The second was the onset of the agrarian revolution in Britain and its subsequent spread to other parts of Europe, making crop rotation more scientific and resulting in larger yields. The third was the greater exploitation of vegetables of American origin, including maize, the potato, the pumpkin and various types of bean.[11] Although these vegetables had been introduced into Europe in the sixteenth century, it had taken nearly two hundred years to overcome the strong initial resistance to their partial replacement of traditional European staple crops.

Two examples of the changes brought by population growth to the economic life of Europe can be cited. The first was the increased pressure on land and foodstuffs, which combined with the influx of American bullion into Europe to create the Price Rise. The price index, taken as 100 in 1471–2, grew slowly to 111·5 (1473–86) and fell slightly to 106·6 (1487–1514), before soaring to 161·6 (1515–54), 265·2 (1555–75) and 627·5 (1590–8).[12] The second was a basic change in the pattern of trade in the late sixteenth century. The countries of Southern Europe, including Spain, were no longer able to feed their growing populations and became dependent on other sources of grain supply. In acting as middlemen, bringing grain from the surplus-producing areas of Northern Europe to the needy states of the Mediterranean, the Dutch established themselves as Europe's major traders, building up a merchant fleet which was larger than those of all other European countries combined.

Population growth and contraction were closely related to the political fortunes of many European states. Spain in the sixteenth century was a major European power partly because she had a healthy rate of population growth, while her decline in the seventeenth century was undoubtedly connected with a serious population contraction due largely to plague. France replaced Spain as the greatest power on the Continent by the middle of the century and managed to sustain a slight population growth, with the exception of the period 1700–15. England's political and military importance had greatly increased by 1700, and during the eighteenth century she became one of the world's superpowers. This would have been impossible had her population not increased substantially (from 4·8 m. in 1600[3] to 6·5 m. in 1750 and 9·6 m. in 1800).[8] Russia, comparatively insignificant for much of the seventeenth century, became an integral part of the diplomatic scene in eighteenth-century Europe, and gained more than any other state from the numerous wars of the period. Her population, a mere 15·5 m. in 1600, had struggled upwards to 17·5 m. by 1700[4] and, partly because of natural increase and partly thanks to territorial acquisitions, had risen to 27 m. by 1780.[9] Sweden, with a tiny population in the seventeenth century, could not sustain herself as a major power at a time when armies were growing ever larger in size, and her decline was sealed by an estimated loss of 30 per cent of her male population[13] in the struggle with Russia between 1700 and 1721. Prussia had the similar disadvantage of a small total population, but the Hohenzollern dynasty managed to remedy this and make Prussia a major power in the eighteenth century by developing a bureaucracy geared to maintaining the army. Prussian militarism was, therefore, partly the outcome of a population deficiency.

It has been suggested that the upward movement of population had some influence on the development of the Enlightenment, which originated in England in the late seventeenth century and spread to France in the eighteenth. The philosophers' belief in the attainability of the perfect human society must have been encouraged by the reduction of natural calamities soon after 1700. Condorcet, Turgot and Goodwin all emphasized that human progress in the future would encompass the arts, sciences and political institutions, and that a steady population growth would be essential for a healthy society. It was not until the end of the eighteenth century that the notion of crisis through overpopulation crept into European thought. By 1798 the idealistic optimism of Condorcet and Mercier was replaced by the warnings of Malthus that the relationship between people and resources would eventually reach a critical

European Population Growth 1500–1800

stage. Indeed, his assertion that resources increase only by arithmetical progression while population increases by geometrical progression has been widely held down to the present day.

European population changes should not be seen in total isolation from those in other parts of the world. Europe was continuously affected by diseases emanating from Asia, and she herself had the most terrible impact on the virgin continent of America, which had been cut off for millennia from any extensive contact with the rest of the world. As Spain acquired colonies and spread her cultural and religious influences, she also transmitted disease on a massive scale. The *Conquistadores* infected thriving Indian civilizations in Mexico and the Andes with smallpox and other diseases previously unknown to the American continent. As a result, Cortes was able to conquer Mexico with six hundred men, while Pizarro captured Peru with even fewer. Other adventurers hacked their way into the interior, spreading measles, typhus and influenza, and wiping out their opponents. The demographic effect was appalling. Recent estimates place the American Indian population on the eve of the Spanish Conquest at 100 m.,[14] with the Andes and Mexico possessing about 25 to 30 m. each. By 1568 the population of central Mexico had been reduced to 3 m. and, by 1620, to 1·6 m.[14] A century after the Conquest the Indian population had declined in many areas by 95 per cent, a loss far worse than that caused in Europe by the Black Death. It is hardly surprising that the Spaniards, who had some natural immunity acquired from continuous contact with the diseases in Europe, should have dominated Central and South America so effectively. As they opened up and exploited the continent's resources, however, they became increasingly concerned about the declining pool of labour, and so resorted to importing negroes from West Africa. The slave trade, to which most maritime countries in Europe (particularly Britain) eventually contributed, caused another massive upheaval; between 30 and 40 m. people had been removed from their homeland by the nineteenth century,[15] in what must have been the greatest forced population movement in history.

13
The Holy Roman Empire
1493–1618

The origins of the Holy Roman Empire can be seen in the reign of Charlemagne, whose Carolingian territories were the basis of his claim to be the direct successor of the Imperial Caesars. Gradually, however, the structure of the Empire weakened until, in the well-known phrase of Voltaire, it was neither Holy nor Roman nor an Empire. Three developments between 1493 and 1618 greatly contributed to this process. Attempts to provide a workable constitution failed miserably, leading to political disintegration by 1608. Constitutional crises coincided with the emergence of two sides with strongly opposed religious views, providing the potential for direct conflict. The actual outbreak of war was caused by the situation in Bohemia, badly mishandled by the Habsburgs in the second decade of the seventeenth century.

The constitutional structure of the Empire had already been loosened in the Middle Ages with the growth of regional autonomy within its borders. The major landmark in the rise of individual states was the Golden Bull of 1356, which created seven Electorates within the Empire, conferring the privilege of electing all Emperors on the Archbishops of Cologne, Trier and Mainz, the King of Bohemia, and the princes of the Palatinate, Saxony and Brandenburg. These were the main rulers within the Empire but, also under the ultimate authority of the Emperor, there were, by the fifteenth century, over 2,500 administrative units. These included 2,000 imperial knights, 50 ecclesiastical princes, 30 secular princes, 70

The Holy Roman Empire

prelates and 66 Free Cities,[1] all of whom aspired to independence while, at the same time, expecting to be defended against external enemies and to receive other benefits of association. Unfortunately, the Empire possessed no effective institutions. The central legislature was the Diet (*Reichstag*); this represented the Electors, princes and Free Cities in three separate Curias, but had no means of enforcing its decisions since the Empire lacked both executive and judiciary. All authorities, great and small, agreed that existing arrangements were unsatisfactory and that certain basic constitutional changes were essential.

The precise nature of these changes was the subject of a prolonged and, at times, acrimonious dispute between, on the one hand, some of the Electors and many of the princes, led by Berthold of Henneberg (Elector Archbishop of Mainz) and, on the other, the Emperor Maximilian I (1493–1519). Berthold's reform party supported the establishment of a supreme court and a common system of taxation, in the belief that these would tighten up the structure of the Empire without increasing the authority of the Emperor. Maximilian, however, as head of the House of Habsburg, had dynastic as well as imperial interests and had no desire to be restricted in any way. Berthold's motive, after all, was to ensure that the resources of the Empire would be used for the benefit of the Empire and that the individual states would be able to exert more influence on the decisions and policies of the Emperor. This was precisely what Maximilian wished to avoid. By marrying Mary of Burgundy in 1477 he had greatly extended the territorial interests of Austria and committed the Habsburgs to a long struggle with France in the future. Naturally he hoped to finance this struggle and the defence of his Burgundian acquisitions with imperial resources. Any constitutional reforms would, therefore, be imposed by him, from above, with the specific intention of bringing these resources more definitely under Habsburg control.

This fundamental disagreement over the purpose of reform ruined any opportunity of establishing permanent institutions. The period between 1493 and 1519 was certainly one of experimentation, and more reforms were introduced then than at any other time in the Empire's thousand-year history. Nevertheless, they reflected the two divergent viewpoints and were far from permanent. At first the reformers had their way. Maximilian, involved in the Italian Wars during the 1490s, had to agree to accept new institu-

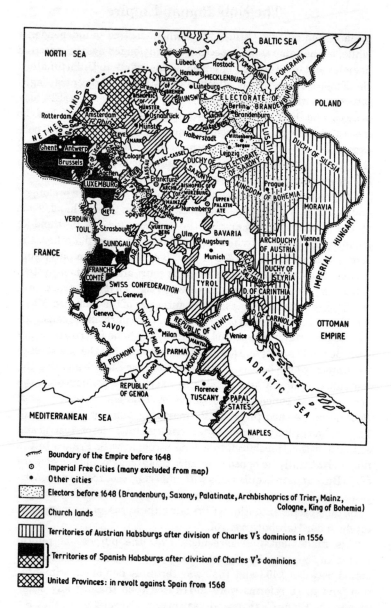

Boundary of the Empire before 1648

⊙ Imperial Free Cities (many excluded from map)

• Other cities

Electors before 1648 (Brandenburg, Saxony, Palatinate, Archbishoprics of Trier, Mainz, Cologne, King of Bohemia)

Church lands

Territories of Austrian Habsburgs after division of Charles V's dominions in 1556

Territories of Spanish Habsburgs after division of Charles V's dominions

United Provinces: in revolt against Spain from 1568

The Holy Roman Empire before 1648

tions in order to obtain the supplies which he so desperately needed. Thus he reluctantly sanctioned an Imperial Cameral Tribunal (*Reichskammergericht*) at the Diet of Worms in 1495 and the Imperial Governing Council (*Reichsregiment*) at the Diet of Augsburg in 1500. The *Reichskammergericht* was the new judicial branch of the imperial constitution, acting as the supreme court. It consisted of a chief justice and several deputies, all nominated by the Emperor, and twenty judges, the choice of the Electors and the various estates of the Empire. The *Reichsregiment* was the executive, again representing the Empire, but this time under the Emperor himself. It operated through six administrative Circles (*Reichskreise*) and its main functions were to enforce the decisions of the *Reichstag* and the decrees of the *Reichskammergericht*. It appeared, therefore, that an effective constitution for the Empire had at last been established, with judicial and executive branches added to the original legislative power.

Then Maximilian took the offensive, altering the whole system to suit Habsburg requirements. Mainly at peace between 1500 and 1508, he no longer needed extra monetary supplies; he benefited also from the untimely death of Berthold in 1504, which deprived the reform movement of its policy maker and chief spokesman. The *Reichsregiment* was ended in 1502; in fact, it had already been replaced by the Emperor's own Aulic Council (*Reichshofrat*), in which Habsburg interests predominated. Recognizing their use, Maximilian retained the *Reichskreise* and increased their number from six to ten. The executive was now firmly in the hands of the Emperor and the states had lost their hope of increased participation in a central government.

Habsburg success was, however, shortlived. Many of the leading princes were not prepared to accept the new situation and therefore sought the first opportunity to cut back the Emperor's power. Herein lies the root cause of the constitutional crisis confronting Charles V between 1519 and 1556, a crisis the more drastic because Charles tried to press his imperial authority further than Maximilian and precipitated open defiance by many German princes.

At the opening of his reign in 1519 there was some prospect of compromise. Charles V's election followed his so-called 'Capitulation', by which he had promised to rule the Empire on the basis of its legal traditions, which could naturally be interpreted by the Electors. The German princes were confident that Charles V could be manipulated more easily than his grandfather and that Berthold's constitutional reforms could be reintroduced. A sad miscalculation! Charles V had more extensive Habsburg interests than Maximilian I: Aragon, Castile and several Italian possessions as well as Burgundy and Austria. In his pursuit of dynastic aims he was hardly likely to allow any weakening of his authority within the Holy Roman Empire. Hence, at the Diet of Worms, in 1521, he startled delegates with the words: 'It is not our mind and will to have many lords, but one, as it is the tradition of the sacred Empire.'[1] Charles was making it absolutely clear that his interpretation of the word 'tradition' was not the same as the Electors'.

What, then, would happen to the reformers and their hopes? At first they managed to bring about some sort of compromise solution because of the difficulties which Charles faced in governing all his dominions effectively. The approach most likely to succeed was for Charles to administer his territories as if he owned each individually, without the added burden of the others. Spain was developing a system of councils which could rule the country without difficulty in Charles's absence. A similar arrangement, some argued, was necessary for the Holy Roman Empire. The Diet of Worms proposed to re-establish the *Reichsregiment* which Maximilian I had abolished in 1502. This was done, with Charles's stipulation that it should operate only during his absence from Germany, and under the supervision of his own representative. It possessed no executive powers other than those delegated to it by the Emperor and it proved to be of little value. By 1530 it had virtually no functions left and the reform movement had clearly come to another halt. More radical and drastic solutions to the Empire's constitutional problems were now being put forward by both sides.

Charles V was determined to impose his authority by force on any recalcitrant states. Conversely, by the late 1520s, many rulers were adopting a less cautious policy and were prepared, for the first time, to defy the authority of the Emperor openly. The situation had, therefore, changed considerably since the reign of Maximilian, and the catalyst which made this possible was Lutheranism. Many princes seized the opportunity provided by a new faith to proclaim their disillusionment with the existing structure of imperial rule. Charles resorted, in the Schmalkaldic War, to military action; partly to eradicate heresy, but also to reimpose his authority on dissident states like Saxony, Hesse, Brandenburg, Pomerania and

The Holy Roman Empire

Brunswick. The Peace of Augsburg (1555), while dealing with the religious issues, made no attempt to solve the underlying constitutional problem.

The imperial regime proved quite unable to deal with any of the crises which arose in the second half of the century. Ferdinand I (1558–64) and Maximilian II (1564–76) concentrated on external threats, ending the Habsburg–Valois struggle and preventing further Turkish encroachments in Hungary. They were, therefore, prepared to let the German states go their own way, fearing that any attempt to apply imperial authority would merely recreate the problems which had forced the abdication of Charles V. Rudolf II (1576–1612), moody, melancholic and unpredictable, was incapable of providing the necessary leadership to reverse this continued decentralization. To make matters worse, the imperial constitution now ceased to function. The *Reichsregiment* had already faded into obscurity by 1530. The judiciary, the *Reichskammergericht*, was seriously weakened in 1598 when the Emperor refused to consult it in an important test case: his decision to remove the Protestant mayor and councillors from their positions in Aachen should have been referred to the *Reichskammergericht*, but this was ignored and the whole process was initiated in the Aulic Council (*Reichshofrat*) instead. Finally, the Diet (*Reichstag*) disintegrated. After the Donauwörth Incident, described in the next section, many Protestant states withdrew their representation from the Diet in 1608. It was a measure of the political anarchy within the Empire that two armed camps, the Evangelical Union and the Catholic League, had come into existence by 1609, clearly anticipating the outbreak of civil war.

These alliances were brought about by a deep religious rift within the Holy Roman Empire, as the Reformation and Counter Reformation reacted upon the constitutional difficulties. The first resulting upheaval was Charles V's attempt to destroy Lutheranism within the Empire. This phase was ended, in 1555, by the Religious Peace of Augsburg, but throughout the rest of the century religious problems only intensified; the most important of these were the inadequacies of the 1555 peace, the growth of Calvinism as a more militant form of Protestantism, and the attempts made by a revived Catholic Church to regain substantial areas in Germany and Bohemia under the Counter Reformation.

Aspects of European History 1494–1789

The Religious Peace of Augsburg, which had been negotiated between Ferdinand and the Lutheran princes of the Empire, was an attempt to draw up a formula for the co-existence of Lutheran and Catholic states. The main principle was *cuius regio eius religio*, acknowledging the sovereign authority of the princes to determine the religion within their states. This appeared a sensible compromise after the previous conflicts between Catholic and Lutheran rulers. The agreement was complicated, however, by two important details. The first was the Ecclesiastical Reservation (*Reservatio Ecclesiastica*), which stipulated that any Catholic prelate becoming a Lutheran after 1555 would lose his political authority and that a Catholic successor would be appointed. Further movement towards Lutheranism was therefore excluded from all Church lands. The second was the *Declaratio Ferdinandea*, a secret guarantee by Ferdinand that freedom of worship would be granted to any Lutheran minorities within these lands. Unfortunately, there were conflicting interpretations of these and other agreements for the next sixty years, and opinions polarized as a result of two test cases.

First, the Catholic Archbishop of Cologne married his mistress and became a Lutheran, intending to introduce a Lutheran Reformation in Cologne. This was clearly a breach of the Ecclesiastical Reservation, all the more serious since the Archbishop was one of the seven imperial Electors. The Pope declared the Archbishop deposed and the Emperor Rudolf II sanctioned the invasion of Cologne and the installation of Ernest of Bavaria as the new prelate. Although the Lutheran states failed to go to the Archbishop's assistance, they acknowledged that the affair created a dangerous precedent, the enforcement of the Ecclesiastical Reservation by military means.

Another important case was the Donauwörth Incident of 1607. When the Peace of Augsburg was drawn up Donauwörth was a Free City under Lutheran rule. In 1607 the Lutheran majority of Donauwörth tried to prevent the Catholic inhabitants from holding processions. The Emperor Rudolf II made a swift decision, allowing Maximilian I of Bavaria to take the city and to restore it to Catholicism. Was this in contravention of the Peace of Augsburg? The Lutherans argued that it was against the spirit of '*cuius regio eius religio*'. The Emperor, however, insisted that there was no legal restraint on his action. Whatever the merits of each claim, the effects on the political situation were serious. The Protestant states feared future encroachments by Bavaria, acting as the instrument of a Counter Reformation Emperor. They realized that the Diet could not prevent this, and consequently many withdrew from it and formed the Evangelical Union in 1608.

Calvinism was the main inspiration behind the defensive organization of the Protestant states. More aggressive from the start than Lutheranism, Calvinism made rapid headway in Germany between 1556 and 1618, and was certainly regarded as a greater threat by the Catholic Church than Lutheranism during this period. Calvinism had not been acknowledged by the Peace of Augsburg and therefore, technically, its spread was in violation of the 1555 settlement. The first German ruler to adopt Calvinism was the Elector Frederick III of the Palatinate, and Heidelberg became the centre of German Calvinist doctrinal development. From the Palatinate Calvinism spread to the former Lutheran areas of Nassau, Hesse and Anhalt. Naturally, the Catholic states regarded Calvinism as a menace, particularly since it had already established itself firmly in the northern Netherlands and was inspiring the Dutch in their revolt against Catholic Spain. Nor were the Lutherans prepared to accept what they regarded as an intruder. Poor relations between Calvinist states (like the Palatinate) and Lutheran states (like Saxony) prevented close Protestant co-operation against the revived power of Catholicism until well after the turn of the century.

The Catholic revival in Germany was one of the manifestations of the Counter Reformation and was centred on Bavaria, with the full sanction and support of the Emperor and the Pope. Three Bavarian dukes pursued a systematic policy of uprooting any form of Protestantism within Bavaria, of enforcing Catholic doctrinal orthodoxy, and of preparing Bavaria as an instrument for the Catholic reconquest of Protestant Germany. Albert V (1550–79) destroyed internal opposition and imposed rigid censorship. William V (1579–97) and Maximilian I (1597–1651) enforced all the decisions of the Councils of Trent and adopted an increasingly aggressive policy towards Bavaria's Protestant neighbours. They prepared Bavaria for the leadership of the Catholic states (under the ultimate authority of the Emperor) and Maximilian I was one of the main instigators of the Catholic or Holy League of 1609, which countered the Protestant or Evangelical Union of 1608. Unfortunately, the Bavarian example encouraged the Emperors Rudolf II and Matthias to turn their attention to Bohemia. The result has been aptly described as 'Imperial Armageddon'.

Political anarchy and religious divisions within the German parts of the Empire were made more dangerous by the deteriorating situation in Bohemia. Every series of crises has its potential flashpoint, whether it be Berlin, Sarajevo or Prague. The Bohemian Revolt, which started the Thirty Years' War, was primarily a nationalist and religious opposition to Habsburg rule and to attempts to tighten up on the administration of Bohemia. The policy pursued by the Emperors was, on the whole, shortsighted and insensitive. In 1609 the threat of a Protestant revolt against Rudolf II's attempts to spread the Counter Reformation in Bohemia forced the Emperor to grant his Letter of Majesty, guaranteeing limited toleration to a section of the Bohemian Protestants. Gradually, however, the Bohemian religious problem became entangled with incautious political manoeuvres. Matthias, who was childless, favoured the candidacy of Ferdinand of Styria for the imperial succession. The usual formal procedure was to gain the election of the candidate as King of Bohemia by the Bohemian estates. This was done in 1617, but in a singularly tactless manner; the Bohemian estates were pressurized into electing Ferdinand, and there was considerable resentment in Prague about the loss of their normal electoral rights and powers. Feelings reached a new peak when, in 1618, Matthias issued a series of decrees withdrawing charters for Utraquist (Protestant) Churches, ending the appointment of non-Catholic priests and banning Protestant meetings. The immediate result of this was the Defenestration of Prague and the Bohemian Revolt against Habsburg rule in 1618. In 1619 Ferdinand was deposed as King of Bohemia. When Frederick V of the Palatinate was elected in his place, the struggle spread into the volatile centre of Germany and was directed against the Emperor, the Counter Reformation and the Catholic states, such as Bavaria, which acted as their agents.

14

Issues Involved in the Thirty Years' War

The term 'Thirty Years' War' was not used by contemporaries, who, in retrospect, tended to refer to the different stages as separate wars (for example, the Bohemian War and the Swedish War). The term was first used nearly twenty years after the Treaty of Westphalia, and seems to be more appropriate than any other; the issues involved were so complex that to use any one of them to describe the entire war would merely obscure the others. The term 'Seven Years' War' to describe the European, maritime and colonial hostilities between 1756 and 1763 was the result of a similar difficulty.

The Thirty Years' War consisted of five major wars and numerous issues which complicated the motives of the diplomats and combatants. The Bohemian War (1618–20), between the Bohemian rebels and the imperial armies, was ended by the Battle of the White Mountain (1620), by which time fighting had spread into central and northern Germany; the Danish War (1625–9) saw the attempts of Denmark to save the German Protestant states from conquest by Tilly and Wallenstein, but her withdrawal was enforced by the Peace of Lübeck in 1629; the Swedish War (1630–48) saw the continual involvement of Sweden, with brief intervals of peace, in a conflict with the Habsburgs for the control of northern Germany and the Baltic, for secular and religious reasons; the Franco-Habsburg Wars (1635–48) were a revival of the Habsburg–Valois struggles of the sixteenth century, only on a larger scale; add to these the worst civil war that Germany has experienced and the scale of the conflict becomes apparent.

Aspects of European History 1494–1789

This chapter will attempt to distinguish some of the basic issues behind these wars. It will examine the reasons for the involvement of the major powers in the Thirty Years' War, the importance of the part played by rebellion, the civil war in Germany, and the role of religion in the war. Finally, it will provide an explanation for the length of the war.

The major powers participating in the Thirty Years' War were France, Denmark, Sweden and the Spanish and Austrian Habsburgs. They fought on German soil for issues which rarely concerned Germany alone, and inflicted far more suffering in the process than they themselves experienced.

The conflict between France and the two Habsburg powers was probably the most direct link between the Thirty Years' War and the struggles of the sixteenth century. Its origins were varied and complex. During the course of the fifteenth and sixteenth centuries the Habsburgs had amassed substantial territory in Europe, some of it in a position which hemmed France in the west. The process had started in 1477 when the head of the House of Habsburg, the Emperor Maximilian I, married Mary of Burgundy, thus preventing France from completing the destruction of Burgundy which she had begun in the early fifteenth century. Subsequently, a complex system of marriages and a degree of historical chance had connected Austria and Burgundy with Spain and her Italian possessions, all of which came under Charles V in 1519. On the abdication of Charles V his brother Ferdinand I became Emperor, and his son Philip II became King of Spain and of the Burgundian and Italian possessions. Before 1559 there had been intermittent but intensive warfare between the Habsburgs and France until the temporary compromise of the Treaty of Cateau Cambrésis.

This agreement never proved to be more than an armistice. The French Wars of Religion occupied France internally during the second half of the sixteenth century, but the revival of France as a major power under Henry IV (1589–1610) brought renewed interest in foreign affairs. The threat to France was still the same: Spain, in the south, a major Habsburg power (which still held much of Italy); to the east, the Spanish territory of Franche Comté and the Netherlands and, further east, the other major Habsburg power, Austria. Henry IV pursued a pacific foreign policy; but his successor, Louis XIII (1610–43) left external affairs to his chief minister, Richelieu,

Issues in the Thirty Years' War

who was determined to weaken the two Habsburg powers and relieve pressure on France. In his own words, he aimed 'to arrest the progress of Spain'[1] and to 'halt the advance of the House of Austria'.[2] He also wanted to win for France her 'natural' frontiers, which meant expansion into Habsburg- (especially Spanish-) held territory along the frontier of the Empire.

Richelieu did not enter the war immediately; instead, he subsidized the enemies of the Habsburgs in the field, especially Sweden (for example, by the Treaty of Barwälde, 1631). He hoped that the result would be the exhaustion of the Habsburgs by the Swedes, so that French military involvement, when it occurred, would be easy and profitable. This was the theory. In practice, the French declaration of war in 1635 was followed by military failure until 1637. The early 1640s, however, saw some spectacular French successes: the defeat of the Spanish army at Rocroi and the occupation of most of Alsace. Between 1645 and 1648, Franco-Swedish armies launched several successful invasions on southern Germany against France's second Habsburg enemy, Austria. Although Richelieu died in 1642, his three aims were substantially realized by the time the Treaty of Westphalia was signed in 1648. French involvement in the war had been carefully calculated and highly profitable. It marked a real turning point in France's status as a major power. Before 1635 she was on the defensive against a massive Habsburg combination. After 1648 she was able to ignore Austria and to demolish Spanish power at her leisure.

Sweden's enemy in the Thirty Years' War was less obvious. Her main interest had been establishing her control over the Baltic, which meant that Denmark and Poland had tended to be her traditional rivals. When Tilly and imperial armies invaded northern Germany after 1625 it was Denmark who intervened on behalf of the Protestants, not Sweden. However, the defeat of Denmark and the arrival of Wallenstein's army on the Baltic coastline by 1627 forced Sweden to re-examine her policy of neutrality. For the first time in the seventeenth century Sweden had come into direct military contact with Habsburg Austria, and Gustavus Adolphus reacted forcefully. In 1629 he said: 'Denmark is used up. The Papists are on the Baltic, they have Rostock, Wismar, Stettin, Wolgast, Griefswald, and nearly all the other ports in their hands; Rügen is theirs, and from Rügen they continue to threaten Stralsund; their whole aim is to destroy Swedish commerce, and plant a foot on the southern shore of our Fatherland. Sweden is in danger from the power of the Habsburg.'[3]

Wallenstein had made no secret of his intention to make Austria a great naval power in the Baltic, and it is therefore hardly surprising that Gustavus Adolphus should have felt impelled to intervene by invading Pomerania in 1630. His initial successes against imperial troops (especially at the Battle of Breitenfeld in 1631) encouraged him to see himself as a crusader on behalf of Lutheranism in northern Germany, and gradually the strategic and religious interests of Sweden merged. To these interests could be added a third: the desire to gain substantial territory in northern Germany so that Sweden could become a German power in her own right. Gustavus Adolphus even formed plans for the reorganization of Germany. In 1631 he drew up his *Norma Futurarum Actionum*, which stated that he intended to destroy the Habsburg grip on Germany and to set up a new Protestant union to defy the power of Catholicism.[4] A Swedish-controlled Confederation would be established, consisting of Protestant states and Catholic states to be conquered in the future. The plan came to nothing because of the death of Gustavus Adolphus at the Battle of Lützen in 1632, but it shows how comprehensive and ambitious Swedish policy had become. From a fight for survival in 1630, Swedish intervention had become a crusade and a threat to dominate Germany. After the death of Gustavus Adolphus, Sweden's fortunes fluctuated. But two things remained constant: her alliance with France against the Habsburgs and her desire for German territory, the latter eventually satisfied by the Treaty of Westphalia.

What of the two Habsburg powers under attack from France and Sweden? What was their motive in fighting such a degrading and expensive war? The short answer is that they were struggling to maintain the status quo, which had been to their advantage, and to overcome a series of rebellions which threatened to upset it.

The two major centres of rebellion were the Netherlands, which involved Spanish military action, and Bohemia, which affected Austria. The Treaty of Cateau Cambrésis (1559) had worked out some sort of compromise between the Habsburg powers and France and, following a period of restless and over-ambitious foreign policy under Philip II (1556–98), Spain had begun to settle down. Austria, too, had no immediate plans for gaining further territory in Europe,

Issues in the Thirty Years' War

and concentrated on consolidating her hold on the Empire and resisting further encroachments from the Turks. The Dutch and Bohemian revolts, however, forced Spain and Austria onto the offensive once more which, in turn, eventually provoked other powers.

The Dutch Revolt had broken out in the 1560s against Philip II's attempts to raise extra taxation, to enforce Catholicism by means of the Inquisition, and to maintain a Spanish army of occupation in the Netherlands, by which means he hoped to destroy any manifestations of rebellion and to give some credibility to Spanish claims to be the military arm of the Counter Reformation. By the time of his death in 1598 this policy had clearly failed and his successor, Philip III (1598–1621) was faced with a revolt which lasted a total of eighty years, overlapping with the Thirty Years' War. At times Spain pooled her resources with Austria in a general campaign against rebellious Protestantism in Germany (for example, Spinola led 24,000 Spanish troops into the Palatinate in 1620), as well as sending armies to the Netherlands. When France entered the Thirty Years' War in 1635 Spain used the southern Netherlands as a base from which to launch an attack on Paris, which failed. By 1648 the defeat of Spain in the western sector of the Empire vindicated the Dutch revolt, and the independence of the northern Netherlands (United Provinces) was recognized by the Treaty of Münster.

Bohemia was less fortunate. Acquired after the Battle of Mohacs in 1526, Bohemia had been one of the wealthiest of the Habsburg dominions. She had been relatively quiet until 1547, when many Czechs joined the Protestant cause in the Schmalkaldic War. They were defeated by Ferdinand (the future Emperor Ferdinand I) who imposed Habsburg rule more firmly on Bohemia while avoiding extreme policies persecution. Resentment accumulated, and was openly expressed in the first two decades of the seventeenth century in the form of Czech nationalism and Bohemian Protestantism, which came into conflict with the intolerant and strictly Catholic policies of the Emperor Rudolf II (1576–1612). Under the Emperor Matthias (1612–19) the situation got out of control, culminating in the famous Defenestration of Prague in 1618, and open Bohemian rebellion against Habsburg rule, German culture and the Catholic Church.

This revolt was the immediate and most easily identifiable cause of the Thirty Years' War, but it did not provide the issues to sustain the war. The Czechs were crushed within two years, unlike the Dutch, and were never again able to challenge Habsburg authority successfully. Before these two years were out, however, the revolt had provided the fuel for a German civil war.

The link between the Bohemian Revolt and the German civil war is relatively straightforward. In 1619 the King of Bohemia, Ferdinand (who became the Emperor Ferdinand II in the same year), was declared deposed by the Czechs as the hated symbol of Habsburg rule. The Bohemian crown was offered to the Calvinist Elector Frederick V of the Palatinate instead. Frederick accepted the title and offered Bohemia the support of the Evangelical Union which had been formed in 1608 and which consisted of several of the more militant Protestant German states. This did not prevent the defeat of Bohemia, and from 1620 the Palatinate, Baden and Brunswick faced conquest and occupation by Spanish troops under Spinola and the imperial armies led by Tilly. Bavaria and other Catholic states had declared for the Emperor, bringing into effect the Catholic League which had been formed in 1609. The Empire was in the process of ripping itself apart.

The Lutheran states of Saxony and Brandenburg were initially unwilling to become involved; they were as suspicious of the militant Calvinism of the Palatinate as of Catholicism itself. However, as imperial troops overran northern Germany between 1625 and 1627 the imperial cause, supported by the Catholic states of Germany, came to be regarded as a dangerous menace. Gustavus Adolphus expressed disappointment when Brandenburg and Saxony failed to welcome the Swedish invasion of northern Germany in 1630. Their reservations about Swedish motives, however, vanished in the wave of horror which followed the sack of Magdeburg by the imperialists; and the troops provided by Brandenburg and Saxony contributed to the Swedish victory at the Battle of Breitenfeld (1631). Although various German states (especially Brandenburg and Saxony) attempted to make peace at various stages between 1632 and 1648, most of them were heavily involved in the most destructive phase of the war. Most were severely mangled, whether they fought for Sweden or the Emperor, whether they were Calvinist, Lutheran or Catholic.

*

Issues in the Thirty Years' War

To what extent was the Thirty Years' War a religious conflict? This question can be answered differently according to two interpretations.

It can be argued that the war was indeed primarily religious in its inspiration, inception and development. Between 1555 and 1618 the absence of war within the Empire had been due to the settlement of the previous religious conflict by the compromise of the Religious Peace of Augsburg (1555), which had been based on the maintenance of the status quo between Lutheranism and Catholicism. The outbreak of war in 1618 was due to three conditions which destroyed this compromise and which precipitated further religious conflict. First, Rudolf II, Matthias and the rulers of Bavaria attempted to enforce the Counter Reformation on the Empire and to win back Lutheran areas in defiance of the Peace of Augsburg. Second, Calvinism, which had been excluded from the Augsburg settlement, established itself firmly in the Palatinate and, from its base in Heidelberg, became increasingly militant and anti-Catholic. Third, Bohemia provided an explosive situation as the Emperors attempted to enforce Catholicism and to remove the religious base of Czech nationalism. The Bohemian response was also motivated by religion; the revolt was followed immediately by the offer of the Bohemian crown to the Calvinist Elector Frederick of the Palatinate.

As the war progressed there were further examples of actions which were religiously inspired. In 1629 Ferdinand II issued the Edict of Restitution to reclaim for the Church property which had been secularized by the Lutherans. When Ferdinand dismissed Wallenstein in 1630, and again in 1634, he was acting under pressure from the Jesuits.[5] There has been a tendency to underestimate the strength of religious feeling in the war because of the subsequent decline of religious influence in diplomacy after 1648, and also to attach too little importance to the influence of Jesuit and Protestant advisers on the decisions made by their rulers.

An alternative argument would be this. Religion played some part in diplomacy and in the deteriorating relations between the German states (and especially between the Emperor and Bohemia). But there are too many inconsistent factors to claim that the war was predominantly a religious one. A few examples should serve to illustrate this. After the Bohemian Revolt of 1618 many Protestant states refused to go to the assistance of their co-religionist, and initially Saxony even declared support for the Emperor – clearly a political decision. When the Protestant states were in general co-operation in the 1630s they were given valuable assistance not only by a Lutheran power, Sweden, but also by the Catholic king of France. While Gustavus Adolphus was campaigning in Germany between 1630 and 1632, threatening the very existence of some Catholic states like Bavaria, one of his admirers was Pope Urban VIII, who was secretly delighted at the discomfiture of the Emperor. During the 1640s Catholic fortunes were still further in decline and the imperial cause appeared to be on the point of defeat. Yet, at this very time, two Lutheran powers, Sweden and Denmark, went to war with each other to settle rival claims in the Baltic (1643–5), thus reducing Sweden's assistance to France and delaying the final thrust. Throughout the war strategic interests were of paramount importance and religion could be seen as a convenient form of justification for devious diplomacy and as a veil for cynical political decisions.

Why did the war last so long? Numerous attempts were made to stop it: there were several peace treaties, for example the Peace of Lübeck (1629) and the Treaty of Prague (1635), as well as the prolonged negotiations at Münster and Osnabrück from 1643 onwards. Yet it continued remorselessly, becoming increasingly destructive and seeming to assume a momentum of its own.

The basic reason was undoubtedly the number of states involved and the complexity of the issues for which they were fighting; war was constantly renewed as more issues came to the forefront. There was another factor of some importance. Usually the rapid conclusion of a war is due to the clear superiority of one of the combatants. The sides of the Thirty Years' War were evenly matched, with France, Sweden, Denmark and the north German states confronting, at various stages, Austria, Spain and the south German states under the leadership of the Emperor. Neither side possessed the advantage necessary for a quick victory and none of the powers resorted to universal conscription or the total commitment of its resources.

Instead, many armies consisted of mercenaries rather than professional troops or conscripts of permanent loyalty. This was not conducive to a rapid military result since mercenaries are one of the few sections of a population who benefit from a prolonged war. The prospect of rapid victory was also undermined by poor military

Issues in the Thirty Years' War

discipline. Only the Swedish troops of Gustavus Adolphus were tightly organized, but after his death in 1632 they, too, wrought destruction on a massive scale.

Meanwhile, the diplomats were in no hurry to settle the issue. France and Sweden refused to attend the same conference and so negotiated separately with the enemy from 1643 onwards at Münster and Osnabrück. All parties feared that they were about to be cheated and so were prepared to fight on for a little longer. After all, the main areas of the campaigns were the German states, not the territory of the major powers themselves. But the cynicism of the diplomats was only to be expected in a war which could produce such destruction and obvious disregard for the welfare of the civilian population.

15
The Effects of the Thirty Years' War on Germany

Before the twentieth century, there was overwhelming agreement among historians that the Thirty Years' War had disastrous effects on Germany. This view of the German 'catastrophe' originated in seventeenth-century Brandenburg, and was passed on to Prussia and the Second Reich. Gustav Freytag (1816–95) expressed the general consensus of opinion about this cataclysmic period of German history: 'When the war ended there was little remaining of the great nation.'[1] During the present century, however, the view that the Thirty Years' War was totally destructive has come in for some questioning, although most historians continued to see it as having contributed much to German decline. The most advanced advocate of a revised view has been S. H. Steinberg, who argued that the war's evil reputation was greatly exaggerated by the 'original atrocity propaganda emanating from Berlin'[2] to enhance the authority of the Great Elector and to provide justification for his measures. The real impact of the war, Steinberg believed, has to be seen in perspective; the struggle was not concerned primarily with the future of Germany, and its impact on Germany has been overstated, particularly since the economy and prosperity of the German cities were already in decline before the main period of the war.

The difference between the two interpretations has been clearly outlined by Theodore K. Rabb, who has labelled the original theory's exponents as the 'disastrous war school' and those who advocate a completely revised view the 'earlier decline school'. Both sides have been thoroughly represented and the dispute persists today,

Germany and the Thirty Years' War

although the majority of historians have tended to accept the most convincing components of each. For some the 'disastrous war' argument has always been conclusive, especially for D. Ogg (*Europe in the Seventeenth Century*) and W. Durant (*The Story of Civilisation*). Many others, however, accept elements of the 'earlier decline' theory, while, at the same time, attaching far more importance to the destruction within the Empire than does Steinberg. Examples are F. L. Carsten (*New Cambridge Modern History*, Volume V), V. H. H. Green (*Renaissance and Reformation*) and A. J. P. Taylor (*The Course of German History*).

The purpose of this chapter is to examine briefly the impact of the war on Germany's civilian population, economy, political structure, and culture. In the course of this composite arguments from both sides will be used and illustrated.

What is not generally questioned is that the war was the most savage conflict seen in Europe before the total wars of the twentieth century. When the effects on the civilian population are analysed there is good evidence for the 'disastrous war' theory. In no European war before 1914 (some would push the date to 1939) were non-combatants so extensively involved as between 1618 and 1648.

There were two main reasons for this involvement. First, each of the several sides in the war made use of mercenary and paramercenary armies who usually lived off the land and who grew accustomed to pillage and violence. Warfare brutalized the population in many areas, to the extent that some armies were actually outnumbered by their civilian hangers-on, who hoped for protection and a share in the spoils of victory. When a town or city was attacked, therefore, the chaos and destruction would be enormous. What made matters worse was that commanders like Tilly, Pappenheim, Wallenstein, Spinola, Gallas and Torstenson were unable to impose military discipline of the type which would have been taken for granted a hundred years later. Second, the war covered virtually every part of Germany. Campaigns were not limited to rapid marches and pitched battles. The complexity of the issues and the number of participants meant that there was an exceptionally large number of smaller armies, who frequently bungled a first campaign and had to repeat it later. Some areas endured twelve or more campaigns during the course of the war; the city of Magdeburg was besieged ten times. The civilian population lost its usual resilience and fortitude in the face of war because the frequent repetition of destruction prevented recovery and reconstruction in many areas. The constant reappearance of armies brought, too, a wide variety of diseases, including the plague itself, which probably accounted for as many casualties as the fighting. Ogg, Wedgwood and Durant have all written evocative passages on the sufferings of German civilians.

There are no really accurate statistics to show the effect of the war on the population of Germany, but there are widely accepted estimates. In 1618 the Holy Roman Empire had the largest population of any political unit in Europe and the Middle East, with the one exception of the Ottoman Empire, the total standing at about 21 m. By 1648 this had shrunk to about 13½ m. The population of Bohemia, within the Empire, was reduced from 3 m. to 800,000 during the same period and 29,000 of her 35,000 villages were deserted during the conflict.[3] Urban centres also suffered severely. Augsburg, the major German city, with 48,000 in 1620, had only 21,000 in 1650.[4] Magdeburg lost 25,000 of her 30,000 inhabitants in the notorious sack of 1631.[5] In general, the areas worst affected were the Palatinate (which, in some places, lost 80 per cent of its population), parts of the Rhineland, northern Brandenburg and Pomerania, Bohemia, and parts of Silesia and Bavaria. These experienced numerous campaigns and came to fear the armies of their allies as much as those of their enemies.

The impact of the war on the total population of Germany was long-lasting. France rapidly replaced the Empire as the most populous European state and German population growth was delayed until the period of the Second Reich (1871–1918), when a population explosion took place.

The impact of the war on the German economy and society is more difficult to assess, and there is considerable scope for the 'earlier decline' theory. During the Middle Ages, Germany had been the meeting ground of European trade, served by the arteries of the great German rivers like the Rhine, the Elbe and the Oder. Italy possessed larger commercial units and cities, but Germany had an enormous number of prosperous towns and a great diversity of interests and products. By 1618, however, Germany was already set into decline. The reign of Charles V (1519–56) had seen the misuse of the Empire's resources in the pursuit of an overambitious foreign policy which was bequeathed to his son, Philip II of Spain (1556–

Germany and the Thirty Years' War

98). Spanish foreign policy after 1556 depended heavily on loans from German bankers, particularly the Welsers and Fuggers, both of whom were adversely affected by the bankruptcies of Philip's reign. Meanwhile, the peripheral powers were gaining increasing control of the main volume of trade: the Hanseatic League, so dominant in the Middle Ages, was being challenged by Sweden in the Baltic, and three major commercial and maritime powers had appeared in the west: England, the Netherlands and France. Trade was now beginning to bypass the Empire altogether.

Economic decline, therefore, predated the war but there can be no doubt that the process was greatly and artificially accelerated between 1618 and 1648. German economic recovery was always a possibility until Germany was trampled underfoot by her neighbours.

The fall in population inevitably affected the economy disastrously. The main result was the decline in the status of the Imperial Free Cities, which became a prey to the less commercially successful surrounding German states. A total new economic network had to be built up, based this time on the support of state rulers (like the Great Elector) rather than on the free enterprise of the cities.

The period of the war created a great commercial vacuum in Central Europe which the other European powers learned to dispense with altogether. The conditions of warfare between 1618 and 1648 rarely favoured the usual practice of conducting campaigns and trade simultaneously, and the destruction was so enormous that the normal trade routes were broken. The peripheral routes, therefore, became more important, as England, the Netherlands, France and Sweden all reduced their volume of trade with Central Europe. Germany was further affected by the Treaty of Westphalia, which gave control over the outlets of major German rivers to foreign powers. For example, the Netherlands controlled the mouths of the Rhine, while Sweden dominated the mouths of the Weser, the Elbe and the Oder. Consequently, where trading contacts were renewed with Germany they were conducted to the advantage of foreign powers, who could impose tolls in the arterial routes under their influence. The general result in large parts of Germany was the decline of the middle classes as entrepreneurs and their tendency to enter bureaucratic service instead. There were, of course, some exceptions to the process of decline. Hamburg, for example, emerged from the war unscathed and proceeded to become Germany's major

113

port. For every Hamburg, however, there were several Augsburgs and Magdeburgs, cities which never regained their previous importance and wealth.

The rural areas of Germany were affected in two fundamentally different ways. F. L. Carsten[6] draws a distinction between southern and western Germany on the one hand and north-eastern Germany on the other. The impact of the war on the peasantry was generally severe: they constituted the majority of the population and they were most affected by the destruction caused by the armies. Yet the long-term effects were more complex.

In southern and western Germany, especially Bavaria and the Palatinate, the war hastened the decline of feudalism, already under way before 1618. The decline in the peasant population reduced the number of tenants available and therefore greatly improved their bargaining power with the nobility. In the north and east, however, the nobility were somewhat more powerful and the decline in the peasant population had the unfortunate result of tightening feudal obligations, as the nobility appealed to their rulers to issue legislation to this effect. In Brandenburg the Great Elector used this situation to gain the support of the nobility to embark upon a programme of political reform and recentralization. In all parts of Germany the nobility were ruined by the war and were thus made more dependent on state rulers; presumably this would have happened anyway as individual rulers gained in power at the expense of the Emperor, but the process was greatly accelerated during the war years. In most states, like Bavaria, the nobility entered state employment. The transition was particularly important in Brandenburg. Here the nobility were encouraged to devote their lives to service in the army and bureaucracy, which became the twin pillars of Prussian autocracy in the eighteenth century.

The effect of the war on German political development again seems to provide qualified support for the 'earlier decline' theory. The main political process, decentralization, had been taking place for centuries, as the princes increasingly challenged the authority of the Emperor himself. The reigns of Maximilian I (1493–1519) and Charles V (1519–56) had seen unsuccessful attempts to reverse the process. The disintegration of imperial authority was increased by the association between the north German states and Lutheranism and between the Rhine area and Calvinism. Freytag's 'German

Germany and the Thirty Years' War

nation' was not, therefore, destroyed by the Thirty Years' War, for the simple reason that there was no German nation to destroy.

Nevertheless, the political fabric of the Empire was, if anything, much weaker in 1648 than it had been in 1618. The Treaty of Westphalia tied the hands of the Emperor and enabled the German princes to conclude their own alliances with foreign powers if they so wished. The Empire had now lost all the characteristics of a sovereign state and was never again to come to a united political decision or to wage war as a unit. Even Charles V had managed to rally the Empire together to face a common external threat in the early 1540s; this could not have been possible after 1648. In the future it was time and time again to be the scene of warfare between member states (for example, the War of the Austrian Succession and the Seven Years' War) as well as between external powers.

The major political effect of the war was to accelerate another earlier development, the growth of large German states. The most extreme case was Brandenburg, who had been slowly consolidating her position in the sixteenth century but was now catapulted into major power status by the Treaty of Westphalia (evidence of an 'earlier rise' theory being combined with a 'beneficial war' theory?). The result was the growth of a major military power in northern Germany to balance the traditional power of Austria in the south. Future conflict between them was inevitable.

Contemporary and eighteenth-century opinion was appalled by the nature of this war, and it was widely regarded as an example of the utmost barbarism. Grimmelshausen's *The Adventures of Simplicissimus* provided a rough and penetrating satire of the period, while Callot's engravings *Les Misères de la Guerre* are a clear and gruesome indication of an artist's attitudes, comparable only with Goya's *Disasters of War* (on the Peninsular War) nearly two hundred years later. The writers of the eighteenth century, especially Voltaire and Diderot, condemned the fanaticism which produced the excesses of brutality and destruction. The war has even provided inspiration for modern writers: Brecht's *Mother Courage and Her Children* uses the Thirty Years' War to analyse the impact of warfare – it provides a direct link between the seventeenth and twentieth centuries.

Literature and art, therefore, tend to support the 'disastrous war' school. How should history see the effect of the war on German culture? Ogg[7] refers to a serious decline, especially in literature, and observes: 'Germany continued to produce great men, but they were mostly great in their isolation, and preeminent in those things – metaphysics and classical music – which influence a small minority.' Some historians go so far as to refer to a greater German affinity to coarseness and violence, part of a bleak picture of cultural decadence.

A more optimistic view, however, could be put forward. It is true that Germany was no longer the cultural focal point of Europe in 1648 and that she came increasingly under French cultural influence in the eighteenth century. As the courts of rulers like Frederick the Great (1740–86) replaced the Free Cities as the cultural centres of Germany, foreign and non-indigenous influences were bound to develop. Nevertheless, there was eventually a revival of German literature, as Goethe (1749–1832), Herder (1744–1803) and Schiller (1759–1805) appealed to a larger cross section of the German population. Together with the many other figures of the German Romantic movement, they influenced the more positive and less militaristic aspects of German nationalism in the first half of the nineteenth century. The ultimate conquest of Germany by militarism and authoritarianism was due less to any cultural deficiencies inherited by Germans from the Thirty Years' War than to the rapid emergence of a new Sparta within the Empire: Brandenburg-Prussia.

16
The Significance of the Treaty of Westphalia

The Treaty of Westphalia is a collective name given to the settlements which the Imperial-Habsburg delegates drew up with France, at Münster, and with Sweden, at Osnabrück. It represents an important landmark in modern European history, as it had a considerable impact on the religious situation in Germany, on the political development of the major powers and the German states, and on international relations for the next hundred and fifty years.

Germany had been torn apart by religious conflict ever since Charles V's Edict of Worms (1521). The princes had attempted to reach a working compromise at the Diet of Speyer in 1526 which had been translated into the *cuius regio eius religio* formula contained in the Religious Peace of Augsburg (1555). Nevertheless, all attempts at co-existence had ultimately failed. Catholic and Protestant unions had been formed for armed combat, contributing to the outbreak of the Schmalkaldic War and the Thirty Years' War. The Treaty of Westphalia definitely improved the religious situation in Germany, and introduced a more rational and stable settlement.

In the first place, rulers were encouraged to show a greater degree of tolerance towards the religious beliefs of their subjects. One of the major defects of the Religious Peace of Augsburg had been that the right to religious choice had been granted to rulers only, which meant that the princes were entitled to impose either Catholicism or Lutheranism as the only religion within their states. The Treaty of Westphalia allowed rulers to maintain the state religion of their choice and to direct the institutions of that religion but, at the same time, urged them to acknowledge the right of their subjects to practise minority religions in private. There were two loopholes in the settlement. No attempt was made to force the Emperor to grant toleration in Habsburg lands, a grave deficiency since it had been the religious situation in Bohemia which had provided the immediate background to the Thirty Years' War. Secondly, any German ruler was entitled to expel religious dissidents who had not been free to practise their faith in 1624; this power was, however, circumscribed by special rules, one of which allowed religious émigrés to own property *in absentia*.[1] Even though these reservations diluted the religious clauses of the Treaty, there was a far greater degree of acceptance of the spirit of toleration and there were no further religious 'test cases' like the Cologne issue (1583–4) or the Donauwörth Incident (1607). The possibility of another intensive period of the secularization of Church property or of winning back Lutheran areas to Catholicism was prevented by a provision of the Treaty that the year 1624 was to be regarded as the criterion for the demarcation between Lutheran and Catholic states. This meant the withdrawal of the unpopular Edict of Restitution (1629) and the restoration to the Protestants of some of the areas conquered by Tilly during the War.

Another shortcoming of the Religious Peace of Augsburg was remedied by the Treaty of Westphalia. The principle of *cuius regio eius religio* had applied only to Catholic and Lutheran princes; other forms of Protestantism had been excluded. Between 1555 and 1618 the most militant form of Protestantism had been Calvinism and the rapid deterioration of the religious situation in this period was due primarily to the conflict between Calvinism and the revived Catholicism of the Counter Reformation. The Peace of Augsburg was, therefore, out of date very shortly after its inception, since it had terminated only the conflict between Catholicism and Lutheranism. The Treaty of Westphalia included Calvinism in its religious clauses, providing it at last with legal status. The territorial distribution which existed in 1648 was now based on Lutheran domination in the northern part of the Empire, Catholic control of the south and important centres of Calvinism along the Rhine.

All Protestant princes, whether Lutheran or Calvinist, had felt insecure before 1618 on political grounds, for the Imperial Diet could always be influenced or swung by an ardent Catholic Emperor.

The Treaty of Westphalia

Ferdinand II (1558–64) and Maximilian II (1564–76) had respected the Protestant princes and had not attempted to use the Diet to exert political pressure on them. The same, however, was not true of Rudolf II (1576–1612), whose attempts to make Germany Catholic by force had destroyed the concept of equal religious representation in the Diet and had resulted in the collapse of the Diet itself in 1608. The Treaty of Westphalia provided more concrete constitutional guarantees for both Protestant and Catholic princes. The Diet could no longer decide upon policies concerning religion by a simple majority; now, Protestant and Catholic deliberations would be conducted apart in the *Corpus Evangelicorum* and the *Corpus Catholicorum*.[1] This removed the possibility of the Emperor passing legislation on the basis of a drummed-up majority in the Diet, since both groups had to be in agreement for any religious issue to be dealt with.

The religious settlement in the Empire was one of the more noteworthy achievements of the Treaty of Westphalia. Religious persecution declined in all but the Habsburg dominions, and rulers who made religious conflicts a base of their foreign policy became increasingly unpopular. For example, both Catholic and Protestant princes joined the League of Augsburg from 1686 to resist the aggressive polices of Louis XIV. The fact that the Emperor, Spain, Sweden, the Netherlands and England also joined the League indicates that religious issues came to be regarded by the majority of states as dangerous when mixed with diplomacy. Although the Treaty of Westphalia did not, as such, end all religious wars, it did provide a settlement which made them anachronistic and which gave stability to Catholics and Protestants in most countries. As far as Central Europe was concerned, the territorial distribution of the main religions was largely undisturbed until the ideological upheaval, frontier changes and massive resettlement of peoples following the destruction of Nazi Germany in 1945.

The major powers participating in the war were affected in fundamentally different ways by the Treaty of Westphalia. For some, like Spain, 1648 began a sharp downward trend into decline. For others, like France, Westphalia was a significant phase in the ascent to military supremacy. There were variations, too, between these extremes. Sweden reached her apex at Westphalia but set into slow decline shortly afterwards. Austria started a downward trend but recovered later in the century and once again became a formidable power.

Spain was excluded from the deliberations between the powers in 1648 because of French resentment at the separate peace treaty concluded between Spain and the Netherlands. The Treaty of Westphalia did not attempt to solve the territorial disputes between France and Spain in Franche Comté; nor did it guarantee peace in the southern Netherlands. The war between France and Spain, in fact, continued until it was concluded by the Treaty of the Pyrenees in 1659 (by which Spain lost substantial territory in Flanders). Nevertheless, the Treaty of Westphalia indirectly weakened Spain in two ways. First, French territorial gains along the Rhine threatened the Spanish hold on Flanders and Franche Comté and drove a wedge into the traditional power bloc of the Spanish and Austrian Habsburgs in Central Europe. Second, the Treaty killed off any remnants of the ambitious foreign policy inherited from Charles V by Philip II, which had been to establish Spanish dominance over Europe and to crush Protestantism and incipient nationalism. Spain had burned herself out as a major power by 1648, and for the rest of the seventeenth century was further weakened in a series of wars with France. By the time of the Treaty of Utrecht (1713) Spain's ties with Austria had been permanently severed and she had lost to the latter those European territories not already annexed by France. Although Spain did experience a period of revival in the eighteenth century (occasioned partly by this reduction of responsibilities), she was never again to reach her earlier peak of power and influence in European affairs.

France, by contrast, entered a period of great prosperity, and of success in diplomacy and warfare. Richelieu had seen her major problem as the combined threat of two Habsburg powers: Spain and Austria. The Treaty of Westphalia destroyed this combination and greatly increased the strength of France along the frontier with the Holy Roman Empire. French gains included Metz, Toul, Verdun, the Sundgau, the two bridgeheads of Breisach and Philippsburg and the control of ten imperial cities along the Rhine. It is hardly surprising, therefore, that France became the most aggressive and successful military power of the second half of the seventeenth century, as Mazarin and Louis XIV pushed back the frontier of the Holy Roman Empire in the west and threatened the independence of the German states in the Rhine area. It is with good reason that

The Treaty of Westphalia

Volume V of the *New Cambridge Modern History* (1648–88) is called *The Ascendancy of France*.

Sweden was one of the victorious powers in 1648 and considered herself the diplomatic equal of France (hence the insistence on negotiating separately). By the Treaty of Westphalia Sweden, too, gained substantial territory, including Western Pomerania, Stettin, Wollin, Wismar, Rügen and the Bishoprics of Bremen and Verden. Having now become a major German power, Sweden was also granted the right to deliberate and vote in the Diet. Her future should have been as promising as that of France. The rest of the century, however, saw her gradual decline and inability to take advantage of her gains. Indeed, the Treaty of Westphalia had a deleterious effect on Swedish power; from 1648 Sweden devoted most of her limited resources to maintaining German territories which were by no means essential for her major power status. She came into conflict with Brandenburg when the Great Elector of Brandenburg (1640–88) prodded at Swedish territory in northern Germany and weakened Swedish military power at the Battle of Fehrbellin (1675). The struggles between Sweden and Brandenburg were one of the unfortunate results of the 1648 territorial settlement and considerably weakened Sweden's capacity to resist the later and much greater threat of Russian expansion into the Baltic. When Peter the Great of Russia joined the Great Northern War (1700–21) Sweden was already in decline; and the Treaty of Nystadt (1721) was a formal recognition of Sweden's 'second division' status.

Austria probably suffered more severely than any other major power from the actual destruction of the Thirty Years' War. By 1648 she was substantially weakened by heavy Franco-Swedish pressure and by her military defeat at the Battle of Zusmarshausen. She gained nothing by the Treaty of Westphalia except the right to withold religious toleration in Habsburg territories. It appeared that the decline of Austrian Habsburg power was inevitable and would possibly be more rapid than that of Spain. For the rest of the century Austria fumbled her way through crises and wars but succeeded eventually in finding a new role. Prevented by the Treaty of Westphalia (and the failure of Wallenstein's plans) from gaining direct access to the Baltic, Austria was forced to expand eastwards instead and, after the rapid decline of Ottoman power from 1683 onwards, succeeded in reconquering much of Hungary. The War of the Spanish Succession provided Austria with further scope for recovery and, by the Treaty of Utrecht, she took over most of Spain's continental possessions.

The German states were affected in different ways by the Treaty of Westphalia, but the general trend was for the larger ones to grow more powerful at the expense of the smaller and weaker administrative units. Saxony, for example, received Lusatia, Brunswick was given the negotiating centre of Osnabrück, and Bavaria was enlarged to include the Upper Palatinate and received the honour of an Electorate (bringing the total number within the Empire to eight). But undoubtedly the main beneficiary of the settlement was Brandenburg. The Great Elector had used his troops in the 1640s to gain territory rather than to play a direct part in the war, with the result that Brandenburg was in a strong negotiating position in 1648. She eventually received eastern Pomerania (the Great Elector expressed great disappointment that western Pomerania was given to Sweden), the Archbishopric of Magdeburg, the Bishoprics of Halberstadt and Minden, and the Duchies of Cleves and Ravensberg.

The Treaty thus unintentionally released from the Empire a second German power, in addition to Austria. Brandbenburg initially concentrated her attention on the Baltic area, as the nature of her territorial gains in 1648 dictated, and came into conflict with Sweden. The enormous strengthening of Brandenburg in 1648 had still more significant long-term ramifications when her rulers eventually looked southwards. Prussia's rise created chaos in Central Europe in the eighteenth and nineteenth centuries as she vied with Austria for the control of a substantial part of Germany.

The increase in the powers of the handful of more important German states was accompanied by a decline in the power of the Emperor. Ever since the thirteenth century, attempts had been made to recentralize imperial authority and to overcome separatism; both Maximilian I and Charles V had devoted many of their resources to this, without success. The Treaty of Westphalia ended the prospect of any further attempts on the same lines. The Emperor now had to obtain the consent of the states to declare war on behalf of the Empire, to impose taxes or to raise troops. The individual rulers were empowered to make separate treaties with other countries provided that they did not threaten the integrity of the Empire. Decentralization became a standard feature of the Empire and Germany, as a result, became, like Italy, a 'geographical express-

The Treaty of Westphalia

ion'. The Treaty of Westphalia weakened the constitutional arrangements of the Empire beyond repair. Napoleon destroyed the Holy Roman Empire in 1806 but no one sought to revive it after his downfall in 1815.

Can the Treaty of Westphalia be seen as a diplomatic turning point? According to C. V. Wedgwood this term is too strong, as the Treaty was, like most others, 'a rearrangement of the European map ready for the next war'.[2] On the other hand, for Georges Pagès the epoch represents 'the transition from medieval to modern times in Western and Central Europe'.[3] It is unlikely that any of the diplomats present at Münster or Osnabrück intended the arrangements to be permanent. The powers which had increased their territories would anticipate further gains in the future. Mazarin, as a pupil of Richelieu, intended to alter the French frontiers to destroy forever the Habsburg threat to France. The unsuccessful powers, like Spain and Austria, naturally aimed at recovering and extending their territory as quickly as possible. Some of the conflicts contained within the Thirty Years' War extended, therefore, beyond the Treaty of Westphalia.

In retrospect, however, it is possible to see in Westphalia one of the definitive treaties of modern history. Most international treaties between 1648 and 1789 were modifications of Westphalia, and concentrated on reversing its imperfections or hammering home advantages gained from it. Furthermore, diplomacy tended to drift for a time away from ideology, concentrating less on religion and more on territorial gain and dynastic consolidation. Many territorial adjustments were made to the Treaty of Westphalia; for example, the Treaty of Utrecht (1713) reallocated many of Spain's possessions to Austria, and the Treaties of Aix-la-Chapelle and Hubertusburg (1748 and 1763) confirmed Prussia's acquisition of the Austrian province of Silesia. What made it possible for the major powers to involve themselves in dynastic wars was the settlement of the main religious issues in 1648 and the consequent removal of some of the fanaticism from diplomacy for the next hundred and fifty years.

17

The Spanish and Portuguese Empires

The first major impetus towards colonization in Africa, Asia and America came from the Iberian Peninsula, which had promoted the most significant of the Voyages of Discovery in the fifteenth and early sixteenth centuries. The dual motive for imperialism was ideology and wealth, aptly expressed by Bernal Diaz, who accompanied the *conquistadores* into Mexico in 1519: 'We came here to serve God and also to get rich.'[1] Both Spanish and Portuguese imperialism had, therefore, the characteristics of the medieval crusade against Islam and heathendom, while also assuming the more modern role of openly exploiting the capital wealth of overseas dependencies. These possessions bordered on the three major oceans. For Portugal they included the Atlantic islands of Cape Verde, Madeira and the Azores; the coast of Brazil; fortress settlements in East Africa (like Mombasa) and West Africa (like São Jorge); more continuous stretches of African coastline like Angola and Moçambique; bases in the Indian Ocean like Ormuz, Goa, Calicut and Colombo; and scattered posts in the Far East in Macao, Malacca, Java, the Celebes and the Moluccas. Spain's possessions, rather more compact, included the Canaries, most of the West Indian Islands, the whole of Central America and a substantial area of South America and, almost as an afterthought, the Philippines.

The purpose of this chapter is to point to comparisons and contrasts between the empires of the two Iberian powers, concentrating on their origins, their administrative structure, and their reaction to external and internal threats.

*

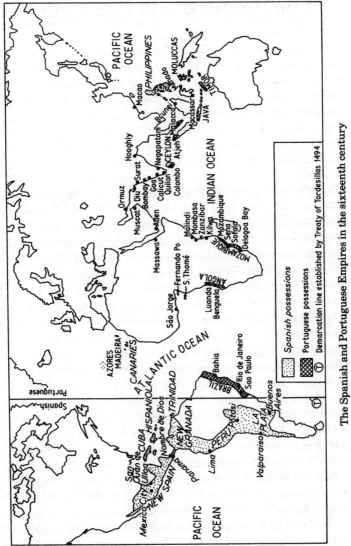

The Spanish and Portuguese Empires in the sixteenth century

Aspects of European History 1494–1789

The origins of Iberian imperialism reveal a basic paradox. Portuguese exploration was far more systematic and carefully planned than the Spanish voyages, yet, once discovery had been converted into conquest or annexation, it was Spain who introduced the more efficient administrative structure.

Portugal was able to make an earlier transition into maritime reconnaissance than Castile because she had accomplished her part in the *Reconquista* from the Moors by the mid-fourteenth century, whereas Castile was still confronted by the substantial Moorish enclave of Granada until 1492. For Portugal the next and natural step was to strike at Islam in North Africa, and the capture of Ceuta in 1415 was the beginning of a carefully planned strategy. Under the guidance of Prince Henry the Navigator (d. 1460) Portuguese mariners explored the West African coastline with the ultimate aims of capturing the supplies of gold from south of the Sahara, one of the sources of the Moors' wealth, and of attacking Islam from the rear, making possible a two-pronged crusade. For most of the fifteenth century Castile had no equivalent aims, being content with the acquisition of the Canary Islands. The Portuguese grand design became even more ambitious in the second half of the century. John II (1481–95) dispatched advance explorers like Pedro de Covilhão to report on the feasibility of achieving maritime contacts with India, of breaking into the Indian Ocean spice trade, and of establishing an alliance with supposed foreign Christian potentates like Prester John in order to complete the encirclement of Islam. Thus, when Vasco da Gama made his epic voyage to India (1497–8), he may well have been acting on fragments of information gradually pieced together in Lisbon. These were sufficiently encouraging to commit Portugal to a policy of eastward expansion round the southern coast of Africa. Castile had no such information and was therefore forced to rely more upon luck and conjecture. Hence her eventual interest in Columbus, whose hope to prove that the Orient could be reached by sailing due west had less significance in the Portuguese scheme. The voyages of Columbus (1492, 1493–6, 1498–1500, 1502–4) were at first considered disappointing, and the Portuguese appeared to have established the only really useful imperial possessions because they alone possessed obvious wealth. Yet, within fifty years the Spanish possessions had grown rapidly, with settlements being established far into the interior, while the Portuguese colonies remained essentially coastal.

The Spanish and Portuguese Empires

This sudden acceleration of Spanish energy was due to two main factors.

First, the Spaniards found that their main source of wealth was in the interior of the spheres of influence allowed to them by the Treaty of Tordesillas (1494); they were therefore forced to focus their attention beyond the coastal areas and offshore islands. Initially the main activities were those of the *conquistadores*: Cortes in Mexico, Pizarro in Peru, Alvarado in Guatemala, Quesada in New Granada and Montejo in the Yucatan. Their search was primarily for the gold reputedly amassed by the Indian civilizations. Once the Spanish Crown had assumed partial responsibility for the administration of the new areas a second rush into the interior began, this time to the enormously rich silver deposits of Zacatecas and Guanajuato, discovered in New Spain (1543–8), and of Potosi in Bolivia (1545). This necessitated further administrative changes to cope with constantly expanding frontiers and settlements. By contrast, Portugal's wealth continued to be derived through coastal entrepôts and, since the products were more diverse and varied, it would have involved enormous effort to take control of them all at source. What really mattered was that the outlets like Goa, Kilwa and Malacca continued to be supplied by the producers. Where gold was discovered in the interior some efforts were made at conquest; for example, expeditions were sent, without success, from Moçambique into the empire of Monomotapa in the sixteenth century. Alternatively, some attempt was made to establish permanent settlements, especially in the Minas Gerais area of Brazil during the gold rush of 1693. On the whole, however, bullion was never more than a secondary source of wealth to Portugal, while to Spain it was fundamental.

Second, the depth of penetration was decided by the degree of resistance from the indigenous populations. The Spanish conquests in Central and South America were made at the expense of civilizations which were culturally sophisticated but totally unprepared militarily for the type of warfare conducted by the *conquistadores*. Both Cortes and Pizarro took maximum advantage of the novelty of firearms and horses, exploited civil wars at the expense of the rulers, and resorted to kidnapping their respective opponents, Montezuma and Atahuallpa. The Portuguese, on the other hand, encountered greater difficulties beyond the coastal areas, particularly in the East. The main force in the Indian Ocean was Islam which, in its various political manifestations, was far more resilient than the American Indian empires. The Muslims of the East African interior fiercely resisted Portuguese attempts to enlarge their coastal settlements, and the ports of Mombasa and Malindi were eventually recaptured by the Swahili and the Omani Arabs by the end of the seventeenth century. Portuguese settlements in India faced constant threats in the sixteenth century from the newly established Mughal Empire in the north, while the East Indies Portuguese bases were set up at the very time that militant Islam was in the process of driving Hinduism out of Sumatra and Java. Elsewhere, several other powers possessed enormous resources and could not be subdued by a mere handful of adventurers: the Hindu states of southern India, the Ming and Manchu dynasties of Imperial China and the Shogunate of Japan. Generally the Portuguese recognized their limitations as conquerors, and preferred to establish diplomatic relations with rulers of the interior while guarding their coastal interests and shipping lanes. The result was that the Portuguese Empire, outside America, consisted of numerous widely scattered bases and coastal enclaves, very different from the much larger colonies of Spain.

The early stages of both Spanish and Portuguese imperial expansion owed much to private enterprise. In America and Africa a series of semi-feudal states emerged, the owners of which were given extensive privileges and powers by the Crown. By the *encomienda* system, established in New Spain and Peru, the *conquistadores* acquired huge areas of land, together with the right to extract tribute and labour services from the inhabitants. Hernando Cortes, for example, owned 25,000 square miles and 100,000 Indians. A similar method developed in Portuguese Brazil after 1533. Prominent settlers were granted vast estates, some of which actually exceeded Portugal in size, and the owners (*donatarios*) possessed extensive political, judicial and military powers. Asia and the East Indies were exceptions to this scramble for private land by soldiers of fortune. Since the nature of Portuguese activity in these areas was entirely commercial, land tenure on such a massive scale was considered impractical. Another barrier, of course, was the military strength of those indigenous civilizations from which such concessions would have to be extracted.

Private enterprise gradually gave way to direct rule by the

The Spanish and Portuguese Empires

mother power. This involved a transition from imprecisely defined feudalism to a new bureaucracy. Spain led the way in the sixteenth century, setting up a uniform system in her American colonies. Portugal followed more slowly and hesitantly, experimenting with different methods before moving towards the Spanish system in the early seventeenth century.

The apex of the bureaucracy consisted of the Kings of Spain and Portugal (the thrones being combined between 1580 and 1640) and the institutions which served them in Europe. The Spanish system developed along conciliar lines. The principal administrative innovation was the Council of the Indies (set up in 1524 by Charles V), which co-operated with the *Casa de Contratación* (1503). Between them they directed every aspect of colonial government and fiscal organization, appointing and issuing instructions to officials at the upper level of the colonial bureaucracy. Portugal eventually adopted a similar system, headed, from 1643, by the Overseas Council. The influence of Spain on Portugal was obvious; the search for a conciliar solution to administrative difficulties was a typically Spanish resort.

The colonial level comprised the principal overseas officials, who deputized for the King. The Spanish colonies were gradually divided into Viceroyalties: for New Spain (1535), Peru (1569), New Granada (1717–24 and 1740) and La Plata (1776). The Portuguese Empire had a less uniform system, the titles conferred often varying between Viceroy and Governor or Captain General. Brazil, for example, was made a Captaincy General in 1549 and changed to a Viceroyalty in 1640, although the latter term was not used permanently until 1763; while the most important post of responsibility overseas in the sixteenth and seventeenth centuries was the Viceroyalty of Goa (1505), which supervised Portuguese settlements throughout the Indian Ocean and the East Indies. Spanish Viceroys were much more under the control of the home government in the sixteenth century because of the constant checks exerted by the Council of the Indies. When the Portuguese equivalent became operative in the seventeenth century the semi-independence of the Captains General was partially curbed, but they always retained a far greater degree of initiative and freedom than the Spanish Viceroys.

The administrations of both empires had a lower range of officials which included Governors, Captains and *Corregidores*. The home governments and the Viceroys had considerable difficulty in controlling those who were responsible for the more inaccessible areas of Spanish America and Portuguese Brazil. Corruption was therefore more pronounced at this level. More important, the indigenous population was often badly treated, in defiance of regulations issued from Madrid and Lisbon. In 1542 the Spanish government promulgated the New Laws, which banned the enslavement of Indians. But the reaction of local estate owners was so hostile that many officials were unwilling to enforce them and, after 1550, thousands of Indians were seized and put to forced labour on plantations and in mines. The decrees of King Sebastian of Portugal in 1570 were equally unsuccessful. The authorities could not, or would not, enforce the ban on Indian slavery and, during the seventeenth and eighteenth centuries, unscrupulous frontiersmen made their fortunes by becoming slave hunters. The inability to prevent the maltreatment of Indians was undoubtedly the greatest single failing in the administration of both empires.

The Portuguese Empire faced more persistent and prolonged difficulties than the Spanish Empire and showed earlier signs of decay. Yet its remnants lasted longer. A survey of the external and internal threats will show that Spain's loss of empire was more sudden and traumatic and therefore more difficult to combat with renewed imperialism.

External threats were far more dangerous to Portuguese possessions. The Portuguese maritime empire was vulnerable to any other European power which chose to concentrate on achieving naval supremacy in the East. During the seventeenth century the Netherlands rapidly overtook Portugal as a ship-building nation and developed a strategy for conquering Portuguese colonies and taking over the spice trade. Making Batavia their focal point for the extension of their dominion and commerce in the Orient, the Dutch appropriated the entire East Indian archipelago, with the exception of New Guinea, Portuguese Timor and the Spanish Philippines, and also drove the Portuguese out of India and Ceylon, leaving only Goa intact. During the 1630s and 1640s the Dutch also captured Brazil and Angola, but their resources had been overstretched, and internal revolts won these back for Portugal. Nevertheless, by the end of the seventeenth century Portugal had lost half of her imperial possessions – those which could be dominated by the range of a ship's

The Spanish and Portuguese Empires

cannon. Spain also experienced continual threats to her coastal possessions, islands and maritime commerce. These were the result mainly of French and English unwillingness to accept the Spanish monopoly in South America and the Caribbean confirmed by the Treaty of Tordesillas in 1494. Francis I, King of France between 1515 and 1547, summed up this feeling: 'I should be very happy to see the clause in Adam's will which excluded me from my share when the world was divided.'[1] English privateers launched a series of attacks in the West Indies in the 1570s and 1590s, forcing Philip II to spend large sums on strengthening coastal defences. But there was never any real possibility that the whole of the Spanish Empire would be conquered. No European country possessed resources (or, indeed, the inclination) to launch major land expeditions into the interior of Central and South America and then to overcome the rebellions which would inevitably follow. Spain's losses, therefore, were confined to several West Indian islands and the coast of Florida, captured by Britain when Spain unwisely committed herself to the side of France in the Seven Years' War in 1761.

Internal threats were infinitely more damaging to Spain, for these destroyed her dominion in continental America and broke the sometimes tenuous links between the metropolitan and colonial halves of the administration. Portugal also suffered loss in the form of Brazil, but the retention of her African possessions was some consolation. The major problem confronted both countries was the emergence of a proto-nationalism in the colonies. This was the product of accumulated resentment against the grip of the *peninsulares* on the administration and against the restrictive economic policies exercised by the mother country. The catalyst for open revolt was the French occupation of Spain and Portugal from 1808. One by one the colonies seceded, having no desire to be ruled by a foreign European power. The process continued after Napoleon's downfall and the defeat of France. Between 1811 and 1825 Mexico, Colombia, Peru, Bolivia, Chile, Paraguay and La Plata declared themselves independent from Spain, while Brazil and Uruguay broke away from Portugal. What had once been the major strength of Spain's colonial dominance, the enormous land area, now became its greatest liability. There was no possibility of any large-scale reconquest, particularly since Britain and the United States expressed open hostility to any such scheme. Portugal survived the crisis more effectively. Forced to abandon Brazil, she managed to strengthen her position in Africa. The Portuguese inhabitants of Angola and Moçambique had no similar secessionist ambitions, largely because they were greatly outnumbered by Africans and relied upon Portugal for economic and military support.

The first two decades of the nineteenth century killed the spirit of Spanish imperialism. True, the colonies of Cuba and the Philippines were retained until 1898, but Spain made little effort to enter a second period of imperialism, unlike Britain and France who, at various stages, had suffered similar reverses. Portugal, on the other hand, developed a new colonial impulse towards the end of the nineteenth century when she joined in the scramble for Africa and extended Angola and Moçambique deep into the interior. This imperial revival was harnessed by the Salazar regime from 1932, and was not recognized as an anachronism until the Portuguese Revolution of 1974.

18

The Impact of the Spanish Empire on Spain's Economy in the Sixteenth and Early Seventeenth Centuries

By far the most important product of the Spanish Empire in the New World was bullion, which was brought to Spain by annual fleets from San Juan de Ulloa and Nombre de Dios. The gold and silver mines had once been owned by the Crown, but most were leased to individuals and companies, the Crown taking a portion of the treasure as rents. Hence each shipment contained both private and royal shares. Allowing for periodic fluctuations, the output of treasure increased steadily between 1530 and 1570, accelerated between 1571 and 1580, and reached a peak between 1586 and 1600 and again in the early seventeenth century. Thereafter, decline set in, becoming increasingly rapid after 1625. This process is illustrated in Fig. 2.

At first the treasure shipments had beneficial effects on Spain; Seville became one of Europe's major ports, and shipbuilding in northern Spain received a considerable impetus from the growing demands for merchant vessels. It seemed that Spain should become the major economic power in the world, controlling, as she did, most of the known reserves of bullion. Yet the reverse happened. After a brief spell of prosperity and prestige the Empire and treasure shipments slowly but inexorably induced a state of economic crisis which actually overlapped the period of greatest wealth in terms of bullion, the 1580s and 1590s. Spain never recovered, and her decline as a major power accelerated during the course of the seventeenth century. It was a classic example of the gross misuse of resources and of the mistaken belief that bullion inevitably means wealth and prosperity. Why did this decline take place?

*

133

Aspects of European History 1494–1789

Spain was one of the least suitable states of Europe to be flooded by vast quantities of bullion, since she had a simple and unsophisticated economy which could absorb and benefit from only relatively small amounts of treasure. Above all, she had a poor and undeveloped agricultural base which was the result partly of large infertile areas and partly of primitive agricultural methods. England, France and the Netherlands came to realize that agriculture was the basis of any sound and balanced economy, as did their colonists in America and Africa. Industries also needed to be developed and foreign markets progressively and permanently exploited. Spanish industrial output in the sixteenth century was small and required a major stimulus. At first the influx of bullion benefited selective industries which related to its exploitation and carriage (like shipbuilding). But ultimately it prevented or undermined the development of others, as it became easier to import articles from other countries, using bullion as a means of exchange. The result was that a primitive economy became a distorted, rather than a developed, economy.

The relationship between Spain and her colonies was also unnatural and damaging. The system of mercantilism, upon which it was

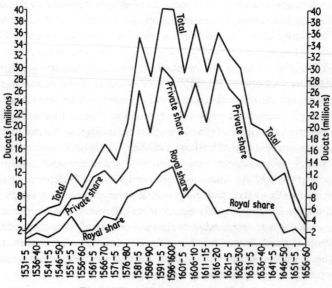

Fig. 2   Treasure imports into Spain

134

supposedly based, was not in itself at fault: a connection of mutual benefit could have been established on the basis of the colonies providing a variety of raw materials and Spain catering for all the needs of the colonists. This balance was not, however, achieved. For one thing, Spain concentrated heavily on the exploitation of bullion (which always accounted for over 80 per cent of the exports from the New World and actually reached 95·6 per cent).[1] Inadequate attempts were made to diversify the products of Central and South America. Seville could have become the entrepôt in Europe for spices, cochineal, maize, cassava, beans, sugar and cocoa, and this might have contributed to the solution of Spain's growing balance of trade difficulties. But the opportunity was not taken and the initiative passed to the Netherlands in the seventeenth century, Amsterdam becoming one of the great redistribution centres for tropical goods. The other side of the relationship also failed to develop. Spain could not meet the demand of the colonists in the New World for food and manufactured goods; indeed, the deficiency became so serious that special cargoes had to be obtained from elsewhere in Europe, particularly from England, France and Flanders. In failing to use the needs of her colonies to stimulate home industries, therefore, Spain relinquished one of the main benefits of mercantilism, a mistake which was not repeated by England, France and the Netherlands when these acquired empires.

The blame for this misuse of resources must lie partly with the Spanish Crown. Yet there was worse to come. The most glaring example of the dissipation of Spain's new-found wealth was the unrestrained foreign policy of Charles V (Charles I of Spain between 1516 and 1556) and Philip II (1556–98). Charles V's involvement in the Habsburg–Valois struggles and the conflict with Lutheranism were incredibly expensive: in 1540 he told Ferdinand: 'I cannot be sustained except by my kingdoms of Spain.'[2] Philip II's wars against England, the Netherlands and the Turks created unbearable demands on the Spanish economy; between 1586 and 1588 he spent 10 m. ducats on the Armada and a great deal more over a longer period in trying to suppress the Dutch Revolt. The basic and disastrous mistakes made by both rulers were to overestimate the amount of bullion available to finance foreign policy and to assume that the increase in the quality of treasure would continue indefinitely. (Philip II was greatly misled by the dramatic but temporary increase in the output of treasure during the 1580s which was due not to the discovery of richer veins but to the use of mercury in the recovery process.) In actual fact the royal share of the treasure was fairly small. Between 1546 and 1550 Charles V received 2 m. ducats out of a total amount of 6·6 m., and in the critical years of 1586–90 Philip II received 9·6 m., out of 28·6 m. (far less than the amount needed to finance the Armada and campaigns in the Netherlands). The solution of both monarchs was simple. They both assumed the future would bring vast returns and raised enormous loans from foreign bankers on the security of the next treasure shipments. The royal share was therefore mortgaged many years in advance and the debts sometimes could not be paid; the Crown was four times bankrupt during the reign of Philip II: in 1557, 1560, 1575 and 1596.

By the end of the sixteenth century it had become clear that much of the treasure from the New World was going straight through Spain to other European countries. This occurred in three ways. First, the private shares of the treasure shipments were used increasingly to pay, usually illegally, for the import of foreign-manufactured goods and corn. Jean Bodin, the French writer, observed in 1568: 'The Spaniards . . . being compelled to secure from us grain, linens, cloth, woad, paper, books, even carpentry and, in short, all manufactures, sail to the end of the world to fetch for us gold, silver and spices.'[3] Second, the royal shares of the shipments were used to pay foreign bankers for loans to finance Spanish foreign policy. At first these benefited the old banking systems of the Fuggers and Welsers and then, as these were affected by the bankruptcies of Philip II, the networks of France, the Netherlands and England. A third outlet for Spanish bullion was the army in the Netherlands; the coinage paid to the troops attempting to subdue the Dutch Republic soon leaked out into Central and Western Europe. In all respects, therefore, Spain acted as a sieve, a deplorable situation which did not escape the notice of contemporaries. In 1617, for example, the Cortes of Castile complained that the silver from the New World 'immediately goes to foreign kingdoms, leaving this one in extreme poverty'.[4]

Spain had, therefore, extracted, imported and re-exported vast quantities of bullion, which adversely affected her economy and left no tangible benefits. The sixteenth century had seen growing financial crisis and a deteriorating balance of trade. During the seventeenth century the situation worsened as the quantity of treasure manifestly began to give out. Shipments into Seville declined from

Spanish Economy and the Empire

42 m. ducats (1591–5) to 29 m. (1611–15), 21 m. (1631–5) and 9 m. (1651–5). Three main reasons have been advanced for this. First, the mines became less productive as the veins became poorer. Second, more treasure was retained by the colonists themselves and was sometimes exported illegally. Third, treasure shipments were increasingly vulnerable to attacks by foreign privateers who managed, for example in 1628 and 1656, to reduce the quantity of bullion actually reaching Seville.[5]

The effects on the Spanish economy in the seventeenth century were devastating. For one thing, the decline in the quantity of bullion affected the price pattern. During the course of the sixteenth century there had been a general rise in prices, affecting Spain and the rest of Europe. A combination of population pressures and the widespread circulation of precious metals had helped push up the price index sixfold between 1500 and 1600, inflation following the routes across which the treasure was dispersed. The connection was not readily accepted by the Spanish monarchy, even though a theologian at Salamanca University explained, as early as 1566, that 'money is worth more where it is scarce than where it is abundant'.[6] Inflation was undoubtedly most pronounced in Spain, bringing both positive and negative effects to the economy. On the positive side, certain select industries were stimulated while, negatively, high costs reduced Spain's competitive strength in Europe. The vital point, however, is that the Spanish economy as a whole had adjusted itself to rising prices. Once the treasure shipments fell away in quantity, and prices throughout Europe stabilized, Spain experienced a prolonged cycle of depression. The more advanced and balanced economies of France, the Netherlands and England, by contrast, made a relatively successful adjustment to the new conditions.

The reduction of the inflow of treasure combined with the colossal debts incurred by Philip II to threaten the security of the currency itself. The coinage was debased on several occasions during the reigns of Philip III (1598–1621) and Philip IV (1621–65); by 1665, indeed, silver had given way almost entirely to the base metals. Also, the decline of the royal share of the bullion resulted in a desperate search for alternative sources of revenue; to a debased coinage, therefore, was added a huge fiscal burden. The increase in taxation, mainly through the *millones*, *alcabala*, *centos* and *octrois*, affected most severely the peasantry and manufacturing and commercial sectors, rather than the unproductive and parasitic nobility. Nor was there much evidence of increased tax returns. The royal treasury became more and more deficient so that, after Charles II's death in 1700, it was barely able to meet the funeral expenses.[7]

The whole story shows a lack of leadership, awareness and economic planning by the central government and it is difficult to envisage so extreme a situation today. The role of government in the economic structure of the state has obviously changed enormously but even by the standards of the sixteenth and seventeenth centuries the general policies of the kings of Spain can only be regarded as incredibly haphazard, piecemeal and unconstructive.

More general changes in Europe emerged as a result of the colonization of America and the import of treasure – there was a fundamental shift in the balance of political and economic power. This appears to have developed in two phases.

In the first three-quarters of the sixteenth century the balance of power shifted from the Mediterranean and Central Europe firmly in favour of the Iberian Peninsula. As the Ottoman Empire established a stranglehold in the fifteenth century on the medieval overland trade routes to the Far East, Italian ports began to decline in importance as redistribution centres and the advantage lay with Spain and Portugal, who established new oceanic trade routes and empires. The treasure shipments for a while confirmed Spain's supremacy. Under Charles V and for the first half of Philip II's reign Spain was unquestionably Europe's major military power, even if she was unstable economically.

The end of the sixteenth century and the first half of the seventeenth saw a further tilt in the balance of power: this time away from the Iberian Peninsula and into north-west Europe, to the advantage of England, France and the Netherlands. This was due to the steady commercial development of these countries, the economic strangulation of Spain, and the disastrous involvement of Spain in the Thirty Years' War. Spain had overreached herself militarily as well as economically; although in a position of bankruptcy, she continued to aspire to a major role in international relations. As a result she fell a prey to more stable and fundamentally prosperous powers like France.

19
Sweden as a Major Power
1611–1721

Many countries in Europe have, at some stage, become major powers, enjoying a period of territorial expansion and military success after modest beginnings. For some the condition has been sustained over long periods – for example, France, Britain and, since 1700, Russia. Their resources and economic development ensured that their influence over European affairs should normally be considerable and that any retraction or decline should be a temporary departure from this norm. For others, being a great power was an exceptional phase in their historical growth, due, perhaps, to an unusually favourable international situation and to a highly effective leadership making the most of limited resources. Such powers included Burgundy and Switzerland in the late Middle Ages, and Sweden in the seventeenth century. This is, however, a strong feeling of inevitability about their eventual military eclipse. Having reached one peak, it seems impossible that they could ever share the experience of Britain, France and Russia in achieving others.

This chapter will examine the factors which made possible the period of Swedish ascendancy and those ultimately responsible for her decline. In many instances they were contemporaneous, but they can be separated for the purpose of analysis.

Swedish power would have been impossible without the military leadership of the Vasas, especially of Gustavus Adolphus (1611–32) and Charles XII (1697–1718), both of whom possessed exceptional abilities when compared with the majority of the commanders of their time. Gustavus Adolphus built the basis of the finest army in Europe by introducing a modified form of conscription and by ensuring that his troops used advanced weapons, notably shorter pikes and lighter firearms, both of which enhanced the manoeuvrability of Swedish columns in battle. Above all, he showed a thorough knowledge of the advanced military strategy of the Dutch school, as expounded and applied by Maurice of Nassau in the 1590s. He went further than any of his predecessors or contemporaries in experimentation, achieving greater co-ordination between pikemen and musketeers, and reintroducing the notion that the cavalry should be used to weaken the enemy by the impact of sabre charges rather than merely add to the firepower of the infantry. With the advanced degree of discipline instilled into his troops, Gustavus Adolphus was able to achieve notable victories in the Thirty Years' War, particularly over Tilly at Breitenfeld (1631). The obviously superior quality of the Swedish troops, tactics and leadership compensated, for the time being, for their relatively small numbers. The Swedish 'magic' carried over into the eighteenth century as well, even when Sweden was no longer the unquestionable mistress of the Baltic. In a last great effort to preserve Sweden's status as a major power, Charles XII took on a formidable coalition consisting of Russia, Denmark, Saxony and Poland. He could not have done this without being supremely confident of inflicting swift defeats and achieving a series of decisive military results in true Swedish tradition. For a while, this expectation appeared to be justified, especially after his victory over a numerically superior force of Russians at Narva in 1700. But Charles was unable to cope with the subsequent change in the character of the Great Northern War from swift offensives to prolonged attrition.

The first half of the seventeenth century produced a confused situation in the Baltic and Central and Eastern Europe, which could only benefit a militarily sophisticated state. Denmark, the major Baltic power of the sixteenth century, was in gradual decline, weakened by a rebellious nobility and an elective monarchy. She was also becoming increasingly unpopular with other European powers because of her grip on the Sound, the entrance to the Baltic. Muscovy was in internal disarray before 1613, during the so-called *Smutnoe Vremia* ('Time of Troubles'). Even when Michael Romanov ascended the throne in 1613, Muscovy remained preoccupied with the threat from Poland's final attempt at eastward expansion. The

Sweden as a Major Power 1611–1721

internal chaos in Germany and the diplomatic attempts of France to outflank the Habsburgs made Sweden a particularly important participant in the Thirty Years' War and provided her with the opportunity to establish complete control over the north German coastline. In these circumstances a state with the discipline of Sweden, no matter how limited in its resources, could hardly fail to make an impact. Gradually, however, Sweden's rivals on the Baltic littoral, particularly Brandenburg and Russia, increased their relative military capacity and began to threaten Sweden's hold.

As Sweden became more deeply involved militarily in attempts to dominate Northern and Central Europe, more intensive exploitation of her resources was essential. Her main advantages included a plentiful supply of iron ore and Europe's only large copper deposits, at Falun. The latter gave Sweden a virtual monopoly in the European markets until copper production declined from the mid-seventeenth century onwards. Under Gustavus Adolphus Sweden produced enough iron to sustain her military growth; the Swedish brass cannon were famous on the battlefields of Germany. The Swedish economy remained unsophisticated and uncomplicated. Sweden was not one of Northern Europe's great commercial nations, although Gustavus Adolphus encouraged Dutch entrepreneurs like Louis De Geer to establish companies and develop trading links with the Netherlands. On the whole, Gustavus Adolphus concentrated on satisfying military requirements, and the main industries therefore geared themselves to warfare, thus prolonging the character of Sweden as a spartan and specialized military power.

One of Sweden's great advantages in the seventeenth century was her ability to achieve internal political stability in her search to remain a major power. This process occurred in two clearly defined periods: the reign of Gustavus Adolphus (1611–32) and the majority of Charles XI (1680–97). The former saw the smooth functioning of constitutional monarchy, as promised in the Accession Charter of 1611. Gustavus Adolphus achieved harmonious relations with the *Riksdag* (legislature) and the *Riksrad* (Council). He was served by one of the ablest ministers of the seventeenth century, Axel Oxenstierna, and he evolved a bureaucracy which was the most advanced in Europe, eventually to be imitated by Peter the Great of Russia. The final version, laid down by Oxenstierna in the 1634 Form of Government (two years after Gustavus's death), consisted of five administrative colleges: the Supreme Court, the War Council, the

Aspects of European History 1494–1789

Admiralty, the Chancery and the Exchequer. Local administration was made up of 23 Districts, or *Län*.Despite its efficiency, this system tended, at times, to work badly, particularly during the Regencies for Christina (1632–44) and Charles XI (1660–79). This was due largely to internal aristocratic wranglings in the *Riksrad* and conflicts with the *Riksdag* over the source of money for Sweden's aggressive foreign policy. Hence Sweden switched to the common Continental expedient of absolutism, and was able to see the seventeenth century out with revived efficiency and even a touch of glory. This transition was accomplished smoothly and with the full consent of the *Riksdag*, which actually conferred upon Charles XI greatly increased powers in 1682. In a Resolution of 1693 the *Riksdag* affirmed that 'he and all his heirs have been set to rule over us as absolute sovereign Kings, whose will is binding on us all, and who are responsible for their actions to no man on earth'.[1] The Crown did not, however, convert this into permanent prerogative rule, and constitutional monarchy was ultimately restored after the reign of Charles XII (1697–1718). Absolutism served to prolong Sweden's military power, but it could hardly be considered a natural condition.

When one examines her basic resources what really surprises is not that Sweden declined but that she clung to her supremacy for so long. As a major power Sweden, with a population of 1·5 m. (0·75 m. in Sweden proper) had to compete with France (21 m. by 1700) and England (5·2 m.).[2] Her economy was based firmly on agriculture and her commerce was less developed than that of almost any other western state. She possessed no great ports (except on the north German coastline) and was one of the few countries of Protestant Europe not to benefit materially from the influx of Huguenot refugees from France after the Revocation of the Edict of Nantes in 1685. Nor did she participate in the general increase of trade in Europe that followed the dispersal of American gold and silver from Spain. She possessed few consumer or luxury industries, unlike England, France, the Netherlands, the German states and Italy, and consequently drew little bullion from the Iberian Peninsula. This meant that Sweden had a serious shortage of coinage for the maintenance of her armies, a problem which was aggravated by the limited possibilities of extracting revenue from trade and industry.

To raise funds to pay for a standing army, Swedish rulers,

whether Kings or Regents, had frequently to resort to alienating Crown lands and revenues for cash. This caused several constitutional conflicts. The *Riksdag* demanded, on many occasions, the resumption of Crown lands (by 'Reductions'); the Crown would forgo the advantages of large sums and, instead, draw a regular income from its restored estates. The main crises occurred between 1632 and 1680. After a period of Regency government the lower Estates of the 1650 *Riksdag* pressed Christina for a series of Reductions to lighten their own load, but she was more interested in other issues and refused to implement them. The second Regency, between 1660 and 1680, alienated further land, and it was only in 1680 that Reductions became effective. The whole story shows a serious dilemma: if the King or Council sold Crown lands and revenues for cash the result was the loss of more continuous supplies of cash. If, on the other hand, these lands and revenues were regained, the *Riksdag* showed every expectation that the King should finance his government and foreign policy without recourse to extra taxation. In 1680, for example, the *Riksdag* observed of the first major Reductions: 'and the Estate of Nobility presume that when all this has been executed and properly carried out, the country will have thereby been given such powerful assistance that it will be possible hereafter for Your Majesty's subjects to be relieved of the necessity to make contributions.'[3] This blithe optimism did not, however, answer the perennial question: who or what would guarantee a regular financial backing for Sweden's foreign military adventures?

Faced by a continual struggle for financial solvency, Sweden suffered what was, arguably, her greatest defect. She failed to back up her military power and success by strong and positive diplomacy. Such consolidation of military gains by diplomacy is essential for the success of a major power since it creates permanence from the transitory and provides an overall aim and sense of purpose. But the essential point about diplomacy is that it must be many-sided and flexible, capable of using different kinds of strength as occasion demands. In addition to being able to use force, it is somtimes essential to maintain a convincing appearance of military threat without actually reaching the point of war. This was precisely what Sweden could not do, and her great difficulty in holding the twilight zone between war and peace greatly weakened her position. The reason was entirely financial. Sweden at war was solvent; her armies lived off enemy territory and the government managed on subsidies paid by those states who used Sweden for a diversionary attack on their own enemies. During the Thirty Years' War, for example, Sweden had exploited the revenues and resources of northern Germany and had been financed by Richelieu's subsidies from the Treaty of Barwälde (1631). Sweden at peace could adapt, although reluctantly, to different forms of supply. But Sweden at peace, maintaining a standing army for use in diplomacy, was an impossibility. As the *Riksrad* observed in 1654, once Sweden raised regiments and refrained from actually going to war 'it will be as good as making war upon ourselves: think how much will have been wasted on maintaining them'.[4] The result was a cumulative lack of finesse in diplomacy. This, in itself, made Sweden a ready prey for more fortunate and devious courts, like that of Louis XIV.

There were attempts to enter the diplomatic scene, but these were largely unsuccessful. In 1661, for example, Bonde (the Treasurer) assessed Sweden's primary need as being one of security based on peaceful relations with other powers. But he soon discovered that neutrality and a show of power were incompatible, and therefore had to resort to accepting subsidies from other powers. Charles XI tried to elevate Sweden to the position of an arbiter in international relations but he succeeded only in making her a mediator between the two sides in the War of the League of Augsburg. A mediator sought by the powers because of its non-involvement rather than its strength: this was an indication of Sweden's future role rather than an affirmation of her past one. Meanwhile, there were two periods when Sweden stood in very great need of sustained diplomatic activity. In 1658 Charles X had successfully concluded a war against Denmark and embarked upon a complex design, involving Austria and Russia, aimed at attacking Poland and relieving her of a substantial part of her province of Prussia. The diplomacy required, however, meant a considerable time-lag. Since his army needed financing at enemy expense, he turned his back on this project and began another round of warfare with Denmark. For the rest of the century Sweden slipped from one war to another without consolidating intervening periods of peace. During the Great Northern War (1699–1721) Charles XII personified Sweden's diplomatic ignorance. He refused to consider any type of settlement after his defeat at Poltava by Russia in 1709, and even antagonized the western powers by ordering attacks on neutral shipping in the Baltic because they were maintaining normal commercial contacts with

Sweden as a Major Power 1611–1721

Russia. By 1715 all of Sweden's possession on the south shore of the Baltic had been lost; yet, even now, Charles refused all offers of mediation, convinced that a military solution could still be applied.

Commanders like Gustavus Adolphus and Charles XII had enormous confidence, based on the certain conviction that Sweden possessed advantages which other powers did not. Under Gustavus Adolphus this was certainly true; under Charles XII, however, confidence became arrogance and developed into an inability to recognize that conditions had changed. Sweden had, by now, lost her earlier advantages over other European powers. The advanced military tactics once used by Gustavus Adolphus became common property and were extensively applied by French commanders. Furthermore, the discipline of the Swedish troops was offset by the enormous increase in the size of the armies of other countries, with which Sweden could not compete. Gustavus Adolphus took 30,000 men into Germany in 1630, but Louis XIV raised the largest armies seen in Europe for a thousand years, and Peter the Great worked on the assumption that he would eventually wear Sweden down by outnumbering Swedish troops by at least 2 to 1. When the Continental states also developed their own bureaucracies to finance and supply these armies, Sweden lost her pre-eminence here as well. During the Great Northern War, for example, Russia's eventual success over Sweden was due partly to the extensive administrative reforms of Peter the Great, borrowed unashamedly from the Swedish model.

Sweden's decline has few, if any, tragic connotations. It was not accompanied by disintegration or internal chaos, nor by invasion from other powers. In the eighteenth century, Sweden achieved a more natural balance and harmony which was reflected by the further development of constitutional monarchy and the increasing diversification of the economy. The military tradition, however, has never been entirely eradicated as, even today, Swedish neutrality is based upon a strong standing army.

20
The Dutch Republic in the Seventeenth Century

The Dutch Republic owed its inception to the Union of Utrecht (1579) by which Holland, Zeeland, Friesland, Utrecht, Groningen, Guelderland and Overyssel, together with several states from the southern Netherlands, combined their resources to defy Spanish rule. Although Spain succeeded in detaching the southern Netherland, thanks largely to the military ability of Alexander Farnese, Duke of Parma, the Seven Provinces retained their independence. They signed an armistice with Spain in 1609 but did not receive full recognition until the Treaty of Münster in 1648.

The rise of the Dutch Republic to prominence in the seventeenth century was rapid. It can be attributed largely to a highly intensive use of its resources, an administration which encouraged free enterprise, and an initially favourable international situation. Unfortunately, the vulnerability of the United Provinces was already apparent by the mid-seventeenth century as these favourable conditions began to change. An examination of the Dutch economy, the administration and the international situation will show that there was always a narrow margin between strength and weakness, between rise and decline.

Dutch power was, above all, economic. Already, under Spanish rule, the seaward provinces of Holland and Zeeland had developed a strong commercial potential, making the most of their control over the mouths of the Rhine, Maas and Scheldt. Although they did suffer economic depression in the 1560s and 1570s, they were presented with a unique opportunity for further commercial expansion in the 1590s. This they seized with remarkable speed. By the last few decades of the sixteenth century Europe was experiencing an accelerating population growth. This coincided with a series of bad harvests, especially in the 1590s, to produce a serious shortage of food in southern Europe, although the grain-producing countries of the Baltic (especially Poland) continued to yield a surplus. The Dutch merchants from Amsterdam and Rotterdam proceeded to develop an enormous bulk trade, conveying Baltic grain to areas of need like Spain and Italy. In 1591, for example, 200 shiploads entered the Mediterranean. At the same time, there was an increase in trade in other articles: timber, iron and copper from the Baltic to western and southern Europe, and salt from France and Portugal to the Baltic. Hence the United Provinces became a major European entrepôt. Cities like Amsterdam, Leyden and Utrecht developed industries which turned raw materials into finished articles for re-export. The Dutch also succeeded in breaking into the Spanish and Portuguese imperial monopolies with the establishment of the East India Company in 1602 and the West India Company in 1621, and became Europe's major dealers in tropical wares, especially in spices and cochineal. Daniel Defoe later expressed the redistributive nature of the Dutch economy by describing the Dutch as 'the Middle Persons in trade, the Factors and Brokers of Europe'.[1] A similar view had already been expressed by the French merchants of Nantes, who complained to the King's Council in 1645 that the Republic 'is made to serve as a way station and storehouse', the purpose being 'to distribute and sell to other nations'.[2]

Economic growth was sustained by a no less remarkable capacity for building ships and providing credit. A significant advance in ship design occurred in the 1590s when the Dutch, always conscious of the shallow water of their ports, developed the *fluyt* or flyboat. This could be used in river mouths as well as at sea, and had the additional advantages of being cheap to build, of having a large cargo-carrying capacity in proportion to its size and of requiring small crews. It gave the Dutch a head start over every other country in Europe, and by 1670 the total of Dutch shipping amounted to 568,000 tons, larger than that of all the other major powers combined. If this provided the machinery to sustain the flow of trade, the lubrication was ensured by the availability of credit and of convenient methods of exchange. This was due primarily to the establishment of the Exchange Bank at Amsterdam (1609), an imitation of the system used in some Italian states, especially Venice. Throughout the seventeenth century Amsterdam remained the unquestioned banking and financial centre of Europe.

Success, however, brought vulnerability: the Dutch Republic became the target of jealous rivals, especially England and France. In the commercial struggles of the seventeenth century, the Netherlands had the disadvantage of limited natural resources, long and vulnerable lines of communication, and a small population. English retaliation occurred first, taking the form of the 1651 Navigation Acts and the Treaties of Westminster (1654 and 1674) and the insistence that Dutch fishermen in English waters take out licences. French resentment of Dutch success expressed itself in the 1660s and Colbert, in an effort to smash the Dutch economy, imposed high French tariffs in 1664 and 1667. From the middle of the century onwards the Dutch economy was under constant pressure. The Dutch fought back and thwarted the efforts of their rivals to break into their commercial network. But eventually the strain took its toll. Security for Dutch shipping could be guaranteed only by convoys, which involved considerable expenditure. As the Republic became involved in wars with England (1652–4, 1665–7 and 1672–4) and with France (1672–8, 1688–97 and 1702–13) the administration had to resort to heavier taxation until, by the end of the seventeenth century, the average rate of taxation, most of it indirect, was three times larger than that in France. The full effects of this became apparent in the eighteenth century. Wages were forced up by the rising cost of living. This raised the price of Dutch manufactures which had previously been low enough to give the Republic a competitive edge in its export trade. Although there was no rapid decline after 1713, the Dutch economy ceased to expand and it did not take its share in the overall increase in world trade. In maturing it seemed to have lost some of its aggressive characteristics.

The Dutch Republic provided one of the first examples in modern history of the rejection of dynasticism by revolution, and the formation of a voluntary federal union. The drift towards republicanism occurred after the failure to establish an alternative monarchy to the Habsburgs, but there is no doubt that the regime was effective in keeping the Seven Provinces together during the period of severe external pressure between 1574 and 1648. It also maintained a generally tolerant atmosphere, apparently influenced by the belief of Erasmus that 'he does not sail badly who steers a course between two several evils'.[3] Despite the victory of militant Calvinism at the Synod of Dort (1618), the government always contrived to prevent it from establishing a stranglehold on thought and economic activity. The United Provinces became a haven for immigrants, many of whom brought with them valuable economic skills. They also

The Dutch Republic in the seventeenth century

reached a high level of cultural achievement in the seventeenth century; a few of the more important figures included such artists as Rembrandt, Steen, Cuyp, Van Goyen, Vermeer, Brouwer, Ostade, de Hoogh and Vouwermans; the poet van den Vondel; the philosophers Descartes and Spinoza; and Huygens, Leeuwenhock and Boerhaave (scientists). In more ways than one the concepts of free enterprise and minimal government interference seemed to be firmly vindicated.

There was, however, a price. Two fundamental problems connected with the administrative system soon became apparent.

The first was the effect of decentralization. The Union of Utrecht (1579) contained an inherent contradiction which the Republic never solved. Although the member states were to form 'an alliance, confederation and union . . . as if they constituted only a single province', each, nevertheless, should retain 'undiminished its special and particular privileges'.[4] The attempt to carry out these two principles produced a weak constitution. Each province was largely autonomous and possessed its own legislative bodies (States). The central legislature, the States General, met at the Hague, but important issues required unanimity, and delegates frequently had to refer back to the Provincial States for further instructions. As a result, the conduct of foreign policy became increasingly inefficient through the loss of speed and secrecy. There was no officially constituted central executive; although the Grand Pensionary of Holland tended to act on behalf of the Republic as a whole, each of the other provinces jealously guarded its local privileges. The Netherlands therefore remained one of the exceptions to the growing centralization of government which was taking place throughout Europe.

The second was a prolonged conflict between two interest groups: the Regents (who included the Grand Pensionary) and the Stadholder (normally the head of the House of Orange). The Regents wanted to avoid any possibility of the Republic drifting towards a monarchy ruled by an Orangist dynasty; for monarchy, according to the writer de la Court, would be 'a death from which there is no resurrection'.[2] The Stadholder, on the other hand, offered more obvious leadership in times of emergency as, for example, during the French invasion of 1672. During the seventeenth century the Republic oscillated from one side to the other, with little chance of a permanent constitutional settlement. Before 1619 the Regents were

The Dutch Republic 1600–1700

in control but, following the execution of Oldenbarneveldt, the Grand Pensionary, the Orangist Stadholders ruled the country (Maurice of Nassau 1619–25, Frederick Henry 1625–47 and William II 1647–50). The Regents dominated the scene again from 1650 to 1672, until Johan de Witt was overthrown during the war with France and replaced by the Stadholder William III (1672–1702). The latter's assumption of English responsibilities from 1689, however, prevented him from giving his attention to the Dutch scene. Similar swings of the pendulum occurred in the eighteenth century, and by the 1770s and 1780s Dutch patriots were expressing their hostility to the lack of definition in the constitutional structure and asserting that 'The Republic must be one and indivisible.'[5]

The rise of the Dutch Republic was connected directly with the international situation. In the first stage Philip II was preoccupied with a series of problems between 1585 and 1598, of which the Revolt of the Netherlands formed only a part (see Chapter 9). He divided his resources between the reconquest of the Low Countries and the Enterprise of England and, from 1592, pressure on the Dutch was further decreased by Spanish involvement in the French Wars of Religion. The second stage saw the further weakening of Spain; this time Dutch survival was made possible by the involvement of all Habsburg resources in the enormously destructive Thirty Years' War (1618–48). The Republic was able to take advantage of Spanish preoccupation in Germany to launch attacks on Spanish and Portuguese colonies. Even in 1648, the Republic was in a favourable position. Western Europe was in a hiatus, between the decline of Spain and the rise of France, and Central Europe was in a state of confusion. Finally, at this stage, the Republic was still not regarded by the other powers as a potential threat. France, for example, was much more concerned with the apparent military strength of Sweden, who seemed the most aggressive of all the Protestant countries.

The Republic benefited from being underestimated and suffered no grievous damage in its struggle for nationhood. Indeed, it was sustained on the rapid weakening of Spain; Dutch ascendancy was in direct relationship with Spanish decline. This situation, however, could not be expected to last. Inevitably the Republic reached a stage in its development where war became thoroughly undesirable. De la Court, giving his priorities for Holland's welfare, observed: 'War is much worse than an uncertain Peace. And among all pernicious things, except the intolerable slavery of being govern'd by the Will of a single Person, nothing is more mischievous than a War.'[6] It was in the second half of the seventeenth century, the period in which the Dutch were struggling to maintain their commercial supremacy, that the most bitter conflicts occurred. The first was with England. The First, Second and Third Anglo–Dutch Wars (1652–4, 1665–7 and 1672–4) sapped some of the Dutch energy at sea and resulted in the capture of large amounts of shipping. But it was the rivalry with France which proved most damaging. During the first half of the seventeenth century, France and the Republic had co-operated in dealing with Spain, the common enemy. The turning point, however, came in 1668, when Johan de Witt, fearing that the complete destruction of Spanish power would release an even greater store of energy from France, was instrumental in forming the defensive Triple Alliance against Louis XIV. The French king now turned on the Republic in an effort to destroy it. This was a situation with which de Witt found it impossible to deal. William of Orange, who assumed the leadership of the Netherlands after the lynching of de Witt in 1672, conducted an effective defensive strategy but saved the country only by the ruinous expedient of cutting the dykes. French resentment was not checked by the Treaty of Nijmegen (1678), and the Republic found itself ranged against France in the War of the League of Augsburg (1688–97) and the War of the Spanish Succession (1702–13). The tables seemed to have turned. The Spanish hold on the northern Netherlands in the sixteenth century had been weakened and lost because of the enterprise and determination of the Dutch partisans and Sea Beggars. By the end of the seventeenth century, however, the Dutch themselves were confronted by a new military power with the largest armies seen in Europe since the time of Augustus. Although Louis XIV was eventually checked by a European coalition and the Netherlands were given a long respite in the eighteenth century, the spectre of a French invasion remained. When the troops of a rejuvenated France poured into the Netherlands in 1795, the Republic, politically disunited and economically weakened, collapsed under the strain.

21
France During the Administration of Cardinal Richelieu

The administration of Cardinal Richelieu (1624–42) was of paramount importance for the development of royal absolutism in seventeenth-century France. But his achievements were not the result of a carefully formulated design; rather they were introduced when required, their timing decided by his own practical experience. As far as possible, Richelieu sought to control the ideological preferences which he undoubtedly possessed and relied on proven remedies. He derived much of the inspiration for his reforms from the past but made extensive adjustments to correspond with his vision of the future. It does not, therefore, diminish his importance to say that he was a dominant force in a long period of evolution rather than the active formulator of revolution. His methods were based on selection and synthesis rather than on invention.

The extent to which Richelieu referred back to the past, together with the impact which he actually had on the future, can be examined in three sections: constitutional developments; the condition of the economy; and his policy towards the three Estates of France.

For Richelieu the linchpin of any constitution was the king, whose power must be absolute in both theory and practice. Furthermore, this authority had a religious base, for 'Kings are the living images of God'. This concept, generally labelled 'Divine Right of Kings' certainly preceded Richelieu and was expressed, for example, in the works of Bodin in the late sixteenth century. Absolutism was also

153

claimed by the monarchy in its legislative process long before Richelieu became Principal Minister; the traditional way of ending royal edicts was with the phrase 'car tel est notre plaisir'.[1] Nevertheless, the second half of the sixteenth century was a period of constitutional dislocation for France, when both the theory and the practice of absolutism suffered a severe blow. The Wars of Religion undermined the reputation and prestige of the monarchy, and it required the reign of Henry IV (1589-1610) to restore the credibility of kingship. When the assassination of Henry IV was followed by a period of regency on behalf of Louis XIII, the position of the monarchy was again uncertain and virtually anything could have happened. The importance of Richelieu at this precise moment was that he recognized the weaknesses of royal power in practice, and concentrated on using traditional ideologies and previously tried methods to enable it to rise from its ashes, fully restored for the future. Richelieu achieved this by developing ministerial absolutism in the name of the Crown. He undertook the process of reform with the full authority and cooperation of Louis XIII, observing: 'The ability to let himself be served is not among the least qualities of a great king.'[2] The success of Richelieu's aim became apparent by 1661. Mazarin, Principal Minister between 1643 and 1661, overcame the anti-absolutist movements known as the Frondes and, by 1661, Louis XIV felt sufficiently confident to assume full control of his administration. Incomparably more powerful than any of his predecessors, Louis XIV owed the security of his absolutism to Richelieu, whose very success meant the future redundancy of the office of Principal Minister.

The growing power of the Crown was exercised through an evolving bureaucracy. This was not created by Richelieu; he merely defined it more carefully and provided a more systematic structure at the centre. The precedents went back to the twelfth century, when the original *Curia Regis* had contracted into an inner Royal Council. By the end of the sixteenth century this had been subdivided into more specialized units which included the *Conseil d'Etat*, the *Conseil des Parties* and the *Conseil des Finances*. When Richelieu became Principal Minister in 1630, after the *dévots* and Marillac had fallen from favour, the trend was towards tighter control over the conciliar system by the king and a few key ministers in the *Conseil d'en Haut*, contact with the provinces being maintained by the *Conseil des Dépêches*. Richelieu continued the process of elevating a few ministers and reducing the size of the decision-making bodies, a trend which had begun under Sully and Henry IV and was completed by Louis XIV. Yet, at the same time, Richelieu had no pre-arranged blueprint for reform, regarding piecemeal measures as more likely to be effective in the long run. He even opposed sections of Marillac's *Code Michaud* in 1629 because he considered that the proposed institutional changes which it contained would be unworkable. Richelieu's methods proved successful in the immediate future; the conciliar system was not substantially altered by Mazarin and was therefore inherited as Richelieu had left it by Louis XIV. It proved quite capable of sustaining royal absolutism, although Louis XIV liked to work more directly with individual ministers, and avoided further subdivisions of the councils already in existence. On the other hand, Richelieu provided no guidance as to the long-term direction which the councils should take in their relationship with absolutism. As a result they were, by the end of the seventeenth century, becoming ossified and in need of substantial overhaul.

Richelieu's administration also increased royal authority over the provinces. This, too, was neither without precedent nor based on systematic planning. The powers of the provincial governors had already been partially curbed by, for example, the Ordinance of 1545 and by the reforms of Henry IV. Richelieu went further. He used the power of the Crown to dismiss any governors who resisted royal absolutism, and his task in identifying them was eased by a tendency for families like the Vendômes of Brittany to participate in plots. By the end of Richelieu's administration twelve of the original sixteen governors had been replaced. The powers of the traditional authorities were gradually conferred on the *intendants*, agents representing the Crown in the provinces and responsible for the enforcement of royal edicts. These officials were by no means a new creation; they had been in existence since the mid-sixteenth century. But Richelieu regarded them as an ideal means of dealing with local disorder and maladministration. Since these problems were expected to be temporary, the position of *intendant* would not be a permanent appointment. Nor would any appointee be allowed to establish permanent connections with the area under his jurisdiction. As Richelieu's administration progressed, however, the *intendant* played an increasingly important role, assuming control over the raising of troops, the administration of justice and the implementation of decrees. By 1637 these 'temporary' officials had been established over most of France and were in control of provincial subdivisions known as *généralités*. Richelieu's successor, Mazarin, continued the process of transferring local powers to the *intendants* by making them responsible for tax assessment and collection. Although the backlash of the Frondes resulted in their temporary withdrawal, the *intendants* were reinstated during the 1650s and, by the time Louis XIV assumed personal power in 1661, there were no fewer than thirty of them, under the systematic supervision of Colbert. More than any other official, the *intendant* came to typify the administration of the *ancient régime* in France, the direct, if unintentional, result of Richelieu's reforms.

A major potential source of resistance to the growth of absolutism was the Paris *Parlement*, which regarded itself as the traditional guardian of laws and liberties. The predecessors of Louis XIII had always been careful to avoid a direct confrontation, and compromises had usually been arrived at whereby the *Parlement* registered royal edicts after a token delay and nominal remonstrance. Richelieu saw that the *Parlement* could easily become an obstructive organ within the constitution, and concentrated on reducing its powers without destroying it altogether. His methods were not carefully calculated but were more or less related to the needs and opportunities of the moment. In 1631, for example, he established the *Chambre d'Arsenal* which assumed the power to conduct trials of major political offenders, thus bypassing the judicial powers of the *Parlement*. In 1635 Richelieu used a traditional expedient of placing major offices for sale, applying this to the *Parlement* itself. The result was that twenty-four new *conseilleurs* of *Parlement* were created, the funds being used to assist the French war effort. The process was repeated in 1637. As Richelieu had anticipated, the prestige of the Paris *Parlement* suffered from the new association with venality, and Richelieu was able to make use of this discomfiture. In 1641 he confronted it with an order that all edicts were to be registered before any remonstrance would be permitted. Richelieu did not live to see the attempt of the *Parlement* to regain its rights and privileges in the First Fronde, but his measures set the pattern for the future policies of Louis XIV. Again, the *Parlement* was gradually weakened, and the 1673 Letters Patent imposed a restriction on its powers which was virtually identical to the Order of 1641. Richelieu could not, however, provide a long-term solution to the

The Administration of Richelieu

counter claims of absolutism and the *Parlement*. He merely deferred the climax of the struggle, which occurred well into the eighteenth century.

Richelieu was confronted by greater difficulties with the finances and the economy. The entire fiscal structure was unbalanced and, to make matters worse, France was experiencing a period of serious economic depression, part of what some historians have referred to as a general European crisis. Richelieu's administration provided no major advances or reforms, but it was an important phase in the development of the financial system so characteristic of the *ancien régime*.

The fundamental problem was the lack of a uniform structure. Most of the revenue was derived from direct taxes, like the *taille*, and indirect taxes, like the *gabelle*, both of which were unequally assessed and distributed. There was no shortage of criticism of the exemptions of the nobility and clergy from a substantial number of taxes. Bodin, the writer, and Bullion, the *Surintendant des Finances*, added their voices to the demand for a more systematic method of assessment. There is no doubt that Richelieu's personal preference was also for reorganization, but he came to the conclusion that more effective use of the present system was a safer policy, particularly since he confessed his 'ignorance on financial matters' and had no precedents to guide him if he committed himself to institutional reform. Therefore, he resorted to doubling the *taille* and *gabelle* and to removing blockages from the existing structure. This course of action was continued by Richelieu's successors, D'Emery, Colbert, Louvois, Pomponne and other finance ministers who served Louis XIV. All sought to maximize the yield of existing taxes and some introduced new taxes (like the *dixième* and the *capitation*). But none was able to overcome the inherent inequalities and lack of justice which had eaten into the whole fabric and which contributed directly to the crisis of 1789.

France's financial difficulties were accentuated by a venality which was common throughout Europe. This was of two types: personal enrichment from public revenues, and political advancement from the sale and purchase of offices. The first was restrained but not actually stopped by Richelieu; it would have been impossible to eradicate it altogether since leading ministers from Sully to Pomponne all benefited. The second was dealt with more systematically. At first Richelieu urged Louis XIII to 'banish the sale of offices'.[3] Gradually, however, he came round to the view that this would be impractical. 'Venality of office would be a crime in a newly established republic but prudence does not allow us to act in the same way in a monarchy, whose imperfections have passed into habit and whose disorder is part of the state.'[4] If the sale of offices could not be eliminated it could at least be conducted for the greater benefit of the Crown. Recognized as a form of revenue since 1522, the sale of offices had been made more attractive by the *paulette* of 1604, which allowed offices to become hereditary, subject to regular payments. Richelieu made more extensive use of the *paulette* and greatly increased the range of offices for sale. Sometimes this could be used as a political weapon as, for example, in his attempts to reduce the prestige of the Paris *Parlement*. Richelieu's approach devalued many offices and caused the duplication of others. No doubt this enhanced the authority of the Crown in relation to its servants. But, at the same time, it increased dependence on this form of revenue until it eventually became an addiction; between 1689 and 1715 Louis XIV's government relied on the sale of offices to raise the huge sum of 900 m. livres.

In his policy towards commerce and manufactures Richelieu was one of a line of mercantilists extending from Sully to Colbert. He fully subscribed to the view expressed by Henry IV that royal edicts were the best method of stimulating growth, although he redefined one or two major priorities. According to Sully, the main emphasis should be placed on the development of agriculture, whereas Richelieu concentrated on commerce, which he regarded as 'the creator of new values, the generator of wealth for all peoples'.[4] As Superintendent of Commerce and Navigation from 1626, he had a vision of France as a major seapower, second to none in the volume of her trade and the wealth of her colonial possessions. Unfortunately, he was obliged to reduce the scope of his aspirations because of the practical difficulties involved, particularly the widespread resistance among French merchants to policies so obviously formulated and dominated by the central administration. He also lacked the necessary personnel to enforce orders banning all imports into France in foreign ships. Nevertheless, Richelieu did provide a clue as to the way in which the economy could expand in the future. Some of his ideas were implemented by Colbert after 1664, the navy being increased from 20 to 196 ships and a series of commercial companies being established to organize trade with the West Indies, the East Indies, the Levant and Northern Europe.

The official social structure of France constituted the clergy as the First Estate, the nobility as the Second Estate and the bourgeoisie and peasantry as the Third Estate. Richelieu was connected with the First Estate by profession and the Second by birth. The Third remained something of an unknown quantity to him, and his policy towards it lacked the subtlety which displayed his confidence in dealing with the other two.

In his attitude to the Church, Richelieu is often projected as a materialist, basing his whole approach on a pragmatic and Machiavellian concept of the utility of religion as a social cement. Yet Richelieu was fundamentally in harmony with the approach of his predecessors. He followed Henry IV and Sully in departing from the mentality of the Wars of Religion and tried to prevent the *dévots* from establishing the full force of the Counter Reformation as official government policy in the 1620s. He was by no means radical in his attitude to the relationship between King and Church; he pursued a cautiously neutral line between Gallicanism and Ultramontanism, although he put pressure on the Assembly of Clergy to conform to his policies on financial matters (for example, he persuaded the Assembly in 1635 to increase its annual subsidy). Mazarin followed a similar diplomatic course, avoiding commitment to either side, and it was not until Louis XIV's majority that Gallicanism and Ultramontanism became contentious issues. When this did occur, the result was so complex that it would be difficult to perceive any direct influence exerted by Richelieu. A clearer pattern emerges over Richelieu's attitude to minorities, particularly the Huguenots. He followed the official policy of Henry IV, as laid down in the Edict of Nantes (1598), and reaffirmed some of the guarantees in his Peace of Alais (1629). Nevertheless, he had no sympathy for the basic principle of toleration nor for the Huguenots as a group. He abhorred heresy and he urged Louis XIII to reduce any political autonomy which Protestants had acquired in France. 'As long as the Huguenots retain their position in France, the King will never be master within the realm.'[5] It is possible that Richelieu envisaged the time when concessions to the Huguenots could be withdrawn. Louis XIV later believed that this time had arrived in 1685, when he was informed that Protestantism was in such a weak state that the

Edict of Nantes could be revoked without the danger of massive resistance. On the whole, Richelieu was an orthodox Church leader, devoid of mysticism and aggressive fervour for reconversion, but also anxious to prevent heresy from gaining any permanent position of strength.

Richelieu lived in a period when the nobility had high hopes of restoring their status and privileges after the restraining rule of Henry IV by taking advantage of the power vacuum during the Regency of Marie de Medici (1610–23). Richelieu, himself an aristocrat, sympathized with what he regarded as 'one of the principal sinews of the state'.[6] But, at the same time, he was fully aware of France's long history of aristocratic plots and revolts. His basic policy, therefore, was to allow the nobility to retain their privileged social position, but to weaken their political influence by making full use of already tried methods. His main concern was to stamp out *coups* wherever they occurred, the main examples being the Chalais Revolt (1626), the Montmorency Revolt (1632) and the Cinq-Mars Revolt (1641). Richelieu made full use of the powers given in the *Code Michaud* (1629) to deal with *lèse majesté*. These, in turn, were a reaffirmation of the Royal Declaration of 1610, the Ordinance of Blois (1579) and the 1539 Ordinance of Francis I, which had pointed to the dangers of 'conspiring, plotting or moving against our person or children or against the state of our realm'.[7] In his search for security Richelieu often proceeded harshly against those accused of *lèse majesté*, believing that 'public utility often benefits from injury to individuals'. It is hardly surprising that Richelieu was thoroughly detested by the entire *noblesse d'épée*, and that the administration of Mazarin saw the backlash in the form of the unsuccessful Second Fronde. Nevertheless, Richelieu's measures had been effective. The nobility were increasingly isolated from the real source of political authority, a process which was taken to its logical conclusion in the next reign. During the entire period of his majority (1661–1715) Louis XIV selected most of his ministers from outside the ranks of the *noblesse d'épée* and carefully neutralized the latter by requiring their attendance at Versailles from 1683 onwards.

The Third Estate covered a huge spectrum of French society, and two examples can be used to show that Richelieu's attitudes and policies fit into a general pattern of evolutionary development.

At one extreme, the Third Estate overlapped into the Second since those members of the bourgeoisie who aspired to political power could merge into the nobility, either by buying offices or by genuine appointment. This process was well under way by the beginning of the seventeenth century, when the growing bureaucracy was recruited partly from the ranks of the bourgeoisie. Richelieu encouraged this as a means of reducing the political influence of the *noblesse d'épée* and of increasing the royal revenues through the sale and proliferation of offices. During the reign of Louis XIV the blurring of the distinctions between the two Estates was complete. As the top level of the Third Estate passed into the Second, upward mobility would be sought by new aspirants.

At the other extreme the Third Estate remained downtrodden and exploited. None of the seventeenth-century ministers had any basic concept of social justice which would relate the level of taxation to the degree of wealth. Richelieu tended to echo traditional views that the role of the peasantry was purely productive. 'All politicians agree that when the people are too comfortable it is impossible to keep them within the bounds of their duty . . . they must be compared with mules, which, being used to burdens, are spoiled more by rest than labour.'[8] Any protest or rising was, therefore, to be treated severely, and Richelieu observed of the *'Nu-pieds'* rebellion of 1639: 'We cannot make too great an example in this instance.'[9] He inherited and perpetuated the assumption that the productive sections of the Third Estate were capable of sustaining frequent increases in taxation. The lesson offered by the numerous rebellions of the 1630s and 1640s was lost, as violence came to be accepted as normal in the provinces. There is no evidence, for example, that Louis XIV's taxation policy was ever moderated because of popular uprisings, even though these occurred virtually every year during his reign.

Richelieu once stated that his first concern was the prestige and power of the king, the second the strength of the kingdom. This is an apt comment on his overall achievement. He succeeded in rescuing the authority of the Crown from possible oblivion and made available some of the resources used by the *'Roi Soleil'* after 1661. At the same time, however, his methods were dependent on the use of traditional expedients which tended to damage French society as much as they benefited the French monarchy.

22

France Under Louis XIV

The peak of French absolutism was reached during the personal rule of Louis XIV (1661–1715). His authority was fully enshrined in the concept of the Divine Right of Kings as expressed by Bossuet: 'The person of the King is sacred . . . all the state is in him; the will of the entire people is contained in his.'[1] This hinged on the precept that 'It is God who establishes Kings.' Louis XIV was determined to act the part of absolute monarch to the full, referring to kings as 'fathers of their people' and emphasizing the importance of a government 'that is directed by Kings whom God alone can judge'.[2] He departed from the more passive role of Louis XIII, who had been content to entrust the use of his prerogatives to a leading minister.

Yet it is possible to oversimplify the significance of Louis XIV's powers in practical terms and to exaggerate the actual range of his authority. Even the theory of Divine Right was circumscribed. Bossuet, for example, warned that 'Kings, like all others, are subject to the equity of the laws.'[1] When they were applied, the prerogative powers frequently came up against the forces of tradition and privilege. Louis XIV soon came to realize that the changes he sought to impose from above could rarely be carried to their logical conclusion, and that absolutism would have to accept certain boundaries in practice as well as in theory. Indeed, the very security of his position depended on his being able to establish a degree of balance and harmony within French society. Absolutism was the elevation of royal power above all other levels, but it could be accomplished only by the maintenance of everything in its 'natural and legitmate order'.[3] To destroy all obstacles would upset this balance and would invoke the accusation of tyranny. Louis XIV therefore accepted the continuation of many privileges and traditional powers which actually militated against absolutism.

The main theme of this chapter, the development of royal power encountering the resistance of tradition, can be illustrated by Louis XIV's administrative, economic and clerical policies.

Louis XIV exercised more complete personal authority over the process of government than had any of his predecessors. He openly acknowledged his enjoyment of responsibility and power: 'Le métier de roi est grand, noble, delicieux'[4] and, according to Voltaire, he had 'trained and inured himself to work'.[5] He was, therefore, careful not to appoint a successor to Mazarin, and he insisted that ultimate reference for instructions should be made 'à moi'. Where Louis XIII had used a Principal Minister, Louis XIV employed Secretaries of State, none of whom were allowed to become too elevated. Colbert, Le Tellier, Louvois and Pomponne did not possess the range of authority entrusted to Richelieu; this was now exercised by the King himself. Nevertheless, there were certain inevitable limitations to his authority. Louis made no major structural alterations in the Royal Councils, which comprised the *Conseil d'Etat*, the *Conseil d'en Haut*, the *Conseil des Finances*, the *Conseil des Dépêches* and the *Conseil Privé*. He attempted, as far as possible, to tighten up on the membership of the *Conseil d'en Haut*, the central body, but the whole system was too well lubricated by the purchase of offices for Louis to consider destroying it. Unlike Frederick the Great of Prussia (1740–86), he made no attempt to stamp his own imprint on the structure or to cut through the upper bureaucracy to ensure more direct control at all levels. The conciliar system remained, even if it was weakened, and Louis XIV's absolutism depended ultimately on what information the ministers chose to feed to him. Total personal supervision was, therefore, out of the question, particularly when Louis XIV removed the centre of his administration from Paris to Versailles. Indeed, one of the many criticisms levelled against Louis towards the end of his reign was that his rule was becoming increasingly disjointed.

In local administration the dichotomy between advancing royal power and the resistance of tradition was even more apparent. On the one hand, it was evident that the *intendants* were being given greater authority and discretionary powers over the provinces and towns. Under Colbert they had become regular royal agents, thirty in number, supervised by the Royal Councils and assuming financial, military and judicial control over the *généralités* in which they served. The result was a parallel decline in the powers of the governors and other traditional provincial officials. On the other hand, no attempt was made to reconstruct the local administrative system. Many traditional positions were retained and offered for sale; these included the financial *officiers*. Nor was there any systematic reorganization of urban government. Although the 1692 statute abolished the right of towns to elect their own officials and extended the powers of the *intendants*, the former municipal officials were kept to satisfy local aspirations. In general, the new royal officials did not replace the old provincial functionaries. They overlapped them, with the result that two bureaucratic layers were built up, the one impeding the progress of the other.

The reign saw no radical change in the nature of the Paris *Parlement*. Louis XIV certainly intended to assert his authority over any institution claiming a share in the legislative process and he referred to the Paris *Parlement* as being 'in possession and enjoyment of usurped authority'.[3] Furthermore, 'The rise of the *Parlements* in general had been dangerous to the entire Kingdom during my minority. They had to be humbled, less for the harm which they had done than for that which they might do in the future.'[3] By the 1673 Letters Patent the Paris *Parlement* was ordered to register edicts without discussion, thus confirming Richelieu's treatment in 1641. But Louis XIV was careful not to destroy the institution altogether – it was a potential source of danger if provoked too openly, as the First Fronde had proved. The real attempt to overcome the *Parlement*'s challenge to royal authority did not occur until Maupeou's abolition of the *Parlements* in 1771.

French law experienced a similar combination of royal encroachments and the persistence of tradition. New legal codes introduced, mainly during the administration of Colbert, included the Civil Ordinance (1667), the Criminal Ordinance (1670), the Ordinance of Commerce (1673), the Ordinance of Marine (1681) and the *Code Noir* (1685). Despite these examples of innovation, considerable local diversity remained, especially between the northern region's common law and the Roman law applied in the south. Absolutism did not, therefore, confer legal uniformity. This was to be the achievement of the French Revolution and Napoleon I.

The increase in royal authority had mixed effects on finances. There were considerable improvements in the methods of tax collection, but not in the structure of the fiscal system. Under Louis XIV France was taxed as if she were permanently on a war footing, but the numerous inconsistencies and privileges resulted in chronic wastage.

Louis XIV authorized and supported the extensive reforms of Colbert. These included the use of *intendants* to assess the level of taxation in the *généralités*, frequent surveys to reduce the incidence of petty corruption, and the increase of indirect taxes, like the *gabelle*, in order to extract more revenues from the wealthier sections of society. Careful planning, and the removal of numerous blockages, resulted in a series of balanced budgets, virtually unheard of in the seventeenth century. But Colbert's proposals for more radical reform were ignored by Louis XIV. The result was that the inequalities and privileges remained basically untouched. The Church escaped direct taxation on payment of an annual 'free gift'. The nobility claimed exemption on the ground that they served France militarily. Louis was reluctant to challenge the status quo, for fear of provoking the First and Second Estates into active resistance to absolutism. He was also opposed to interfering with local exemptions and the uneven application of the *taille*, *gabelle*, tariffs and excise duties. When, in the 1690s, Vauban proposed a basic solution to the financial problems of France by the assessment of an income tax at 7 per cent on all classes, Louis was predictably hostile. Faced with this unwillingness to challenge the system, Colbert's successors had to make do with hand-to-mouth methods in dealing with ever increasing war debts. The result was a state of constant financial crisis. Between 1708 and 1715, for example, the total expenditure of the government was 1,915 m. livres, while the revenue collected was not more than 461 m. By 1715 the total deficit probably stood at 3,000 m. livres. Louis XIV's failure to push absolutism through the barrier of economic privilege created an intolerable situation of prolonged semi-bankruptcy for the eighteenth century, which had much to do with the eventual destruction of royal absolutism.

Between 1667 and 1683 French commerce and industry were

under the capable direction of Colbert, as Controller General. He adopted the view that the best means of increasing 'the power and the glory of His Majesty and lowering that of his enemies and rivals'[6] was by a policy of mercantilism involving more extensive state controls. This was achieved by a variety of methods. Colbert stimulated the growth of the French merchant marine and imposed heavy tariffs on imports in an effort to eradicate English and Dutch competition. To encourage French commercial expansion he established several Royal Companies, directed by the State. These included the East India Company (1664), the West India Company (1664), the Northern Company (1669) and the Levant Company (1670). He also increased the scope of state intervention in industry, greatly diversifying the range of manufactures and forming a series of *Manufactures Royales*. It might be thought, therefore, that Louis XIV's reign provided a thoroughly effective mercantilist system. There were, however, two serious shortcomings. One was that the reforms of Colbert and the policies of his successors failed to overcome either the numerous privileges of the trade guilds or the inconsistencies of internal customs barriers which enabled some of the eastern provinces to trade more easily with Germany than with the rest of France. Another was that royal intervention was frequently of the wrong kind, being concerned with the quality of manufactures and the quantity of exports rather than with the encouragement of a more efficient capitalist system. Consequently, the regime failed to liberate fully the productive forces of French industry and commerce. As Adam Smith later observed: 'The industry and commerce of a great country he (Colbert) endeavoured to regulate upon the same model as the departments of a modern office.'[7] This was seen as early as 1685 by Des Gilleuls, who believed that 'le plus grand secret est de laisser toute liberté dans le commerce'.[8] The natural conclusion, therefore, was that the reign failed to destroy the anomalies and restrictions of the commercial and industrial sectors while at the same time imposing excessive restraint on free enterprise.

What was Louis XIV's attitude to French society? He was determined to prove that he was unquestionably in authority over all classes. But in his concern to eliminate the possibility of rivalry and criticism from any source he contributed to the growth of an unbalanced and stratified system which could not be maintained indefinitely as the basis of absolute monarchy. He created a neutralized but potentially dangerous aristocracy. His attempts to withdraw all offices of state from the grasp of the *noblesse d'épée* and to concentrate its leading members at Versailles meant that a substantial sector of the Second Estate became increasingly non-productive and was regarded as parasitic by the rest of society. The structure of the Third Estate was also adversely affected. Louis XIV carried to its logical conclusion Richelieu's promotion of members of the bourgeoisie into state offices as a new nobility. This beheaded the productive body of the bourgeoisie by encouraging a scramble for offices among those who had achieved commercial successes. It also heaped upon this new nobility the accumulated resentment of the *noblesse d'épée*. Saint Simon, for example, referred to Louis XIV's choice of officials as 'la règne de vile bourgeoisie'. The lower section of the Third Estate, the peasantry, continued to be regarded as the inexhaustible source of direct taxation, and Louis XIV ignored the warnings provided by the numerous rebellions which occurred during his reign. If anything, the conditions of the peasantry worsened. Absolutism, far from conferring benefits by destroying the remnants of feudalism, actually allowed it to regain ground between 1660 and 1670 as the nobility were enabled to increase their seigneurial powers; this forestalled the possibility of aristocratic revolt, but the eventual price was rural upheaval such as occurred in 1789.

The most complex sequence of events during the reign concerned religion. As a Gallican, Louis quarrelled with the Pope; on becoming an Ultramontanist, he opposed Gallicanism; and, as a devout Catholic, he attacked minority movements like Protestantism and Jansenism. The nature of these conflicts and the shifting ground upon which he stood are an indication that firm, decisive and consistent royal policy was lacking.

The Crown was quite capable of increasing its authority by draconian measures, as can be illustrated by three examples. First, Louis ensured himself a firm base of support by nominating only Gallican bishops and by insisting on extending the right of *régale* to all dioceses within France. This precipitated a conflict with the papacy which was not finally resolved until 1693. Second, the Revocation of the Edict of Nantes (1685) imposed extremely harsh punitive measures against the Huguenots at a time when most other European monarchs had accepted a more enlightened and moderate policy. The Edict was the culmination of a long campaign against Protestantism which had included the expulsion of Huguenots from all offices and trade guilds (1681) and the use of the Dragonnade system (1684). Louis clearly believed that he was acting from a position of great strength and that the removal of a compromise agreement (such as the Edict of Nantes) with a dissident minority would be an open indication of the success of absolutism. Bossuet seemed to uphold this view when he enthused: 'The work is worthy of your reign and of yourself . . . Heresy is no more. May the King of Heaven preserve the King of Earth.' Third, Louis XIV tried similar measures against Jansenism, on the assumption that royal absolutism had an inherent obligation to prevent the growth of further heresy in the future; his destruction of Port Royal in 1711 was an indication of the lengths to which he was prepared to go to maintain orthodoxy.

Yet Louis XIV always seemed to stop short of full clerical control and often retreated, after a while, to a less authoritarian position. For example, he had an ambivalent attitude to the activities of the Assembly of the Clergy in 1682. On the one hand, he secured the passage of the Four Articles, guaranteeing basic Gallican liberties. On the other, he prevented the discussions on separatism from going too far and he promptly disbanded the Assembly when the issue of a separate Patriarchate in France came up. This apparent inconsistency is easy to explain and it shows the limits to which royal power was prepared to go. Too extreme an assertion of Gallicanism would benefit the Assembly of Clergy and the Paris *Parlement* rather than the king himself. This was because the direct transfer of power from Rome to Paris would inevitably be followed by demands from the Assembly and the *Parlement* for greater control over the Church than the king would wish to grant. Louis therefore sought safety, by moving deliberately towards an Ultramontane position, and blocked the aspirations of the Assembly and the *Parlement* by reintroducing some of the influence of the Pope by 1693. At no time, therefore, did Louis XIV ever attempt to push absolutism to the point of a direct challenge to papal supremacy, and he stopped well short of the policies of Napoleon I.

Louis XIV did not say 'l'état, c'est moi'; this myth was probably started by Voltaire. It would not even have been true. The very isolation of the monarchy, the supposed guarantee of its power, was a major source of weakness. For, while the king balanced the classes against each other, juggled with his ministers and retained certain privileges as safeguards against protest, he lost the opportunity of establishing a more systematic bureaucracy. As Frederick the Great later proved, it was only by means of carefully structured and integrated layers of officialdom, shorn of traditions and venality, that a king could exercise the kind of personal control to which Louis XIV aspired.

23
French Foreign Policy in the Seventeenth Century

During the seventeenth century France became the leading power in Europe, in a process made up of two main phases. Henry IV (1589–1610), Richelieu (1624–42) and Mazarin (1643–61) all concentrated on the traditional view that the major enemy was the Habsburgs in their twin manifestations of Spain and Austria. Then, after attaining his majority in 1661, Louis XIV (1643–1715) extended the scope of French foreign policy and made the maritime powers (initially Holland and then England) the main opponents of France. By the last quarter of the seventeenth century France reached the peak of her power and influence but also became universally detested and increasingly vulnerable. This was the result of the inconsistencies of Louis XIV himself and his departure from the caution and restraint of Richelieu and Mazarin.

It is hardly surprising that in the reign of Henry IV (1589–1610) France was less aggressive towards her neighbours. After the destructive Wars of Religion the main priority was internal reconstruction and the reconciliation of warring factions. Although Henry IV resumed the old Valois campaign against the Habsburgs which had dominated French policy before Cateau Cambrésis (1559) he concentrated after 1598 on diplomatic rather than military activity. He succeeded, for example, in weakening the Spanish war effort in the Low Countries by providing subsidies to the Dutch in their continuing struggle for independence. He also concluded alliances with some of the Protestant princes of Germany, with the Swiss cantons

French Foreign Policy 1600–1700

and with Sweden – all designed to deter the Spanish and Austrian Habsburgs from displaying further aggression towards France. According to Sully, Henry IV had even more extensive ambitions: a project for European stability known to history as the Grand Design. This envisaged the destruction of Spanish power in Italy and the Netherlands, together with an end to Austrian control over Hungary, Bohemia and the Holy Roman Empire. Once the Habsburg threat to Europe (and, of course, to France) had been removed, Europe could settle down to a new stability based on balance and harmony between the six hereditary monarchies, six elective monarchies, three republics and three religions (Catholicism, Lutheranism and Calvinism). The whole structure would be upheld by a regular conciliar system and guaranteed by general disarmament. What really distinguished the Grand Design from the normal run of French policy was the assumption (derived, no doubt, from the bitter memory of civil war) that French interests could be served only by building order in Europe, not by profiting from disorder.

In the first half of Louis XIII's reign there was a temporary reconciliation with the House of Habsburg as the French government, under the influence of the *dévot* party, now thought in terms of an alliance of Catholic powers to deal with revolution and sedition attributed to a renewed Protestant offensive in Europe. Richelieu, however, was convinced that France could not co-exist safely with a powerful Habsburg combination. On receiving the title of Principal Minister in 1630 he therefore urged Louis to abandon the *dévot* policy and to reopen the struggle to 'arrest the progress of Spain'[1] and to 'halt the advance of the House of Austria'.[2] This would be accompanied by the gradual eastward expansion of the French frontier to a position along the Rhine where it could serve, simultaneously, as a defensive line and as a series of bridgeheads for future offensives against the Holy Roman Empire.

Richelieu's method was based on the judicious combination of diplomacy and military force. The former tended to predominate until 1635, by which time Richelieu believed that France had recovered sufficiently to enter the Thirty Years' War with prospects of immediate success. He fostered close relations between France and the maritime powers, drawing up the Treaty of Compiègne with the Dutch in 1624 and arranging the marriage between Henrietta Maria and Charles I of England in 1625. He was constantly active in Central Europe. In 1625, for example, he was instrumental in diverting the campaigns of Ernst Mansfeld from the Palatinate to the Netherlands, since he feared that Spain might gain the upper hand against the Dutch rebels and subsequently threaten the French frontier; with his encouragement, Mansfeld provided Spinola with an additional obstacle at a critical time. In his relations with the German states Richelieu was assisted by a somewhat sinister intriguer, Father Joseph, who achieved a measure of success at the Diet of Ratisbon in 1630. Richelieu's major instrument against the Habsburgs, however, was Gustavus Adolphus of Sweden, who invaded Germany in 1630. Richelieu reasoned that Sweden possessed the military prowess to bring the Habsburg offensive to a standstill but that she lacked the resources to inflict total defeat and thereby win control over the Empire. France could, therefore, benefit from a stalemate in which Sweden and the Habsburgs would exhaust each other, leaving Richelieu with the initiative when he chose to enter the struggle. The Treaty of Barwälde (1631) was the basis of this policy. In return for a guarantee of French material aid and subsidies for six years, Gustavus Adolphus agreed to maintain 36,000 troops in Germany, although he undertook not to invade Bavaria, which Richelieu was hoping to detach from the Habsburg-Imperialist camp.

On the whole, Richelieu was remarkably successful. France had succeeded in maintaining a coalition against the Habsburgs and in destroying the initiative gained by Spain and Austria in the 1620s. There were, however, miscalculations in his policy. He lost control over the Swedish offensive in Germany from 1632 as Gustavus Adolphus followed his own design and invaded Bavaria. Richelieu feared, for a while, that Sweden might force a victory in Central Europe after all, and he expressed relief at hearing of the Swedish king's death at the Battle of Lützen in 1632. Richelieu's policies of checks and balances could now be resumed, but only because of a stroke of luck. Moreover, he committed France to the Thirty Years' War several years too early. In 1635 France was fresh, but also untried. As a result, the performance of French troops was initially unimpressive. It seems that Richelieu had failed to reform and modernize the French army sufficiently. From 1637, however, France began to recover, and the real value of Richelieu's diplomacy became apparent. While the Habsburgs and Sweden were experiencing the strain of years of destructive warfare, France still possessed considerable reserves; these were used in the 1640s in her

French Foreign Policy 1600–1700

search for an advantageous settlement. But Richelieu died in 1642, some time before the final vindication of his policies.

Mazarin proved the ideal successor, trained in the methods of Richelieu but without the urge to experiment with his own schemes. What Richelieu designed Mazarin consolidated, thus introducing to French foreign policy a period of retrenchment. He pursued, with singleminded determination, the humiliation of France's two Habsburg rivals and the strengthening of the French frontier. The results were apparent in the Treaty of Westphalia (1648) and the Treaty of the Pyrenees (1659). The former gave to France Metz, Toul, Verdun, Southern Alsace, Breisach, Philippsburg and authority over ten imperial cities. Austria, by contrast, received no territorial additions and emerged somewhat enervated from the Thirty Years' War. The Treaty of the Pyrenees, concluding France's struggle with Spain, was still more advantageous. France received Artois and Roussillon from the Spanish Netherlands, together with fortresses in Hainault, Flanders and Luxemburg. What had become particularly apparent was the growing weakness of Spain, exposed at the Battle of Rocroi in 1643 and confirmed over the next sixteen years of warfare. By mid-century it was clear that France and Spain were exchanging roles, that the ascendancy of the one was being accomplished by the decline of the other. This was a happy situation for France, but it brought a degree of uncertainty. When Mazarin died in 1661 it was plain that France would continue to exploit Spain's problems in order to extract further territory. But what direction would French foreign policy as a whole now take?

On taking control of French diplomacy, Louis XIV at first kept to the lines laid down by Richelieu and Mazarin. He observed in 1661, for example: 'The state of the two crowns of France and Spain is such today and has been such for a long time in the world that it is impossible to raise one without humbling the other.'[3] The War of Devolution against Spain (1667–8) was a further stage in this traditional conflict, resulting, by the Treaty of Aix-la-Chapelle, in the acquisition of more border areas in Flanders. But the first decade of Louis XIV's absolutism began a major shift in French diplomacy which resulted eventually in the maritime powers (the Netherlands and England) becoming the major antagonists of France. The catalyst for the change was Louis XIV's deep resentment of the apparent ingratitude of the Netherlands 'who, in spite of my recent aid to them, were working to unite all Europe against me'.[3] This seemed to be confirmed by the Dutch participation in the Triple Alliance against France during the War of Devolution in 1668. By 1670 his resentment had become an obsession, and he intrigued with Charles II of England for the destruction of the Netherlands. According to its final article, one of the objectives of the Secret Treaty of Dover was to 'humble the pride of the States General and to destroy the power of a people which has . . . shown ingratitude to those who have helped to create its republic'.[4] This policy was fully supported by the French economist and minister Colbert, who regarded the Netherlands as a major obstacle to French naval and commercial development. 'As we have ruined Spain on land, so we must ruin Holland at sea': this was the new axiom of French foreign policy.[4] The most consistent enemy of Louis XIV was soon to be the Stadholder, William of Orange. He became particularly dangerous after assuming the English crown in 1688, and regarded France in the same light as William the Silent had once seen Spain.

The significance of the switch to an anti-Dutch policy was enormous. The entire pattern of European alliances and diplomacy stretching back over the previous hundred years was substantially altered. The last decades of the sixteenth century and the opening of the seventeenth had seen a situation where some powers, like Spain and Austria, were endeavouring to maintain the status quo to their own advantage in Europe, while areas like the Netherlands and Bohemia aspired to independence, and a series of Protestant states resisted the weight of the Counter Reformation. The eventual result had been the emergence of two armed camps and the complex sequence of events known as the Thirty Years' War. France had usually been identified as one of the forces working against the Habsburgs and therefore as a sympathizer with revolt and Protestantism. The actions of Louis XIV brought about a complete transformation. Dutch diplomacy now projected France as the major threat to European and Protestant security, all the more dangerous since France was potentially more powerful than the Habsburg combination had ever been and certainly more openly aggressive. As the reign progressed the rest of Europe realigned itself, nearly always against France. It was now possible, for example, to see the Netherlands and Spain on the same side, as during the War of the League of Augsburg (1688–97). In this situation French diplomacy necessarily became far more complex; Louis XIV had fewer constant factors upon which to base his policies than had his predecessors. Richelieu and Mazarin had always manipulated a situation which already existed, whereas Louis had created an entirely new one.

Louis XIV responded to this complication in a contradictory way, showing great skill and perception on some occasions and blindness on others. He has had more critics and apologists than any other figure in French history, with the single exception of Napoleon I, and controversy about his aims and methods remains undiminished. But all would agree with Voltaire's assessment that 'this monarch loved grandeur and glory'[5] and that Versailles, with its cult of royal glorification and its lack of constructive criticism, was anything but an ideal environment for the formulation of balanced policies. Paradoxes and inconsistencies therefore multiplied, compounded by an immense degree of self-confidence and arrogance.

These became apparent in his response to religious issues in diplomacy and warfare. Before and after the Wars of Religion French policy had been based on a pragmatic view of Europe which had made possible an alliance with the Turks (1536) and with Sweden (1635), both against fellow Catholic states. When Richelieu had been appointed Principal Minister in 1630 France had become entirely predictable in her pursuit of purely secular objectives. Louis XIV, however, seemed to operate at two separate levels. On the one, he continued to exploit the problems of his co-religionists by maintaining an active interest in the Ottoman threat in Central Europe. In 1683, for example, he refused to provide French assistance for the relief of Vienna, hoping, no doubt, that the collapse of Austria would clear his way to become the most dominant ruler in Europe since Charlemagne. Other powers could point to this policy as the epitome of self-interest, particularly since the Ottoman threat had caused them to sink their own differences and to react with concern to what must have seemed a serious ideological menace. On the other, Louis seemed to be influenced by religious motives which spilled over into his foreign policy. His decision to revoke the Edict of Nantes in 1685 could not be defended on any practical grounds and had serious repercussions. Fifteen years earlier, the Secret Treaty of Dover had actually stated that Louis would assist in returning England to Catholicism, a clear departure from the type of policy pursued by Richelieu. It is doubtful whether Louis XIV ever intended to make religion the base of his aspirations, but the rest of Europe certainly came to see him as an ideological threat, a dangerous anachronism in a more enlightened and less bigoted age. The Dutch and, after 1688, the English, compared him with Philip II of Spain (1556-98), while the papacy and Catholic powers like Austria had no feeling of commitment to him and were seriously embarrassed by his persecutions. He became the object of a powerful propaganda war, initiated by the Huguenot refugees and sustained by hostile governments. The allegations laid against him were inevitably distorted and exaggerated but he had only himself to blame in having provoked so powerful and articulate a minority.

Louis XIV found his role greatly complicated by the unnecessary return of ideology to international relations, and therefore had to call upon all his skills and experience as a statesman and diplomat. How successful was he?

In some ways he showed a remarkable capacity to out-manoeuvre opponents and to extract advantages from unpromising situations. He frequently resorted to legal arguments in attaining his ends, regarding no treaty as permanent: 'No clause is so precise that it is not subject to some interpretation.'[3] The pretexts for the War of Devolution showed a careful manipulation of the domestic law of the Spanish Netherlands, while the legal arguments behind the acquisition of frontier territory from Germany in the 1680s (as *réunions*) made full use of any ambiguities in the Treaty of Westphalia (1648). When occasion arose he was capable of buying up client states by lavish and well-timed use of French cash. For example, he made maximum use of Charles II's financial difficulties and provided him with the subsidies which enabled him eventually to defy the Whig-dominated Parliament in 1681. In return, France was assured a period of English neutrality. Other rulers drawn by the lure of extra revenue were the King of Sweden, the Elector of Brandenburg, and the Rhineland princes. Louis was also adept at isolating his enemies, as he showed before the Dutch War, when he concluded the Secret Treaty of Dover with England in 1670, an alliance with Sweden in 1672, and treaties with the Rhineland princes between 1671 and 1672. He could extract a favourable peace settlement from a position of stalemate, as he demonstrated in 1678. By the Peace of Nijmegen he acknowledged that the Netherlands could not be forced to yield substantial territory and he compensated France at the expense of the debilitated Spain. He observed, with characteristic lack of modesty: 'I fully rejoice in my clever conduct whereby I was able to profit from every opportunity I found to extend the boundaries of my kingdom at the expense of my enemies.'[4]

But whatever his talents as a diplomat, Louis XIV was capable of the most monumental blunders. These were due largely to the intrusion of seemingly irrational impulses which could upset the most carefully prepared designs. The first apparent example was his obsessive hatred of the Dutch nation which altered the direction of French policy and incurred the undying enmity of a new power before the destruction of France's traditional rival, Spain, was complete. His capacity to antagonize was almost unequalled in modern history and can be illustrated by four typical instances. First, he threw away the possibility of a favourable armistice with the Dutch in 1672 by insisting on an annual acknowledgement, through emissaries, of Dutch submission to France. This demand was considered totally unreasonable and negotiations broke down, to be followed by Dutch military revival and six more years of warfare. Second, the methods of carrying out his *réunions* in the 1680s sometimes departed conspicuously from his normal pursuit of legality and amounted to open annexation in defiance of the opinion of German rulers. His capture of Strasbourg in 1681 could only be seen as an act of aggression, particularly when Louis added that 'Alsace was a passage for our troops to Germany'.[6] Third, the decision to devastate the Palatinate in 1688, which produced no material gain, swiftly consolidated the League of Augsburg against France. The resentment of the Empire was still apparent fourteen years later, when the Diet, declaring war on France, stated that 'the King had done all that he could be enfeeble and entirely ruin the German people'.[7] Fourth, he committed a major blunder in 1700. This was not, as is sometimes asserted, his acceptance of the Will of Charles II of Spain, but his unnecessary actions which antagonized France's rivals, and hastened the formation of the anti-French Grand Alliance in 1701. He insisted on occupying the Barrier fortress, which involved the expulsion of Dutch troops; he refused to consider any compensation for the Emperor now that the Second Partition Treaty (1700) had been destroyed; and he immediately asserted French privileges over other nations in all ports of the Spanish Empire. As a result, most of Europe was hurried into the War of the Spanish Succession, provoked once again by an aggressive assertion of French power. This reveals one of Louis XIV's greatest defects, in marked contrast to Richelieu. Success could not merely be seen as implicit in the gain; it had to be publicized to the extent of humiliating the dispossessed. Unable to maintain a low profile, Louis XIV possessed neither the means of preventing conflict nor the ability to effect a reconciliation.

Louis XIV reigned without a Principal Minister for fifty-four years. Of these, thirty were spent in the pursuit of diplomatic objectives by recourse to war. Each time the struggle grew longer; the War of Devolution lasted two years, the Dutch War seven years, the War of the League of Augsburg nine years and the War of the Spanish Succession twelve years. For much of his reign he dominated Europe, but provoked an increasingly concerted opposition. Unlike some rulers who have done this, he did not suffer cataclysmic defeat and he managed to hold his own to the end. But France had been over-exposed to his ambitions and was less powerful in relation to the rest of Europe by 1715 than she had been in 1661. The Treaty of Utrecht (1713) was confirmation that France had been contained, just as the Treaty of Westphalia (1648) had checked the Habsburgs.

24
The Reforms of the Great Elector[1]

During his reign (1640–88) the Great Elector, Frederick William of Hohenzollern, made extensive changes in Brandenburg and established the basis for the Prussian state of Frederick William I (1713–40) and Frederick the Great (1740–86). He inherited a series of semi-autonomous provinces, each of which was under the control of its own Estates (these were representative institutions consisting of the nobility and some of the bourgeoisie from the towns). All the provinces were in economic decline as a result of the destruction caused by the Thirty Years' War. He bequeathed a more cohesive state based on a triangle of power, the three points of which were autocracy, bureaucracy and militarism.

Significant as the reign was, however, it was essentially a transitional period. Many of the reforms introduced by the Great Elector were the result not of an elaborate plan but rather of the necessity of the moment. Just as important, they were not always uniformly applied throughout his dominions. This meant that substantial modification was necessary during the reigns of his successors in order to rationalize and simplify his institutions.

The main political and constitutional change was the breaking of the power of the noble-dominated Estates and the gradual creation of a centralized bureaucracy. Behind this development was the Great Elector's desire to maintain a standing army in time of peace as well as war.

This *miles perpetuus* would require permanent financial support

179

in the form of regular grants from the main Estates: those of Brandenburg, Cleves-Mark and, after 1660, East Prussia. Since the Estates jealously guarded their fiscal autonomy, considering a permanent standing army and the extra financial obligations as an unwarrantable intrusion on their privileges, some conflict was unavoidable. It is unlikely, however, that the Great Elector possessed from the start an overall scheme for the systematic subjection of the Estates. After all, on his accession in 1640, he swiftly brought to an end the despotic rule of Schwartzenberg (George William's principal minister) and gave favourable consideration to the Estates' petitions to the Crown to reaffirm their liberties. On the issue of a standing army, however, the Great Elector was inflexible, and this shaped his future policy. At first he found himself bargaining for supplies from the Estates from a position of weakness and was obliged to grant more concessions than he intended. In 1651, for example, he was forced by intransigent opposition from the Brandenburg Estates to drop a proposed stamp duty, and in 1653 he issued a Recess providing substantial social and political privileges to the nobility of the Estates in return for a grant of 530,000 thaler. Confirmation of existing rights was also given to the Estates of Cleves and Mark in 1649 and 1653. Becoming thoroughly disillusioned by the obstructive policies of the Estates, he took advantage of anything that was likely to undermine their power. During the Northern War (1655-60) he levied heavy taxes without consulting the Estates and, after the Peace of Oliva, he withdrew some of his previous concessions in a new Recess in 1660. As time went on he appeared to gain confidence and, from 1661 onwards, he confronted the Estates with proposals for an entirely new system of revenue extraction based on excise. (This will be examined in the next section.)

The end result of this conflict was the decline of the Estates. It would be a mistake, however, to assume that their power was uniformly and evenly reduced. The methods used and the results gained varied considerably in the three main areas of the country. The Brandenburg Estates had their authority whittled away gradually by the introduction of excise in 1667, 1680 and 1682, and by the granting of extensive social privileges to the nobility to compensate for their loss of local political power. By 1688 they were no longer able to offer any challenge to royal supremacy. The Estates of East Prussia were dealt with more summarily. After the full integration of East Prussia into his dominions in 1660, the

The Reforms of the Great Elector

Great Elector was confronted by a powerful separatist movement, based on the nobility and the town of Königsberg. It required two military expeditions and the exemplary execution of a leading Junker, von Kalckstein, to break the Estates and bring them under central control. Cleves and Mark were more fortunate. The Great Elector bought off the nobility by increasing their social status, but failed to destroy the influence of the towns in the Estates. Cleves and Mark thus retained a degree of watered-down self-government which was denied to Brandenburg and East Prussia, probably because the Great Elector extracted what he wanted in the way of financial contributions and had no desire to use force to impose complete uniformity on an area which was not actually in revolt.

The decline of the Estates was accompanied by the growth of a new bureaucracy. Again, however, policy evolved gradually and with several changes of direction. At first the Great Elector actually seemed prepared to reduce the extent of royal power, dissolving the powerful central institution known as the War Council (*Kriegsrat*), which had been set up by his predecessor in 1630. He changed his mind, however, when Brandenburg was involved in the Great Northern War, and proceeded to establish the *Generalkriegskommissariat*, which was similar to the *Kriegsrat*. Responsible initially for the supervision of military recruitment, the *Generalkriegskommissariat* gradually acquired administrative duties and responsibility for the collection of taxation.

This was the first systematic bureaucracy which the Hohenzollerns had ever possessed, and it was not without faults. First, its influence was not uniformly established. The towns were brought more systematically under its authority than the countryside, and Brandenburg and East Prussia contained far more royal officials than Cleves and Mark. Second, there existed separate institutions for the exploitation of lands owned by the Crown; these included the Domains Chambers, and existed outside the scope of the *Generalkriegskommissariat*. The bureaucracy was, therefore, not completely centralized, and Frederick William I had eventually to streamline the whole system by forming the General Directory in 1722.

Economic changes during the reign were partly the result of a deliberate policy of mercantilism and partly the side-effects of political developments. Considerable short-term rapid progress was made, but at the same time problems for the future were created.

Aspects of European History 1494–1789

The Great Elector gradually came round to the view that government interference in the economy was necessary. Military requirements impressed upon him the need for a more rational system of taxation than the existing method, the Contribution (a direct tax on land and trade in rural areas and towns, which excluded the nobility). He proposed the introduction of a new *modi generales*, an indirect tax based on the Dutch method of excise collection. This would be charged on beer, wines, brandy, flour, meat, salt, corn and craftsmen. Since this would include the nobility within its scope it was generally welcomed by the urban representatives in the Estates and resisted by the aristocracy.

What appears at first sight to be a radical idea had several disappointing results when put into practice. The conflict with the Estates (or, more specifically, with the representatives of the nobility) over the introduction of excise was not followed by any systematic or uniform application. In Brandenburg it was made optional in 1667 and compulsory in 1680. But it applied only to the main towns, the rural areas continuing with the Contribution. This had the undesirable effect of creating a deep division between urban and rural areas, soon to be enforced by internal tolls which survived until the creation of the *Zollverein* in the early nineteenth century. In Cleves and Mark it was not introduced at all; after nine attempts between 1667 and 1687 the Great Elector gave up and contented himself with the revenue already forthcoming from the Contribution. In East Prussia the nobility actually requested the introduction of excise, hoping that this would ensure the support of the towns for their political struggle against Berlin. The Great Elector, discerning and suspicious, insisted on maintaining the Contribution and excise was not, in fact, introduced into East Prussia until 1716, by which time the threat of rebellion had passed.

Government intervention to foster industries and agriculture had generally beneficial results. Again, the Great Elector was influenced by economic ideas prevalent in the Netherlands, and he applied them with enormous energy. He encouraged the construction of canals, the growth of overseas commerce and the development of new industries such as cottons, velvet, linen, silk, paper, lace and iron. Of particular importance was his encouragement of immigrants from other European countries. These were usually persecuted religious minorities, including Jews, Calvinists, Lutherans and Catholics. Brandenburg acted as a magnet to enterprising

The Reforms of the Great Elector

groups who found hope in the Great Elector's assertion: 'We have never thought to arrogate to ourselves the dominion over consciences.'[2] The major influx occurred in 1685, when the Edict of Potsdam made possible the settlement of 20,000 Huguenots driven from France by Louis XIV's Revocation of the Edict of Nantes. Their contribution to the industrial development of Brandenburg in the seventeenth century and Prussia in the eighteenth was incalculable.

One of the major consequences of the Great Elector's political and economic changes was the widening of social divisions, always in favour of the nobility. From the beginning of his reign he faced, in the extension of royal power, the choice of partnership with either the bourgeoisie or the aristocracy. Unlike Louis XIV, he chose the latter, and did whatever he could to confirm the social status and privileges of the aristocracies of Brandenburg, Cleves-Mark, and, once they had abandoned their separatist tendencies, of East Prussia. The nobility paid a price; they were seriously affected by the declining power of the Estates and by the encroachment of the bureaucracy in Brandenburg and East Prussia. But, in exchange, they received the majority of the places in the new *Generalkriegskommissariat*, together with all the commissions in the army. This resulted in a vitally important development: the emergence of a 'service' nobility which underpinned the growth of royal absolutism. Of all the countries in Europe, Brandenburg was the only one which really succeeded in establishing harmony between monarchy and aristocracy.

At the other end of the scale, Brandenburg also became a model for the effective exploitation of the peasantry. The Brandenburg Recess of 1653 confirmed several aristocratic powers which could have lapsed into obscurity if they had been left alone. It revived a particularly rigid type of villeinage called the *Leibeigenschaft* and virtually removed any right of appeal by peasants against their masters. This delayed the emergence of Prussia into modern statehood and placed her among the countries which still had to go through the difficulties of shaking off the remnants of feudalism. The Great Elector introduced political and military changes without which Frederick the Great could not have made Prussia a major power after 1740. These were, however, accomplished by the continuation of social anachronisms which were eventually to be swept away by Stein and Hardenberg after 1807.

25

The Growth of the Prussian Bureaucracy in the Eighteenth Century

The Great Elector (1640–88) had been responsible for developing the power of the ruler in Brandenburg by undermining aristocratic separatism. As Brandenburg evolved into Prussia and assumed her status as a European power the newly established absolutism was backed up by an increasingly complex bureaucracy.

Frederick William I (1713–40) rationalized the institutions which he had inherited and, in so doing, set up the basic structure which was to survive for the rest of the century. Frederick the Great (1740–86), while not intending to destroy this structure, became convinced that it was dangerously liable to malfunction when placed under pressure. He therefore reshaped it in such a way as to allow himself considerable personal influence at all levels. This chapter will examine and comment on the changes made in the mainline administration by both rulers, while excluding any detailed treatment of other institutions like the army and judiciary.

The main achievement of Frederick William I was to create a more harmonious relationship between the monarch and the central institutions of the bureaucracy, and between the central institutions and local government. In so doing, he made extensive use of the principle of collegiality; all decisions were taken jointly by ministers after careful committee consideration and every effort was made to avoid the emergence of powerful heads of departments of the type which had become common in France. At the same time, he ensured that collegiality did not reach the very top. Royal autocracy was

The Growth of the Prussian Bureaucracy

unaffected and the king still exerted personal influence over the bureaucracy by issuing Instructions. In fact, he never departed from his general observation in 1714 about the duties of his officials and subjects: 'One must serve the King with life and limb, with goods and chattels, with honour and conscience, and surrender everything except salvation. The latter is reserved for God. But everything else must be mine.'[1]

The compromise between collegiality and autocracy can be seen in the administrative reorganization which followed Frederick William I's Instructions of 1722. Aware of the conflicts about overlapping functions between the two main existing institutions, the *Generalkriegskommissariat* and the General Finance Directory, he recast them into the single body known as the General Directory (*General-ober-Finanz-Kriegs-und-Domänen-Direktorium*). This

(1) After the reforms of Frederick William I (1713-40)

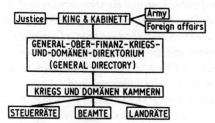

(2) After the reforms of Frederick the Great (1740-86)

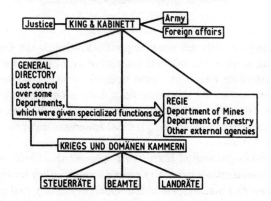

Fig. 3   The Prussian bureaucracy in the eighteenth century

185

consisted of four departments and was headed by a president and five vice-presidents (or ministers), served by fourteen councillors. The vice-presidents conferred regularly in collegial fashion (as a board) and kept in regular (written) contact with the president – the king himself – who made the ultimate policies. Local government was also remodelled; it now consisted of a series of Provincial War and Domains Chambers (*Kriegs-und-Domänen-Kammern*). Each of these was headed by a president and was staffed by councillors, who supervised the activities of three main types of local official: the *Steuerräte* in the towns; the *Landräte* in the rural areas; and the *Beamte* on the royal estates. Responsibility was collective, and orders were handed to the Provincial Chambers by the General Directory after being approved by the king. Throughout the new structure Frederick William I emphasized the opening of careers to talent and the maintenance of a close link with the army; retired officers frequently found their way into administration either at Provincial Chamber or General Directory level.

While collegiality became clearly established in the General Directory and Provincial Chambers, autocracy remained firmly positioned at the apex of the bureaucracy. Despite being president of the General Directory, the king governed mostly from his *Kabinett*, issuing Instructions through his private secretaries. He also ensured that the army, the judiciary and foreign affairs remained outside the jurisdiction of the General Directory. He seemed generally satisfied with his reforms, and his main fear was that his successor might be weaker and allow collegiality to encroach on autocracy instead of maintaining the harmony which he had created.

What happened was the exact opposite. Frederick the Great, far from being prepared to delegate his authority, developed what was little short of an obsession about preserving every vestige of his autocratic powers. At the same time, he placed the bureaucracy under a greatly increased strain and the important modifications he found necessary extended the personal intervention of the king at all levels.

From the beginning of his reign Frederick the Great departed from his predecessor's generally pacific foreign policy and plunged Prussia into the mainstream of European diplomacy and warfare. The General Directory, according to Frederick, was unable to meet

The Growth of the Prussian Bureaucracy

the demands of this transition, operating slowly during the First and Second Silesian Wars and grinding to a virtual halt during the Seven Years' War. The main problem was that the collegiate system could not operate swiftly without royal supervision, particularly when the king was away on campaigns. In addition to this, the bureaucracy had to find enormously greater financial resources to save Prussia from being overrun by French, Russian and Austrian armies during the Seven Years' War (1756–63), and had to cope with Austrian and Russian occupations of Berlin, and the frequent interruption of normal communications with the Domains Chambers resulting from enemy invasions.

Frederick the Great was swift to criticize the performance of his officials and tended to underestimate the problems which confronted them. Despite his reputation as an enlightened despot, he had a generally misanthropic attitude to humanity and was harsh in his condemnation of his own subjects: 'This nation is heavy and lazy. These are two defects against which the government has to strive without ceasing.'[2] He felt that the quality of the bureaucracy was open to constant reproach and his replies to reports sent to him by his officials frequently contained phrases like: 'The whole lot of you deserve to be given the boot.'[3] Faced with the prospect of reprimand, dismissal and even impeachment, ministers in the General Directory began to co-operate in anticipating the areas of royal displeasure. This incurred further condemnation: 'His Majesty has discovered with the greatest displeasure that a kind of hate, animosity and *ésprit de parti* exists among the ministers.'[4] His distrust became so acute that he greatly extended the *Fiscal* system of administrative spies which had been introduced by Frederick William I.

From the outset Frederick the Great faced a difficult problem. How could he improve the system of Frederick William I without ending up with one like Louis XV's? How could he remove the worst defects of the collegiate method of government without introducing a series of far more powerful ministers, who would have scope for extensive individual initiative? About the undesirability of the latter he had no doubts; in his *Anti-machiavel* he had stated: 'There are two kinds of princes in the world: those who see everything with their own eyes and who really govern, and those who depend on their ministers, allowing themselves to be led by those who have gained influence over them.'[5] Frederick's search for a solution resulted in

187

the growth of several new institutions which operated alongside the traditional bureaucracy but which were more firmly under the king's control and functioned more rapidly.

The General Directory was Frederick's main target. At first he tried to improve its efficiency by adding new departments to oversee the economy, to stimulate trade and industry, and to administer the provisioning of the army. Unfortunately, because of the conflicts between the new departments and the original four over the precise demarcation of duties, the reforms were less effective than Frederick had hoped, and he adopted a different approach after 1763. This can be described as an attempt to acquire more direct personal influence over each detail of administration by reducing the role of the General Directory. The Departments subsequently established were allocated specific functions and, although they were theoretically connected with the General Directory, in practice they were separate ministries, corresponding directly with the king. The process began in 1766 with the introduction of the *Regie* (*Administration générale des accises et des péages*), which took charge of the administration of finances and revenue collection. The king employed its staff from outside the General Directory, entrusting the execution of policy to a superintendant and four deputies. The Department of Mines and Metallurgy, also virtually autonomous from the General Directory, was set up in 1768, and the Department of Forestry in 1770. Other external agencies dealt with specific aspects of the economy, such as the tobacco monopoly. By this reorganization Frederick increased the scope of autocracy, cutting through the upper layers of the bureaucracy without actually removing them completely.

The same principle of close royal supervision influenced changes in local government. Frederick had no intention of abolishing his father's Provincial War and Domains Boards, but he did consider it necessary to reduce their power of initiative and to ensure the more rapid execution of royal Instructions. Therefore new provinces like Silesia (appropriated from Austria in 1740) were given Domains Boards which were responsible not to the General Directory but to Frederick himself. The same applied to West Prussia after its incorporation as a result of the First Partition of Poland (1772). The degree of this supervision was made apparent in 1783, when Frederick the Great informed the Chamber of Breslau (Silesia): 'You have no right of initiative whatsoever. All matters must be

The Growth of the Prussian Bureaucracy

reported to me directly.'[6] Even the original Domains Chambers set up by Frederick William I found that they were expected to keep in constant and direct communication with the king, which usually meant bypassing the General Directory in the process.

The more direct involvement of the king in the administrative structure was accomplished, paradoxically, by his withdrawal into *Kabinett* government in order to deal with the enormous amount of paperwork. He no longer maintained even the fiction of being president of the General Directory and spent most of his time reading reports from the Departments and Provincial Chambers and issuing Instructions and orders (sometimes as many as forty in one day). The only direct contact which he had with officialdom was the inspection tours through the different provinces, which he undertook between May and August. He remained very conscious of the impossibility of exercising personal supervision, and he continued to fear opposition and intrigues from within the bureaucracy. He therefore ensured that of all the personnel governing Prussia he alone had the power, information and knowledge to maintain an overall perspective and balance. This involved a greatly exaggerated workload but this was something that Frederick the Great never attempted to avoid. After all, a year before coming to the throne he had referred to his prospective role as Prussia's *premier domestique*.

How effective was the Prussian bureaucracy in the eighteenth century? The main motive for administrative reorganization was the more rapid exploitation of Prussia's resources for the benefit of the army, which was of vital importance for the preservation of what was essentially an artificial state. The successful accomplishment of this can be seen in the emergence of Prussia as one of the world's leading military powers and in her capacity to survive simultaneous wars with Russia, Austria and France. Frederick the Great expressed considerable dissatisfaction and complained that the General Directory and Provincial Boards were incompetent. Yet, when placed in the context of other bureaucracies in Europe at the time, they were markedly superior. For all its faults in 1756, the Prussian administration managed to collect as much in revenue as that of Russia. Austria had consciously imitated the Prussian structure, and Frederick's system was regarded with envy in France. In a social sense the Prussian bureaucracy was also highly effective;

together with the army, it made full use of Prussia's aristocracy and prevented a slide into degeneracy and uselessness of the type which afflicted the nobilities of France and Russia.

There is, however, another side to the story. In becoming a major power, Prussia accepted absolutism more completely than any other European state apart from Russia. At no stage was there any room for a bureaucracy which was related to, or in any way overlapped, representative institutions: these had been undermined by the Great Elector in the seventeenth century and were not to reappear in any significant form until the nineteenth. The administration was in every way the tool of the king and, as such, developed a very serious deficiency. Frederick the Great constantly emphasized that his ministers were to have no initiative, that they were employed 'to carry out my orders, not to interfere . . . they must obediently let themselves be governed and must not take over the government'.[3] The system worked under the personal, at times obsessive, super-vision of Frederick the Great. But his less able successors, Frederick William II (1786–97) and Frederick William III (1797–1840) found that they were unequal to the task and that the reformed structure began to come apart. As Baron Stein observed in 1807: 'As long as a great man was at the head of the state, guiding it with spirit, strength and uniformity, the system produced good and brilliant results which hid from view much that was patched up and unfinished.'[7]

26
Prussian Foreign Policy
1740–1786

Mirabeau once observed: *'La guerre est l'industrie nationale de la Prusse.'*[1] Prussia's close connection with militarism was deliberately fostered by her rulers to compensate for her vulnerability in Europe. She was badly fitted by nature to be a major European power, in contrast to other states like England, Sweden, Spain, France and Russia, all of which possessed certain advantages. Prussia had no major resources until she acquired Silesia in 1740 and Rhineland-Westphalia in 1815, and her soil was of average to poor quality. It would have come as little surprise, therefore, if this artificial state had suffered the same fate as Poland and had been torn apart. That this did not happen was because, in Mirabeau's phrase, Prussia was not a state which possessed an army but an army which possessed a state.

After 1740 Prussia became a predator, under the control of Frederick the Great, probably the most devious statesman of the eighteenth century. More than any other ruler he was regarded by Europe as an upstart, and he earned for himself the reputation of being treacherous in his diplomacy. The main reason for this was that his foreign policy was fundamentally unpredictable. His measures were entirely pragmatic, and he seized opportunities as they arose. At the same time, he always sought to justify his actions by carefully prepared utterances designed to convince other rulers of his good faith and the justice of his cause. In his *First Political Testament* (1752) he wrote: 'The great art is to conceal one's designs, and for that one must veil one's character and reveal only a firmness

191

measured and tempered by justice.'[2] The ruler, he wrote, in his *Second Political Testament* (1768), should always display 'suppleness and resource'. Furthermore: 'What fails at the first attempt matures with time, and the way to hide secret ambitions is to profess pacific sentiments till the favourable moment arrives.'[3] This sounds thoroughly Machiavellian, but Frederick was swift to deny that he had derived any inspiration from that source; in his other major work, *Anti-machiavel*, he referred to Machiavelli's *The Prince* as a dangerous book for ambitious men. The general impression, therefore, is that, perhaps because he was so much the opportunist in his policies, Frederick felt it necessary to project an image of morality. His *Political Testaments*, intended for the use of his successor, were secret, and could, therefore, be frank; whereas his *Anti-machiavel* was clearly written for public consumption. In historical terms, Frederick the Great came half way between Charles V and Bismarck. He lacked the ideological emphasis of the former but was not prepared to adopt too openly the *Realpolitik* measures of the latter. As a result he employed a curious mixture of opportunism and moral self-justification in all aspects of his foreign policy.

The reign seems to divide into three main phases of diplomacy and warfare. The first period, between 1740 and 1745, saw Frederick's acquisition of Silesia from Austria, followed by the War of the Austrian Succession, in which he conducted some thoroughly devious diplomacy. Then, by 1755, he was beginning to fear isolation in Europe, and a series of disastrous diplomatic blunders on his part resulted in the emergence of a powerful coalition against Prussia by 1757. Between 1756 and 1763 Prussia was forced to fight for survival, and Frederick made up for some of his previous diplomatic mistakes by displaying highly effective military leadership. Finally, after 1763, he attempted to keep Prussia out of any major wars but, at the same time, continued in an aggressive type of diplomacy. This had mixed results; although Prussia acquired substantial territory from Poland, Frederick again found himself in isolation by the 1780s.

When Frederick the Great came to the throne in 1740, the rest of Europe expected a continuation of the pacific and unadventurous polices of Frederick William I (1713–40) and was, therefore, totally unprepared for what happened. Within weeks of his accession Frederick had involved himself in intensive diplomatic activity, the

Prussian Foreign Policy 1740–1786

main aim of which was to secure the province of Silesia for Prussia. Silesia belonged to Austria and, under normal circumstances, Frederick might have thought twice before undertaking such a major task. But 1740 was an ideal year for a Prussian king with nerve. Charles VI (Archduke of Austria and Holy Roman Emperor) had just died without leaving a male heir. He had spent the last years of his life trying to persuade the European powers to sign the Pragmatic Sanction, which would guarantee his daughter Maria Theresa as ruler of the Habsburg dominions. He had also hoped that the Imperial Electors would choose Maria Theresa's husband, Francis, as Holy Roman Emperor, so that the two positions could be reunited under any male issue in the future. On becoming Archduchess of Austria, Queen of Bohemia and Queen of Hungary, Maria Theresa found herself challenged by the Elector of Bavaria, who advanced his candidature for the Habsburg dominions. Frederick seized the opportunity which this difficult situation offered. He stated that he would give Prussia's guarantee that Austria's territory would not be violated; in exchange he wanted part of Silesia. In order to press his point he sent Prussian troops across the border. Since they encountered little resistance, they were soon in occupation of Silesia. Frederick immediately provided justification for his action, referring to the 'chaotic' situation in Austria and the Empire: 'I have been compelled to send my troops into the Duchy [Silesia] in order to prevent others seizing it. . . . I have no other purpose than the preservation and the real benefit of Austria'.[4]

What were his real motives? He later provided a clue in his *First Political Testament*, in which he asserted: 'By our geographical position we are neighbours of the greatest Princes of Europe; all these neighbours alike are jealous of us and secret enemies of our power.'[2] Of these Austria was the most dangerous and Silesia acted as a springboard from which could be launched an invasion into the heart of Prussia. In Prussian hands, Silesia would be a definite military advantage since it would greatly increase the distance which Austrian armies would have to march in hostile territory before threatening Berlin. Strategically, it would separate Saxony from Poland, both of which were under the same ruler and friendly towards Austria. Silesia was also desirable for commercial reasons, since it contained the main trade routes down the Oder River valley to the Baltic and was the pivot of east–west trade in north Central

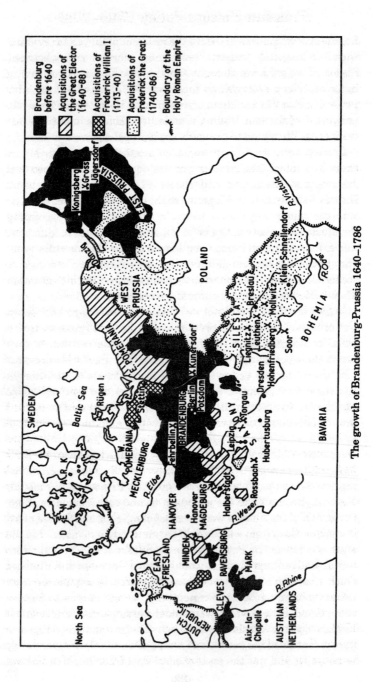

The growth of Brandenburg-Prussia 1640–1786

Brandenburg before 1640

Acquisitions of the Great Elector (1640–88)

Acquisitions of Frederick William I (1713–40)

Acquisitions of Frederick the Great (1740–86)

Boundary of the Holy Roman Empire

SWEDEN

North Sea

Baltic Sea

Rügen I.

DENMARK

MECKLENBURG

W. POMERANIA

E. POMERANIA

Stettin

EAST FRIESLAND

HANOVER

Hanover

MINDEN

RAVENSBURG

MARK

CLEVES

DUTCH REPUBLIC

Aix-la-Chapelle

AUSTRIAN NETHERLANDS

R. Rhine

R. Weser

R. Elbe

MAGDEBURG

Halberstadt

Rossbach X

Hubertusburg

S

Leipzig X X N Y

Torgau

BRANDENBURG

Fehrbellin X

Berlin X
Potsdam

X X Kunersdorf

WEST PRUSSIA

Brahe

EAST PRUSSIA

Königsberg X Gross-
Jägersdorf

POLAND

SILESIA

Breslau

Liegnitz X

Leuthen X
Dresden
Hohenfriedberg X
X Mollwitz

Soor X

Klein-Schnellendorf X

R. Vistula

R. Oder

BOHEMIA

BAVARIA

202

Prussian Foreign Policy 1740–1786

Europe. In addition to this, it had valuable mineral resources which were an essential prerequisite for any industrial development. Finally, Frederick was anxious to make use of the army which had been carefully constructed by Frederick William I; he believed that Prussia would have to participate in a war if she was to avoid the possibility of the army falling into decline. And what better opportunity could be expected to arise than in 1740?

Frederick was taking something of a risk in hurling an untried army at a major European power, but it paid off. The Austrians' reaction was slow and the Prussians were able to defeat them at the Battle of Mollwitz in 1741. In the same year a formidable coalition was constructed against Austria, consisting of France, Spain, Savoy, Saxony, Bavaria and Naples. An alliance between Prussia and France came into existence and it seemed that Austria would soon have to make peace. From this time onwards Frederick resorted to a series of complex diplomatic manoeuvres which gave him a reputation for treachery in most of Europe.

In October 1741 Frederick and Maria Theresa formed the Secret Convention of Klein-Schnellendorf, by which Frederick offered to end the struggle with Austria in return for Austria's *de facto* recognition of Prussia's occupation of Silesia. By the beginning of 1742 Austria began to recover and threatened Bavaria and Saxony. Frederick promptly forgot the Convention of Klein-Schnellendorf and resumed contacts with France against Austria. After another round of fighting, Frederick again withdrew from the war, this time by the Treaty of Berlin which followed preliminary negotiations and an agreement at Breslau (1742). Austria again had to grant qualified recognition to Prussia's occupation of Silesia. Frederick attempted to justify his withdrawal by writing to the French government: 'You are aware that since our agreement I have done everything possible to support the designs of your King your master with inviolable fidelity. . . . I yield by necessity alone.'[4] By 1744 the situation had again improved for Austria; the coalition against her had virtually disappeared and she now had the support of England, Saxony and Savoy. Frederick feared that if the pressure were removed totally from Austria, Maria Theresa might be able to concentrate again on Silesia. He therefore re-entered the struggle in 1744, with a characteristic excuse: 'The King feels obliged to inform Europe of the plan which the present situation compels him to adopt for the welfare and tranquillity of Europe. His Majesty, being no longer able to witness with indifference the troubles which are desolating Germany, and after fruitlessly attempting every means of conciliation, finds himself driven to employ the forces which God has put at his disposal in order to bring back peace and order, to restore law, and to maintain the head of the Empire in his authority. . . . in a word the King asks nothing, and his personal interests are not in question. His Majesty takes up arms only to restore liberty to the Empire, dignity to the Emperor and tranquillity to Europe'.[4] His real aim, however, was to encourage France to remain in the war. Over the next year, Frederick won several military victories, including the Battles of Soor and Hohenfriedberg (both in 1745). He now felt that Austria had been weakened again and that his hold on Silesia had been confirmed. Consequently, he concluded another peace with Austria, by the Treaty of Dresden (1745), deserting his French ally for the third time within four years.

Prussia remained a spectator for the rest of the war (1745–8), and by the Treaty of Aix-la-Chapelle (1748) she received recognition of her claim to Silesia. But Frederick was to pay dearly for his success. Maria Theresa would not let the matter rest and conceived a strong personal animosity towards Frederick. She would take the first opportunity to recover Silesia. Frederick was uncomfortably aware of this and noted in his *First Political Testament* (1752) that he considered Austria 'of all the European powers the one which we have offended most deeply'.[2] He would have to spend many years defending his conquest and trying to re-establish his reputation among the European rulers.

This proved more difficult than Frederick had anticipated, and Prussia entered a period of disastrous diplomatic failure which had to be paid for by a long and expensive war. Between 1755 and 1757 several major alliances were reversed in what was to become known as the Diplomatic Revolution, and Prussia suffered severely from the outcome.

Prussia's predicament was due partly to Frederick's short-sightedness. He was neatly outmanoeuvred by the Austrian Chancellor, Kaunitz, who aimed at breaking the connection between Austria and Russia. In 1755 the system of alliances began to change when Austria and Britain failed to agree on a renewal of their commitments. Britain, fearing for the safety of Hanover against

Prussian Foreign Policy 1740–1786

Prussia, formed a Subsidy Treaty with Russia, by which the latter guaranteed to maintain an army in Livonia. Frederick rightly felt that this was threatening Prussia and he proceeded to plan what he considered would be a master-stroke. If he could secure an alliance with Britain, Austria would be isolated, since Prussia would be on the same side as Russia, and France could be relied upon to keep the link with Prussia. He was particularly certain about the latter point, believing that France and Austria could never become allies; it would be against the whole grain of their history over the previous two hundred and fifty years. 'It is an axiom', Frederick asserted, 'that it will never be a French interest to foster the aggrandisement of the House of Austria.'[5]

Thus, when, in 1756, the Convention of Westminister was signed between Britain and Prussia, Frederick expected a considerable diplomatic victory. He was shortly to experience one of the worst shocks of his career. Kaunitz had been working on France to ditch the Prussian alliance, and Frederick's agreement with Britain brought this to fruition. Louis XV roundly condemned Frederick's treachery and made a preliminary agreement with Austria by the First Treaty of Versailles (1756). This was a serious blow, since Frederick had always believed that the connection between France and Prussia was essential to Prussia's security. In his *First Political Testament* he had written: 'Our present interest, especially since the acquisition of Silesia, is to remain united with France.'[2] He had assumed that France was similarly dependent on Prussia in her rivalry with Austria, and completely failed to realize that the main enemy of France was no longer Austria but Britain. To make matters worse, the Empress Elizabeth had a deep personal hatred of Frederick (which was not diminished when Frederick referred to her, Maria Theresa and Mme de Pompadour as 'the three first whores of Europe') and considered that Prussia was Russia's natural enemy. On hearing of the Convention of Westminster, Russia immediately broke with Britain and swung towards Austria. Prussia now faced the prospect of fighting three major powers with the assistance only of British subsidies.

Frederick then made another miscalculation. He felt that a coalition against him was inevitable and that he could retrieve the situation only by a pre-emptive attack against his anticipated enemies. In 1756 he invaded Saxony, hoping to provide Prussia with an area of strategic importance for the manoeuvre of Prussian armies in the coming war with France, Austria and Russia. His excuse certainly lacked originality – he claimed that he was protecting Saxony from the possible depredations of the other powers. The invasion was a serious error of judgement. He gave the rest of Europe the impression that Prussia was the aggressor, thereby destroying any sympathy which might have been felt by uncommitted countries. His action merely hastened the formation of a coalition against him: France formed the Second Treaty of Versailles with Austria in 1757 and Russia signed the Convention of St Petersburg in the same year. Both made the return of Silesia to Austria a solemn undertaking, one to which France had been unwilling to pledge herself in 1756. Furthermore, Sweden joined the coalition in 1757, as did a number of the states of the Holy Roman Empire. Finally, Frederick himself had earlier concluded that a surprise invasion such as this could not benefit Prussia a second time: 'It is not in our interest to reopen the war; a lightning stroke, like the conquest of Silesia, is like a book the original of which is a success, while all imitations of it fall flat.'[2] This assessment now proved correct. Frederick gained nothing by the attack, and found Saxony impossible to hold in the subsequent war.

There can be little doubt that Frederick had failed as a diplomat. Prussia was surrounded by enemies and faced a greater threat to her existence than almost any other state in modern history. Yet during the Seven Years' War (1756-63) Prussia survived against fearsome odds, and for this Frederick must receive much of the credit in his more successful role as a military leader.

Frederick aptly summarized the nature of Prussia's predicament in the Seven Years' War by comparing himself to a man attacked by flies. 'When one flies off my cheek, another comes and sits on my nose, and scarcely has it been brushed off than another flies up and sits on my forehead, on my eyes and everywhere else.'[6] Prussia's only chance of survival lay in making maximum use of her shorter internal lines of communication, and swinging her armies into action against successive enemies as rapidly as possible. One decisive battle was not enough; the armies of France, Austria and Russia each had to be defeated and defeated again. If the three allies had been able to coordinate their strength and plan a simultaneous invasion on different parts of Prussia, Frederick the Great could not have produced a solution. As it was, he took advantage of the delays

Prussian Foreign Policy 1740-1786

which the enemy armies encountered and proceeded to deal with his opponents one by one.

This strategy needed an unconventional approach to warfare and a willingness to abandon all the usual rules. Frederick worked on the principle of avoiding any wastage; Prussian armies were always inferior in numbers to those of the allies and Frederick aimed to achieve just enough to cause the defeat of the enemy, without suffering heavy casualties. The answer was the oblique battle order. Prussian troops were sent in strength against a selected point of the enemy, usually the flank, in order to weaken his defences, cause confusion and precipitate a retreat. Other troops were kept in reserve to follow up the victory or to provide necessary cover if the attack failed.[7] These tactics worked brilliantly at Rossbach (where, in 1757, 25,000 Prussians defeated 50,000 allies) and at Leuthen (where 30,000 Prussians inflicted a crushing defeat on 80,000 Austrians). Napoleon later called Leuthen 'a masterpiece. Of itself it suffices to entitle Frederick to a place in the first rank of generals.'[8]

No less important than his brilliance as a strategist were Frederick's stamina and resilience. On two occasions Prussia was in grave peril; but Frederick broke loose and defeated his enemies, providing an essential breathing space. In 1757 the Prussians were defeated by a Russian army at Gross Jägersdorf, and Berlin was threatened. The Austrians were also moving on Berlin through Silesia, and the French were in Saxony and Hanover. Prussia was saved, however, by Frederick's victories at Rossbach and Leuthen. In 1759 the existence of Prussia was again threatened when Frederick's army was destroyed by the Russians and Austrians at Kunersdorf. Frederick recovered rapidly when the allies failed to make the most of their victory, and in 1760 won the Battles of Liegnitz and Torgau. Time, however, was not on Prussia's side. Frederick had anticipated only a short war. How long could Prussia survive with her limited resources?

The question was rendered hypothetical by one of the great examples of chance operating in history. The Empress Elizabeth died on 7 January 1762 (by the new calendar) and was succeeded by Peter III, whose admiration for Frederick was even more intense than his mother's hatred had been. Peter concluded peace with Prussia in May 1762, and this was followed by Sweden's withdrawal in the same month. Peter and Frederick, meanwhile, were exchanging superlative pleasantries with each other. Peter wrote: 'If the King gives me the order to do so I and my whole empire will make war on hell itself.' Frederick, no doubt, kept this in mind, and enthused, in return: 'If I were a pagan I would erect a temple and altars to Your Imperial Majesty as a divinity.'[6] France and Austria, by contrast, were becoming increasingly cool towards each other, and by 1763 Austria was fighting alone against Prussia. In 1763 general exhaustion brought about the conclusion of the war by the Treaty of Hubertusburg. Prussia had lost half a million of her inhabitants but she still possessed Silesia. She had survived all the attempts to destroy her and she was still recognized as a major power.

The period between 1763 and 1786, the second half of the reign, was less eventful. Prussian foreign policy was based, until 1781, on the Russian alliance. The man who had made this possible, Peter III, was deposed and assassinated in 1762, but Catherine the Great (1762–96) renewed the alliance and turned her back on Austria, Russia's ally since 1725. Frederick soon discovered, however, that this new commitment could rapidly turn into a liability and a source of danger. Joint Russo-Prussian action in Poland excited the mistrust and hostility of Turkey, who declared war on Russia in 1768, in order to protect her northern frontier in the Balkans from Russian encroachments. Frederick tried to evade assisting Russia, but by 1771 it looked as if Prussia might become involved in a general war. Austria had just signed a treaty with Turkey to prevent Russian expansion into the Balkans. If Austria actually declared war on Russia, then Frederick would have to help his new ally. How could he prevent this catastrophe and, at the same time, advance the material interests of Prussia?

The answer lay in Poland. One of the weakest states in Europe, Poland had gradually fallen under Russian influence but had remained intact territorially. Frederick now reasoned that Russia could forgo any large-scale expansion into the Balkans at the expense of Turkey and compensate herself in eastern Poland instead. This would relieve the pressure on Austria to come to Turkey's aid, and a slice of Polish Galicia would be an added incentive for Austrian neutrality. Naturally Prussia, too, would receive her share. Frederick had already considered the importance of the Polish Province of West Prussia in his *First Political Testament*: 'It separates Prussia from Pomerania and prevents us from sending support to the former. . . . You will see this more plainly if you consider that the Kingdom of Poland cannot be attacked except by the Muscovites, that if they descend on Danzig, they cut the army of East Prussia off from any connection with this country'.[2] Frederick therefore pushed hard for the partition of Poland. Catherine eventually agreed to the scheme and the First Partition was carried out in 1772. At last Frederick had moved to avert war rather than precipitate it and had acted on his belief that 'the acquisitions which one makes by the pen are always preferable to those made by the sword'.[2]

Again, however, Frederick paid a price; he had thoroughly alienated Catherine by his actions. Convinced that Frederick would continue to slither out of any military obligations in the future, the Empress eventually decided to dispense with the Russo-Prussian Alliance. In 1778 the Bavarian throne fell vacant on the extinction of the Wittelsbach dynasty. Austria claimed the throne for the Habsburgs and Prussia resisted this claim by military force. In the ensuing War of the Bavarian Succession (1778–9), Frederick received no assistance from Russia. In fact, Catherine now sought closer connections with Austria, forming an alliance with her in 1781 and thus reverting to the position which had existed before 1762.

Frederick now feared that his last years would be marked by another period of Prussian isolation. He tried to reopen the connection with France, but found that Louis XVI was concentrating French resources against Britain and that France was no longer interested in continental conflict. He knew better than to revive the link with Britain, and Sweden he described contemptuously as 'a name without a power behind it'. Almost in despair, Frederick did the only thing that was left. He turned his attention to Germany herself and formed a league of the smaller German states of the Holy Roman Empire under Prussian leadership. Some historians have seen the *Fürstenbund* of 1785 as the first major step towards German unity and the establishment of a German nation. This, however, would be reading too much into Frederick's motives and achievements. Frederick was no German nationalist. Unlike Bismarck, who later made the absorption of Germany into Prussia the main element of his foreign policy, Frederick had always regarded Prussia as self-sufficient without Germany. Many historians, especially German, refer to Frederick the Great simply as 'the King', a fitting title for a ruler whose ambitious foreign policy and diplomacy were never directed towards his elevation to 'Emperor' or 'Kaiser'.

27
The Reforms of Peter the Great

The reign of Peter the Great (1682–1725) is often used to illustrate the prime importance of leadership in the development of nations; another much quoted example is the Emperor Meiji of Japan (1867–1912). Although few would question the influence of their personalities in effecting internal changes, there is inevitably a conflict of interpretation as to the precise nature of their achievements. Peter the Great has been the subject of particular controversy among Russian historians. On the one hand, he is seen as a revolutionary, comparable in his measures with the Bolsheviks. Berdyaev, for example, believed that 'Peter's methods were absolutely bolshevik. He wanted to destroy the old Muscovite Russia, to tear up by the roots those feelings which lay in the very foundation of its life.' To Berdyaev the Petrine and Bolshevik Revolutions showed 'the same barbarity, violence, forcible application of certain principles from above downwards, the same rupture of organic development and repudiation of tradition . . . the same desire sharply and radically to change the type of civilization'.[1] By other historians Peter has been projected as the personification of Russian evolutionary progress. Soloviev believed that Peter's personality and achievements directed the flow of Russian history into a more advanced stage of its evolution and made possible future modernization and progress. 'No people had ever equalled the heroic feat performed by the Russians during the first quarter of the eighteenth century. . . . The man who led the people in this feat can justly be called the greatest leader in history, for no one can claim a place of higher significance in the history of civilization.'[2]

These two important but extreme interpretations provide, between them, a method by which Peter the Great's achievements can be examined. The approach of Berdyaev raises the question: to what extent were Peter's changes really a break with the Muscovite past? Soloviev's thesis lends itself to the question: to what extent were these changes really the basis of future progress and development? The answers are not easy to provide, and depend upon the relative importance of the military, administrative, economic, social and religious reforms of the reign.

Peter assumed full autocratic powers in 1689 and ruled Russia until 1725. During these thirty-six years he involved Russia in twenty-three years of hectic warfare (with Turkey 1695–6 and 1710–11, and with Sweden 1700–21). It is only to be expected, therefore, that military matters would have received absolute priority, and there is some scope for stressing his innovatory role in this area.

Russian military power in the seventeenth century had been tested by a series of costly wars and had been found seriously defective. The main components of the army were: the militia provided by the service nobility (*dvoriane*) in exchange for landed estates (*pomestie*); permanent units like the Cossacks and the Streltsy Guard; and foreign mercenaries, who accounted for over half of Russia's military capacity. Peter the Great introduced Russia's first major national army. Although he had certain precedents to guide him (like Ivan the Terrible's use of foreign advisers before 1584 and the gradual development of a more efficient infantry force by the 1680s) Peter's reforms were, nevertheless, sweeping and fundamental. He was inspired, or obsessed, by an overwhelming desire to defeat Sweden and to annex her Baltic territories of Karelia, Ingria, Esthonia and Livonia. He was prepared to learn from his own mistakes (for example, the defeat of the Russian army at Narva in 1700) and to adapt western technological advances for his own use. His first major measure was the introduction of conscription, and the general levy was fully effective by 1709. This made the use of mercenaries unnecessary, as he was able to maintain a standing army of at least 210,000 regulars. He followed other European rulers in making full use of the flintlock and bayonet and he fully appreciated the need for careful training; hence his intro-

The Reforms of Peter the Great

duction of the Naval and Artillery Academies for officers. He also considered the deficiencies of leadership within the army and, by his introduction of the Commissariat, provided greater co-ordination and contact between the Russian generals. These developments were not the only factor in the eventual victory of Russia over Sweden; Charles XII, after all, made serious mistakes in his Russian campaign. Nevertheless, Russia could not have emerged as the victor without Peter's reforms. She would merely have survived, weakened and depleted. It would be no exaggeration to claim that Peter's military success in the Great Northern War provided the basis for Russia's emergence as a major power in the eighteenth century. This strength was sustained even during the period of administrative crises between 1725 and 1762, and after the accession of Catherine the Great Russia was able to expand her frontiers more rapidly than any other European state.

Muscovite Russia had possessed no fleet, mainly because of the lack of suitable outlets to the Baltic and the Black Sea. Peter the Great can be considered the father of the Russian navy and here he had no precedents to guide him, only his visits to Western Europe, which acquainted him with the principles of naval design. The first six frigates were launched in 1703 (this was made possible by the capture of Swedish territory on the Baltic coast while Charles XII was campaigning in Poland); by 1714 Peter had developed a substantial fleet and inflicted a serious defeat on the Swedish navy at the Battle of Cape Hango. By 1725 Russia possessed 50 battleships and 400 galleys, and was in firm control of the Baltic. Russia's future as a naval power was therefore assured and it was left to Catherine the Great to acquire control over the Black Sea, an area in which Peter was less successful. The extent of Peter's achievement is aptly expressed in Sir Godfrey Kneller's portrait, which shows Peter clad in armour in the foreground, with the fleet which he had created in the distance.

Military developments were accompanied by administrative reorganization. The basic motive was to make the conduct of the war with Sweden as efficient as possible by introducing several western institutions to renovate the creaking Muscovite bureaucracy. There is, however, a strong case against regarding Peter's approach as revolutionary. He operated without an overall design or plan and sometimes made mistakes which he subsequently had to rectify.

Aspects of European History 1494–1789

Nor were many of his reforms of any lasting influence. Far from providing the basis of the administration of Tsarist Russia for the next two hundred years, Peter introduced what turned out to be a series of temporary institutions which were substantially modified by his successors. A brief survey of central and local government should illustrate these points.

The seventeenth-century Muscovite structure of central government was based on the Boyars' *Duma*, the *Zemskii Sobor*, the *prikazi* and the autocracy of the Tsar. The *Duma* was an advisory council, possessing some executive and judicial functions and composed of the upper sections of the nobility. The *Zemskii Sobor* was an irregular institution through which the nobility, on occasions, managed to exert extra influence on the Tsar, but its history is somewhat erratic. The *prikazi* were the government departments, under the control of the *Duma*, and consisting of between forty and fifty members. Unfortunately, the whole system was generally inefficient and many individual functions of the various institutions overlapped. Peter the Great attempted to make the structure more effective. The *Duma* and the *Zemskii Sobor* were replaced in 1711 by the Senate, consisting of nine members, which thus eliminated the advisory influence of the nobility. The Senate supervised the Colleges which Peter eventually set up in 1718 to replace the *prikazi* as the main executive departments. The main contrast between the *prikazi* and the Colleges was that, in the former, decision-making tended to rest with individual officials, whereas the latter used the Swedish method of boards to arrive at collective decisions.

Peter's changes were therefore limited, modernization rather than destruction being his main motive. That he failed to provide an adequate solution to Russia's administrative problems became obvious during the reigns of his successors. The Senate had a complex history after 1725. Peter's immediate successors, Catherine I (1725–7), Peter II (1727–30) and Anna (1730–40) ignored it; its place was taken by a Privy Council which could be regarded as a reversion to the Boyar *Duma*. Elizabeth (1741–62) re-established the Senate, but it had to compete with an institution known as the *Konferents*. Catherine the Great (1762–96) reduced the Senate's powers and ruled through her own Imperial Council. Eventually Alexander I (1801–25) relegated the Senate to a judicial role, and its remaining political functions were absorbed by the Council of State. Peter's Colleges were also gradually undermined. Between 1725 and 1762

The Reforms of Peter the Great

the general tendency was for departmental heads to emerge as petty autocrats, thus, in effect, reverting to the *prikazi* system. Catherine the Great eventually replaced all but three of the Colleges with a new system of ministries directed by presidents rather than boards. This process was continued by Alexander I, who ended the last Colleges in 1802 and 1811. Nineteenth-century Russia, therefore, possessed institutions which owed far more to Catherine the Great and Alexander I than to Peter the Great.

Local government reforms were similarly unimpressive in their lack of radical change and lasting influence. It has often been asserted that Peter the Great brought local government into line with the central government bureaucracy. But this was already under way in the seventeenth century. Michael Romanov (1613–45) made full use of the traditional local government official, the *voevoda*, in extending the range and scope of royal power in the provinces. Peter intended to streamline the system, again mixing traditional institutions with ideas imported from the West. He made two attempts. The first, in 1709, established eight *gubernii*, each ruled by a *voevoda*. The second, in 1718, was influenced, to some extent, by Swedish principles. It consisted of eleven *gubernii*, in charge of fifty *provintsii* (each governed by a *voevoda*), the *provintsii* being subdivided into districts. Neither the 1709 nor the 1718 system worked particularly well and the latter was greatly complicated by the need to maintain a large standing army. Military subdivisions were also introduced, and these were superimposed on the local government boundaries, creating an intolerable confusion. Under the pressure of military commanders the civilian elements of local government gradually declined. The Swedish influence soon disappeared and Russia between 1725 and 1762 possessed a local government structure which lacked any precise definition. Two further reforms were therefore necessary to create some sort of order: Catherine the Great's Local Government Statute of 1775 and Alexander II's Statute of 1864.

The one area in which Peter did attempt to introduce substantial change was municipal government. In his 1721 Edict he ordered each town to establish a council, based on limited elections and possessing a degree of financial and administrative autonomy. The experiment, however, failed, because Peter had miscalculated. He was attempting to impose a western system upon largely undeveloped towns whose inhabitants had, as yet, no desire for political

207

participation or financial responsibility. By the end of his reign failure was already apparent and subsequent conditions of maladministration and uncertainty again necessitated further reforms: the 1785 Municipal Charter of Catherine the Great and the 1870 Edict of Alexander II. As with all other aspects of the administration this attempt indicates a lack of overall planning and a tendency to resort to piecemeal measures.

An essential factor in Russia's war effort against Sweden was the more rational and extensive use of her resources. Consequently, economic reforms were one of Peter's major priorities, although they were geared to achieving military success rather than a balanced economic structure. Again, however, there was no overall blueprint for change and the motives and effects varied.

Industrial development is generally regarded as Peter's major economic achievement, and the usual interpretation is that he forced it upon Russia from above rather than waiting for it to develop from below. Certainly his reign was something of a turning point. Seventeenth-century Muscovite Russia possessed a number of industries, including metallurgical works at Tula, but these were often run by foreigners. Peter brought the most important industries under state control and encouraged their expansion by government subsidies, which were also used to create new industries. He used a modified form of mercantilism (which was the prop of most European economies at the turn of the century), but the real catalyst for change in Russia was undoubtedly the war. He concentrated on heavy industry and the manufacture of articles used by the army. The increase in production was spectacular: for example, the output of pig-iron quadrupled between 1700 and 1720 and the number of manufactories increased from 21 in 1682 to about 200 by 1725.

This rapid growth continued after the death of Peter the Great in 1725, and the rest of the eighteenth century saw the establishment of Russia as the major iron producer of Europe. Industrial development became increasingly diversified, with consumer goods being manufactured in quantity for the first time in the late 1720s. By the end of the century, however, the impetus was slowing down and Russia began to fall behind other countries. The basic reason for this was an inherent weakness in the economic fabric of Russia. Peter's policies of state control were highly successful at the time but laid no foundations for the development of private enterprise or a more

The Reforms of Peter the Great

sophisticated form of capitalism of the type which accompanied, and took advantage of, the industrial revolutions in Britain and Germany. Russia never evolved out of Peter's brand of mercantilism, and even in the 1890s the Finance Minister Witte had to recommend extensive government action to bring Russian industrial development up to date.

Peter's reign saw a considerable increase in commerce with Western Europe. Trading relations had already been developed in the sixteenth century, when Ivan the Terrible (1533–84) had encouraged contacts through the White Sea port of Archangel. Nevertheless, it was Peter who 'opened Russia's window on to the West' by acquiring outlets to the Baltic and establishing the new capital and port of St Petersburg in 1703. The one major defect of his policy was that he was forced to depart from the usual principles of mercantilism, whereby Russian exports to other countries should be carried in Russian ships. Unfortunately, Russia did not possess anything like an adequate merchant marine: Peter had concentrated the whole of his attention upon his powerful navy.

Agriculture was scarcely affected by Peter's reign. He showed little interest in its development and made no attempts to alter practices which had remained unchanged for centuries. His successors seemed to inherit his indifference. Russia was hardly influenced by the agrarian revolution of the eighteenth century, and it was not until the second half of the nineteenth century that the government really began to show concern about the low agricultural production of Russia.

Social changes between 1682 and 1725 were far from revolutionary. Although Peter sought to impose western fashions in clothes upon a largely unwilling population, the basic social structure remained unaltered; if anything, class divisions were intensified. Peter's main ambition was to impose the concept of state service upon the nobility and consequently to reduce their independence. This could be seen as backward looking; Ivan III (1462–1505) and Ivan the Terrible had both sought to increase their control over the Boyars and to develop the *pomestie* (estates granted to the nobility on the basis of loyal service). Then, during the Time of Troubles (1604–13), the nobility had succeeded in regaining some of their privileges. Although further attempts were made by the Tsars of the seventeenth century to limit their authority, the nobility retained an

209

influential role in government; qualifications were based on ancestral purity rather than competent service. Peter the Great's main achievement was to revive the concept of the service nobility, and his Table of Ranks (1722) provided a rigorous means of qualification for state service, removing the previous importance of blue blood. Unfortunately, the effects were limited. Only an efficient autocrat could keep the nobility in subjection without running the risk of a palace revolt. The period after Peter's death, therefore, saw the gradual emancipation of the nobility from the harshness of state service, and a revival of their former powers. Both Anna (1730–40) and Elizabeth (1741–62) granted the nobility special privileges, while Peter III introduced his *Manifesto Concerning the Freedom of the Nobility* in 1762, which undid all the reforms of Peter the Great. Increasingly, the Russian nobility became a semi-independent and reactionary barrier to progress. In 1856, for example, Alexander II actually had to appeal to them to emancipate the serfs and was forced to resort to an Edict when they refused.

The Russian serfs had no reason to regard Peter the Great as an innovator or reformer. During his reign they were treated more harshly than ever, and the period represents another phase in the long process of deteriorating conditions. Peter's contributions to this were twofold. Firstly, he divided the serfs into two official categories: those who served the state and worked in the new industries and those in the private service of the nobility. Secondly, he heaped further burdens upon them, including a passport system which restricted their movement from their owner's estate, a poll tax which increased their financial obligations, and a more systematic method of conscription into the army. His policy was not alleviated by his successors, most of whom seemed to regard the continuation of serfdom as the price which had to be paid for Russian economic development and for a degree of co-operation between the Tsar and the nobility. For once, most western historians would agree with the words of Stalin: 'Peter accomplished a great deal toward the creation and strengthening of the national state of the landowners and merchants . . . and the strengthening of the national status of these classes was carried out at the expense of the serf peasantry, which was being fleeced threefold.'[3]

The soul of Tsarist Russia was the Orthodox Church. Peter regarded this as a thoroughly conservative institution and as a brake upon

The Reforms of Peter the Great

the changes which he intended to introduce (even the shaving of beards was fiercely resisted by the clergy). His Church reforms were far-reaching, but not entirely out of keeping with the aspirations of previous rulers. He succeeded in placing the Church under full state control, something which Ivan III and Ivan the Terrible had wanted to do, but had to leave incomplete.

Peter's most apparent change was to reduce the apex of the Church to the status of a government department. When the traditional head of the Church, the Patriarch, died in 1700, Peter refused to appoint a successor and eventually abolished the title altogether. In 1721 Peter issued his Spiritual Regulation by which the control of the Church was to be exercised by the Holy Synod. This Synod consisted of bishops selected by the government and was presided over by the Procurator General, who was appointed by the Tsar. The basic structure of the Church remained unaltered for the next two centuries and the subordinate role played by the Church inevitably laid it open to the charge that it was the main ideological support of the whole system of autocracy in Russia. In fact, the office of Procurator General became increasingly political. In 1877 Procurator General Pobedonostsev expressed, in a letter to Alexander II, a view which Peter would have found eminently gratifying: 'The whole secret of Russia's order and progress is above, in the person of the monarch.'[4]

Peter's attitude to Church property was consistent with previous Muscovite trends. Ivan III, for example, had systematically deprived Novgorod of a considerable amount of monastic wealth in 1478. Ivan the Terrible, while not actually dissolving monasteries, had taken care to prevent the Church from acquiring any further lands. Alexis I's Code of 1649 had brought the monasteries under the control of a type of secular *prikazi*. Nevertheless, there was scope for greater state influence, which is what Peter the Great provided. He was hostile towards monasticism and ordered the smaller monasteries to be dissolved. The larger ones were heavily taxed and were ordered to play a more useful role in society. His policy was maintained by Catherine the Great, whose Decree of 1764 ordered the closure of over five hundred larger monasteries, making available over a million serfs for state service. Both Peter the Great and Catherine the Great adopted the familiar Western European expedient of transferring part of the wealth of the Church to the coffers of the state.

211

Aspects of European History 1494–1789

There can be no simple overall assessment of Peter's reforms, for the basic reason that he did not adopt an overall plan or even a systematic approach. His reign was of vital importance in the rapid creation of a new military and naval power. This could be interpreted as revolutionary and as the beginning of a whole new vista of active and aggressive foreign policy. His administrative reforms, however, were not fundamentally radical. Although he borrowed ideas from the West he also maintained part of the old Muscovite system, and the Petrine superstructure was frequently discarded by his successors, to be replaced with their own institutions. His economic policies produced spectacular industrial advances, but did nothing to prevent the development of an unbalanced economic structure which it was subsequently found impossible to adapt to more advanced forms of capitalism. Peter's reign had little lasting impact on the class structure. The twin processes of the emancipation of the nobility and the enslavement of the serfs was under way before 1682 and continued after 1725; the former was only temporarily interrupted by Peter, the latter was endorsed by him. As far as the Church was concerned, the period can be seen as a turning point, for it was Peter who ended its independence and made it one of the pillars of Tsarist autocracy.

In his assertion of autocracy, Peter provided a link between the Muscovite state and the Russian Empire of the eighteenth and nineteenth centuries. He confirmed the total authority of the monarchy in a manner which looked backwards to the concept of the Tsar as the heir to the power of the Caesars (with tendencies to arbitrary despotism like that of Ivan the Terrible) while, at the same time, anticipating the concept of service to the state which was to be an essential feature of the 'enlightened despotism' of Catherine the Great.

28

Russia Under Catherine
the Great

The reign of Catherine II (1762–96) opened with prospects of extensive reform, but ended with unrelieved reaction. The change occurred not in the basis of her authority, for she had always insisted
on maintaining her autocratic powers intact, but in the nature of her
aspirations. The purpose of her absolutism was, at first, the introduction of certain policies inspired by the Enlightenment, but it
eventually became merely the preservation of the status quo. The
main reason for this change of direction was that she was subject to a
long process of Russification. Before her accession in 1762 she had
succeeded in implanting the Russian language and Russian customs
upon her own German upbringing; but not until she had been in
power for some time was she fully affected by the force of Russian
tradition and conservatism. Increasingly, she had to adapt politically as well as socially, a process which made her re-examine her basic
beliefs.

This transformation took place in four main stages. First between
1762 and 1767 she had to concentrate on political survival after her
seizure of power, and this certainly modified her youthful idealism;
she still intended, however, to introduce extensive reforms, as her
Instructions to the 1767 Commission show. Second, after 1767, she
had to reduce her reform proposals as the interests represented by
the Commission revealed the strength of Russian conservatism and
hostility to change. Catherine was by now somewhat bemused, but
still hoped to persuade the nobility to agree to some reforms and to
improve the conditions of the serfs. Third, after the Pugachev

Rebellion of 1773 she came to the conclusion that her priority was to protect the existing social structure against revolution; the changes which followed were, therefore, based on conservative rather than progressive principles. Finally, after 1790, she adopted a more rigid and dogmatic approach, condemning all forms of radicalism, both inside and outside Russia.

Catherine commenced her reign with a compromise between certain ideals which were influenced by the Enlightenment, and hard-headed realism derived from her experience of a palace *coup*.

She had developed her links with the Enlightenment during her youth in Germany, and she sustained her interest in the writings of ancient and contemporary philosophers even after adopting Russia as her motherland. She corresponded regularly with the French representatives of the Enlightenment, particularly with Montesquieu (until his death in 1775), Voltaire, Diderot, d'Alambert and the *Encyclopédistes*. She was described in 1745 as 'a philosopher at fifteen' and considered that her mind was 'of a philosophic nature'. There is also reason to suppose that her political views were progressive and she even referred, on occasions, to her *'âme républicaine'*.

When Catherine seized power in 1762 these philosophical influences were diluted by a large measure of pragmatism, based on an instinct for survival. After all, no Russian ruler could feel completely safe, especially after deposing a predecessor. As Herzen later observed: 'The inhabitants of St Petersburg, when retiring at night, knew not under what government they should awake in the morning.'[1] Catherine therefore had to establish herself securely and to manoeuvre politically to maintain her prerogatives without losing the essential backing of the court nobility and the bureaucracy. She felt that she had to be flexible, and wrote: 'I have not based my hopes for success on any one mode of action.'[2]

Thus, between 1762 and 1767, Catherine maintained a grip on the throne by pursuing the normal court intrigues while, at the same time, trying to introduce something new into Russia. The combined influences of the Enlightenment and tradition were evident in the summoning of a Commission in 1767 to rationalize the imperial laws. This was backward-looking in that it reverted to seventeenth-century procedure, whereby the *Zemskii Sobor* had been consulted by the Tsar over the codification of law. But a complete innovation

Russia Under Catherine the Great

occurred when Catherine issued her *Nakaz* or *Instructions*. These contained principles for the guidance of the delegates of the Commission and show that Catherine was determined that there should be a strong theoretical basis for any discussion on future reforms and changes.

The content of the *Instructions* indicated a careful balance between the fulfilment of certain ideals and the maintenance of undiminished autocracy. Catherine acknowledged that much of the *Instructions* was influenced directly by Montesquieu's *L'Esprit des Lois* but she also made sure that the basis of her own power structure was secure. For example, Montesquieu could well have stated: 'What is the true End of Monarchy? Not to deprive People of their natural Liberty; but to correct their Actions, in order to attain the Supreme Good.' (Article 13 of the *Instructions*.) But Article 9 owes nothing to the Enlightenment: 'The Sovereign is absolute.' Nor does Article 19: '. . . the sovereign is the source of all imperial and civil power.' There is some discrepancy in Catherine's concept of the role and rule of law. Article 34 proclaims, with the philosophers: 'The Equality of the Citizens consists in this: that they should all be subject to the same Laws.' Article 57, however, emphasizes the force of tradition: 'The Legislation ought to adapt its Laws to the general Sense of a Nation.' This came to include the continuation of existing inequalities before Russian law.

Catherine's caution was best expressed in Article 513: 'The Supreme Art of governing a state consists in the precise Knowledge of that Degree of Power, whether great or small, which ought to be exerted according to the different Exigences of Affairs.'[3] Yet, with this reservation, Catherine had a strong desire to introduce major reforms. She hoped that the Commission would be an agent for social change which would include an improvement in the conditions of the serfs and the economic development of a strong middle class. She believed, in short, that 1767 would see the beginning of an extensive legislative programme inspired by a politically experienced philosopher ruler.

The result was extremely disappointing. Although the Commission was broadly representative of the population (excluding the serfs) and handled a total of 1,441 petitions from all classes, it soon became clear that it was not an appropriate vehicle for progressive reform. Many of the petitions contained requests for the confirmation of the existing privileges of the nobility, while the bourgeoisie showed strong interest in acquiring property rights over the serfs. The Commission appeared hopelessly divided in its opinion and was eventually ended in 1768. Its most important effect was to convey to Catherine an impression of the rigidity of Russian society. She became increasingly aware of the need to maintain the support of the *dvorianstvo* (nobility); and her instinct for political survival now warned her against attempting to introduce progressive measures against the will of the upper levels of society. The period after 1767 actually saw some evidence of retreat by Catherine. The serfs, for example, were deprived by decree of the right to petition against abuses committed by the nobility, on pain of corporal punishment or exile to Siberia. Nevertheless, Catherine did not, at this stage, yield totally to the demands of the nobility. She still had some reservations about the exploitation of the serfs and hoped to secure modifications in the social structure. She still regarded herself as a potential reformer, even though, in the Commission, she had encountered the obstacle of traditionalism. There was still a possibility that she might find another means of persuading the nobility to accept limited changes for the benefit of the serfs and the administration.

The Pugachev Revolt (1773–5) brought about a major change in Catherine's policies. When the Cossack leader threatened the existence of Catherine's regime by combining a series of social demands on behalf of the serfs with his own candidature to the throne, Catherine came to realize that her own security depended entirely on the support of the nobility and that she might actually jeopardize this by attempting to alleviate the burdens of the other classes. The revolt was eventually overcome with aristocratic co-operation, and the reprisals which followed were an indication of Catherine's further departure from the Enlightenment. Her social conscience now virtually disappeared. She no longer accepted that serfdom and exploitation were problems, and she now decided that all future reforms should be based on the traditional patterns of *dvorianstvo* request.

This change was illustrated by a series of interviews which Catherine agreed to give Diderot between 1773 and 1774. In response to searching questions posed by Diderot about the nature of Russian society, Catherine provided a number of evasive platitudes and grossly inaccurate details. She observed, for example: 'The bread which nourishes the people, the religion which consoles them, these are the only ideas of the people. They will be always as simple as nature.'[4] When challenged about the conditions of the serfs, she claimed that in most areas they dined regularly on chicken and had even developed a taste for goose!

In her institutional reforms after 1773 Catherine granted extensive concessions to the nobility, hoping to integrate the *dvorianstvo* voluntarily into the service of the state, and to form a solid defence for autocracy against future revolution. Catherine was now reverting to the policies of previous Russian rulers and was actually influenced more at this stage by the nobles' petitions to the 1767 Commission than by her own *Instructions* for the Commission's guidance. The Edict reforming local government in 1775 stressed the widely popular principle of decentralization, and consequently continued the process of undermining Peter the Great's collegiate system in St Petersburg. The Charter to the Nobility in 1785 confirmed the extensive concessions which had been granted by Peter II in 1762, extending Catherine's 'solicitude to our loyal Russian *dvorianstvo*'.[5] Noble titles were to be hereditary and more completely protected, the principle of voluntary state service was fully acknowledged, and Associations of Nobles were to be constituted in each district of the provinces as a basic means of representation in local government. During the same period the power of the nobility over the serfs was confirmed and extended; Catherine now abandoned her belief, expressed in the *Instructions*, that no further enslavement should take place. Indeed, she probably contributed more to intensifying that enslavement than any other ruler in Russian history. It has been estimated that she handed over at least 800,000 state peasants to private ownership, and millions of subjects of the areas added to Russia by her active and successful foreign policy were also brought into the system, especially in Poland and the Ukraine. The grip of traditional Russia on Catherine was now almost complete.

The last stage was Catherine's final ideological alienation from the original sources of her inspiration. This happened during the last six years of her reign, and was due primarily to two shocks which she found even more severe than the Pugachev Revolt: the outbreak of the French Revolution and the opposition of Radishchev.

Events in France after 1789 confirmed Catherine's suspicion that the Enlightenment had become perverted and that it had drifted away from the restraint and caution of Montesquieu and Voltaire. Nothing could have been more abhorrent to her than the challenge to absolute monarchy which developed, after 1792, into republicanism and regicide. As a defensive reaction she began a dogmatic condemnation of any demands for reform, and fully agreed with Grimm's description of the French National Assembly as 'fools masquerading as philosophers' and 'bandits who do not even deserve the title of illustrious criminals'.[6] After Louis XVI's abortive flight to Varennes in 1792, Catherine assumed the role of the leading ideological spokesman of the *ancien régime*, encouraging the autocracies to form coalitions, although unwilling to commit Russia militarily.

The case of the writer Alexander Radishchev showed how far Catherine had moved away from her early progressive ideas. Radishchev and Catherine had been in basic agreement at the beginning of the reign in their attitude to the Enlightenment, and Radishchev had been a highly favoured protégé. But her experience of power and her gradual Russification gave Catherine a very different viewpoint from Radishchev who, devoid of political responsibilities and any need to keep a practical perspective, developed into an opposition spokesman. When he published his *Journey from St Petersburg to Moscow* in 1790, he was immediately charged with treason and was sentenced to death, although Catherine had this commuted to exile in Siberia. She considered it necessary to write a detailed condemnation of the whole work, to discredit Radishchev's factual accounts of social conditions in the areas which he had visited and, above all, to accuse Radishchev of appointing himself the leader, 'whether by this book or by other means, in snatching the sceptres from the hands of monarchs'.[7]

In the process of becoming more dogmatic, Catherine had lost the ability to recognize different types of criticism and opposition, and she thought increasingly in absolute rather than relative terms. In her view Radishchev, far from being an articulate spokesman for the oppressed, was 'a rebel worse than Pugachev' and was the Russian manifestation of the French Revolution. In losing her sense of perspective on radicalism, Catherine ended her reign as a typical representative of the Russian monarchy, bent on preserving existing society and institutions. As she observed to Grimm in 1789: 'I shall remain an aristocrat; that is my *métier*.'[6]

Russia Under Catherine the Great

*

Despite her changing political attitudes, Catherine never gave up her intellectual contacts with the West. At first these were largely philosophical, but gradually, as the Enlightenment proved embarrassing to her in its political context, they became more openly cultural, focusing on painting, music, theatre, opera and architecture. The result was the beginning of the cultural development of modern Russia and, as historians like to assert, the addition of a soul to the body formed by Peter the Great. Nevertheless, even here the social structure had a distorting effect. Encouraged by Catherine, the Russian nobility developed foreign tastes which alienated them from their fellow countrymen without making them more susceptible to progressive political influences from the West. The ultimate paradox of the reign was that, while Russia was imposing its will on its ruler, its most traditional élite was in the process of becoming more familiar with the language and literature of France, even while France was becoming a dangerous ideological enemy.

29

sian Foreign Policy in the
Eighteenth Century

Russian foreign policy developed in three main phases between the assumption of autocratic powers by Peter the Great in 1689 and the death of Catherine the Great in 1796. In the first phase (1689–1725), Russia emerged as a major European power under Peter the Great. This had been fully accomplished by the time of his death in 1725 and was due more to military struggle and consolidation than to diplomacy. The second phase, between 1725 and 1762, saw Russia increasingly involved in the mainstream of European diplomacy; this was a period of experimentation and growing contacts with the West. The third phase demonstrated Russia's increased diplomatic importance and, at the same time, produced extensive military conquests. This was the peak of Russia's influence on the Europe of the *ancien régime* and it occurred during the reign of Catherine the Great (1762–96).

The dramatic rise of Russia as a major military power at the end of the seventeenth century and the beginning of the eighteenth was due to the combination of the decline of Russia's main rivals with the emergence of a great leader at exactly the right time.

In the seventeenth century Russia had been hemmed in by three important powers: Sweden in the north and the Baltic, Poland across Eastern Europe, and the Ottoman Empire in the south and the Black Sea. All three had passed the peak of their military capacity by the end of the century. Sweden had benefited territorially from the Treaty of Westphalia (1648) but her new

220

Russian Foreign Policy 1700–1800

German possessions had brought her into conflict with Branden-burg. The victory of the latter at the Battle of Fehrbellin (1675) destroyed the myth of Sweden's military invincibility. When Charles XII came to the Swedish throne in 1697, determined to restore Sweden's reputation by military conquest, he inherited a kingdom already in decline. The final burst of Swedish militarism between 1699 and 1721 was spectacular but doomed to failure. Poland had dominated the Ukraine and much of Eastern Europe in the early seventeenth century, but was severely weakened by a series of wars with Sweden, Brandenburg and Turkey after 1650, suffering serious devastation and heavy population losses. Poland also experienced internal problems; ever since the end of the Jagel-lon line in 1572 Poland had possessed an elective rather than an hereditary monarchy. Although this could produce rulers of out-standing calibre like John Sobieski (1674–96), the general result was the replacement of a powerful monarchy by a divided oligarchy. The Ottoman Empire was another state faced with the double problem of military decline and domestic crisis. The deteriorating quality of the Sultanate between 1566 and 1695 was accompanied by the gradual contraction of Turkish frontiers and serious military defeats at St Gothard (1664), Khoczim (1673), Lemberg (1675), Vienna (1683), Mohacs (1687) and Zenta (1697).

Generally, the position in North-Eastern and South-Eastern Europe by the end of the seventeenth century was highly volatile, with tiring combatants struggling for an elusive supremacy. Bran-denburg sought to displace Sweden as the major power of the Baltic, Sweden tried to gain territory at the expense of Poland, and the Ottoman Empire sought to defend itself against Austria. As yet there was no definite result in any sphere, and the situation was favourable to an emergent power from outside the traditional web of conflict. Furthermore, there was little prospect of decisive inter-vention by any western power because of the struggles in Central and Western Europe generally known as the War of the League of Augsburg (1688–97) and the War of the Spanish Succession (1702–13).

Peter the Great (1682–1725) took full advantage of the situation in Eastern Europe and managed to manipulate the traditional rivalries in the area to the benefit of Russia. His main intention was to give Russia outlets in the Baltic Sea and Black Sea, thus provid-ing her with direct access to the West. The opportunity came in the

Aspects of European History 1494–1789

Baltic with the outbreak of the Great Northern War in 1699. Sweden was confronted by a coalition of Denmark, Saxony and Poland, which Russia proceeded to join in 1700. The first two years of the war were catastrophic for the anti-Swedish coalition; Charles XII defeated the Danes and smashed the Russian army at Narva (1700). By 1709, however, it had become clear that Swedish successes had been transitory, a final burst of military effort. The Russians defeated the Swedes at Poltava and proved to the world that the 'Star of the North' was setting. The Treaty of Nystadt (1721) confirmed Russian possession of all of Sweden's Baltic states between Finland and Poland, notably Karelia, Ingria, Esthonia and Livonia.

The reason for this Russian victory and Swedish decline can be considered as the consequences, partly of the mistakes of Charles XII, and partly of the patient leadership of Peter the Great.

Charles XII committed Sweden to the type of war which the limited resources of that country could not sustain. It has been estimated that Sweden's losses between 1700 and 1721 amounted to 30 per cent of her male population (a higher proportion than the losses suffered by France during the Napoleonic Wars[1]). She also experienced bankruptcy several times, a situation which Charles XII refused to recognize. As a military tactician, Charles XII showed a degree of brilliance which Peter the Great lacked, and his victory at Narva in 1700 is a classic example of a surprise attack with inferior numbers. His overall war strategy, however, was inappropriate. He left Peter the Great a free hand to conquer Sweden's Baltic territories while he himself turned to deal with Poland (1700–7). When Charles returned to Russia in 1707 (in the autumn!) he possessed no clear plan and allowed his army to be drawn southwards by the retreating Russians, instead of pushing northwards to re-establish Swedish control over the Baltic coastline. The very location of the Battle of Poltava, which Charles lost in 1709, shows the extent of his folly. It is deep in the Ukraine, over six hundred miles from the Baltic Sea.

Peter the Great's policy was carefully planned and took full advantage of Charles XII's erratic behaviour. The defeat of the Russians at Narva convinced Peter of the necessity of careful military reconstruction, based upon the more efficient aspects of Swedish organization. He observed: 'I know the Swedes will long continue to be victorious, but in time they will teach us to beat

Russian Foreign Policy 1700–1800

them.'[2] He consolidated Russia's hold on the Baltic coastline during Charles XII's absence in Poland between 1700 and 1707. On Charles's return Peter avoided direct confrontation, knowing that the Swedes would still be likely to win a pitched battle, and resorted to scorched earth tactics. He knew how to make the most of all of Russia's resources and of her space and weather. His retreat deep into the Ukraine stretched the Swedish lines of communication to breaking point, and the Swedish armies were depleted by hunger and frostbite. (The winter of 1708–9 was one of the coldest in modern history and birds were reported dropping dead from the sky.) He was prepared to wait almost two years before turning to face the Swedes; and when he did so, at Poltava, the issue was not in doubt. 40,000 Russians, with ample artillery, defeated 22,000 Swedes, who had only four guns. Peter was able to follow up this victory by reconstructing the Northern Coalition against Sweden, and by defeating the Swedish fleet at Cape Hango in 1714.

Against the Ottoman Empire Peter encountered less success in his search for outlets to the sea. In 1696 he captured Azov on the River Don, but his army was surrounded by a greatly superior force of Turks at the Pruth in 1711. By the Treaty of the Pruth in 1711 Peter was obliged to surrender Azov and to defer the prospect of putting a Russian fleet in the Black Sea. Peter's failure against the Turks is, at first sight, surprising, in view of the extent of Ottoman decline in the seventeenth and early eighteenth centuries. The reason is, however, that Peter probably considered Russia to be primarily a northern power and that her deadliest enemy was therefore Sweden. He decided to concentrate Russia's resources on the destruction of Swedish supremacy in the Baltic and was, therefore, unable to make the most of Turkey's difficulties. On the whole, he preferred to leave the Ottoman Empire alone; the war of 1710–11 was not his doing – it was provoked by the Turks under strong pressure from Charles XII.

Nor was the reign a notable success in the field of diplomacy. Peter was a great military leader but, as is so common, he lacked diplomatic finesse. He failed to come to grips with a particularly complex phase of international relations in the West after 1713. In 1717 he attempted to secure an alliance between France and Russia, only to find that the Regency preferred the Triple Alliance with Britain and the Netherlands (1717). France compromised by drawing up the Treaty of Amsterdam (1717) between France, Russia and Prussia, but this was evidently of secondary importance to the Triple Alliance and carried no military obligations. For the rest of his reign Peter failed to gain full acceptance by the other major powers for Russia as an integral part of the European state system. It was almost as if many statesmen were waiting to see what would happen to Russia after Peter died. Could she maintain her position as a major power?

During the period between 1725 and 1762 Russia was notoriously unstable. Short reigns, palace coups and the revival of the nobility all helped to undermine many of the internal reforms of Peter the Great. But the period was by no means a disastrous one in Russia's external relations. There was much more stability in her domestic affairs, largely because of the continuity of leadership. Russian foreign policy was, for the most part, directed less by rulers than by ministers. Two of these, Ostermann and Bestuzhev, dominated the years between 1725 and 1762. Between them they maintained Russia's established policies of weakening Sweden and Turkey, while at the same time becoming more involved in active diplomacy with the rest of Europe.

Russia's struggle with Turkey and Sweden was on a less spectacular scale than during the reign of Peter the Great. Sweden had ceased to be Russia's major threat, and Russia had not yet rearranged her military resources to deliver a crushing blow on Turkey. Nevertheless, two wars were fought during the period. The first was with Turkey (1736-9), provoked partly by active anti-Russian diplomacy by France with Sultan Mahmoud I. This war ended in only partial success for Russia. Russia gained Azov by the Treaty of Belgrade (1739), but her ships were still denied access to the Black Sea. The Russo-Swedish War (1741-3) was also precipitated by French diplomacy; Sweden was persuaded to take advantage of the instability in Russia at the beginning of the reign of Elizabeth. Russia inflicted several defeats on Sweden, and by the Treaty of Abo (1743), the province of Kymmenegard was added to the Baltic gains which Russia had already made at the expense of Sweden.

Of far great significance than the wars with Turkey and Sweden, however, were Russia's contacts with the rest of Europe. These took various forms and produced a variety of results, ranging from obvious success to arguable failure.

Russian Foreign Policy 1700–1800

The first major link was with Austria. Peter the Great's attempts to form an alliance with France were reversed by his successor. In 1726 Ostermann negotiated the Austro-Russian Alliance, which became the basis of Russian foreign policy until 1762. He considered that Austria was, for Russia, a more natural ally than France, and that French military power had probably been over-estimated by Peter the Great. The result of the Austrian alliance was a period of sustained anti-Russian diplomacy by France, but, as has been seen, Russia overcame those countries which France attempted to use as her instruments.

Ostermann used the Austrian alliance to Russia's advantage in 1733 and, at the same time, opened up another area for Russian influence and diplomacy. Peter the Great's contacts with the West had been established by the military defeat of Sweden. His successors concentrated on continental links now that the Baltic had been won, and one of the objectives was Russian domination of Poland. In 1733 the Polish king, Augustus II, died, and because of the system of elective monarchy there were two rival candidates for the throne. France pressed the claim of Louis XV's father-in-law, Stanislaus Leszczynski, while Ostermann supported Augustus III and sent Russian troops. Austria joined the War of the Polish Succession (1733–5) on Russia's side and absorbed much of the shock of French military intervention. Of the three major powers participating in the war, Russia clearly gained most. France did not mobilize all her resources, as Cardinal Fleury was anxious to end the war as quickly as possible. Austria gained no territory from the war and had to bear the main impact of the fighting. Russia secured the election of her candidate to the Polish throne, and this was to be the basis of her future domination of Poland. Russia also confirmed her reputation as a major military power with a far-reaching strike capacity by sending troops as far west as the Netherlands for the first time in her history.

Ostermann was replaced as Russia's Foreign Minister by Bestuzhev in 1741. Under Bestuzhev's leadership Russian foreign policy entered a staunchly anti-Prussian phase. When Prussia attacked Austrian Silesia in 1740 Bestuzhev was clearly in favour of supporting Austria. He argued that Prussia was potentially a deadly enemy of Russia and that she would threaten Russia's influence in two areas, the Baltic and Poland. In pursuit of a policy which would contain Prussia, Bestuzhev renewed the alliance with Austria in

d eventually committed troops to support Austria in the
the Austrian Succession. The anti-Prussian emphasis of
foreign policy was maintained after the Treaty of Aix-la-
le (1748) and was one of the three basic enmities not reversed
by the Diplomatic Revolution, the other two being Austria's hostility towards Prussia and Britain's towards France. The Empress
Elizabeth (1741–62) was strongly opposed to Frederick the Great of
Prussia and even broke off relations with Britain in 1756 on hearing
that Britain and Prussia had formed the Treaty of Westminster.
Russia then proceeded to confirm the link with Austria by the
Convention of St Petersburg in 1757, finding herself on the same
side as France, who had broken with Prussia and had already allied
with Austria in 1756.

Russia now entered a prolonged and bitter struggle with Prussia.
The Seven Years' War (1756–63) was a major test of Russia's
military strength and saw a mixture of successes, like the Battles of
Gross Jägersdorf (1757) and Kunersdorf (1759), and reverses, like
the Battle of Zorndorf (1758). On the whole, Russian armies posed a
greater threat to the survival of Prussia than did those of either
France or Austria. It is possible that Frederick the Great might have
been worn down had not the Empress Elizabeth died in 1762, to
be succeeded by her son, Peter III. It was in 1762 that the unpredictable happened and Russia experienced her own diplomatic revolution, six years after those of the other powers; this effectively
brought about the end of the Seven Years' War. Peter III, a noted
Prussophile, promptly withdrew Russian troops from Prussian
territory. This was followed by an agreement between Russia and
Prussia which reversed the previous policy of maintaining a close
alliance between Russia and Austria. Russian foreign policy had,
therefore, turned and taken a leap into the unknown. This was not
a calculated risk; it was the whim of a mentally unstable Tsar
obsessed by his hero worship for the King of Prussia.

Because of her early withdrawal from the Seven Years' War,
Russia could expect no territorial gain and, like France, was unmen-
tioned in the Treaty of Hubertusburg (1763). She had spent enormous sums in maintaining the struggle against Prussia and had
suffered heavy casualties. Peter III's armistice of 1762 had probably
deprived Russia of any spoils of victory and it raised several questions. Why had Russia been involved so heavily in the war in the
first place? Could it be that her entry into the diplomatic system of

Russian Foreign Policy 1700–1800

Europe was beginning to misfire? Had Russia been exploited by the other powers?

According to Catherine the Great (1762–96) she had. On coming to the throne after the deposition of Peter III in 1762, Catherine made an immediate decision to pursue a more opportunist foreign policy and to use other states as she believed they had previously used Russia. Her views were amply expressed by Panin, who now headed the Department of Foreign Affairs: 'We will change the system whereby we are dependent on them [other powers] and in its stead we will set up one which will permit us to act without hindrance in our own affairs.'[3] Panin and Catherine did not, however, intend to pursue a more defensive or pacific role. On the contrary, Russia was about to enter the most militant and successful phase of her foreign policy. Diplomacy became more subtle and Russia's military conquest in Europe was more extensive than at any other stage in her imperial history.

What happened during Catherine's reign was so complex that an outline of the main components of Russian foreign policy needs to be provided; these interacted with each other. First, Catherine intended to extract maximum benefit from any country with which Russia was allied and would have no hesitation in reversing any alliance which had ceased to be useful. Hence she made an alliance with Prussia in 1764 and reverted to one with Austria in 1781. Second, Russia was to be supreme arbiter of diplomacy in Europe. Catherine managed to achieve momentary success here in influencing the peace settlement which concluded the War of the Bavarian Succession in 1779. Third, Catherine aimed to gain control over Poland, initially by increasing the extent of Russian political influence, eventually by partition and direct Russian rule over the eastern provinces of Poland. Fourth, she intended to destroy the Ottoman Empire in the south and to provide Russia with direct access to the eastern Mediterranean. Fifth, Catherine cast Russia in an ideological role. During the era of the French Revolution, from 1789 onwards, Catherine emphasized the commitment of Russia to destroying radical forces which challenged the *ancien régime*, although her hatred of republicanism did not prevent her from using the French situation to Russia's advantage in her dealings with Prussia and Austria after 1790.

Catherine did not share Peter III's admiration for Frederick the

227

Great and all things Prussian. But she did respect the military power which Prussia had displayed against enormous odds in the Seven Years' War and considered that Prussia would be a more dangerous enemy than Austria. She therefore recognized Peter III's desertion of Austria in 1762 and drew up an alliance with Frederick in 1764.

This alliance was tested in 1768, when the Ottoman Empire declared war on Russia. Frederick refused to give military assistance, but at least Catherine could rely on Prussian neutrality while Russia prosecuted the war with great military success. The Turkish fleet was annihilated at the Battle of Chesme (1770); but the Treaty of Kutchuk Kainardji (1774) was less generous to Russia than might have been expected. The reason was that Catherine was persuaded to seek territorial satisfaction at the expense of Poland, since the destruction of Turkish power in the Balkans might well precipitate a European crisis and result in another general war.

This suggestion had been put forward by Frederick the Great, who also sought to round off Prussia in Eastern Europe by incorporating West Prussia. Catherine initially opposed partition, since Russian policy was based on keeping Poland intact as a Russian-dominated buffer state. By 1772, however, she decided that this was no longer possible, and she agreed, with Prussia and Austria, to the First Partition. Russia received the lion's share, including White Russia and Livonia. Catherine may have been forced by Frederick the Great to adopt an expedient which she had originally opposed, but she was quick to turn the situation to her advantage and to extend Russia's boundaries to the River Dvina.

By the late 1770s Catherine had come to the conclusion that Prussia no longer constituted a major threat to Russia; Frederick had not succeeded in extending Prussia's military capacity since the Seven Years' War, whereas Russia had become significantly more powerful. It was, therefore, no longer necessary to cultivate the good will of Frederick the Great, whose unreliability as an ally was already notorious. The break came in 1778, the opening year of the War of the Bavarian Succession between Prussia and Austria. Prussia called for Russian assistance but Catherine refused to become involved militarily. Instead, she acted as mediator in the eventual settlement of the Peace of Teschen (1779) and set a precedent at the same time for Russian involvement in the internal affairs of Germany. More important, Catherine formed an alliance with Austria in 1781, thus reversing the policy of the previous nineteen years of her reign.

Why did she do this? The reason was partly that she sensed a desire in Austria for a more active and successful involvement in South-East Europe. Joseph II, who came to the Austrian throne in 1780, was determined to imitate the aggressive foreign policies of Frederick the Great and Catherine the Great, but it was clear to anyone who could read the signs that he lacked their stealth and could easily be duped. Catherine now had further designs for Russia against Turkey; Austria was more likely to be useful to their accomplishment than Prussia. In her so called 'Greek Project' Catherine intended to destroy the Ottoman Empire and restore the Byzantine Empire, which would be ruled by Catherine's grandson, Constantine. Austria would be rewarded by some territorial gain for her participation in the scheme, and a treaty was drawn up to divide the European provinces of Turkey between Russia and Austria. Catherine even succeeded in provoking Turkey into declaring war on Russia and therefore contrived to give the appearance of Russia as the aggrieved power. In the Russo-Turkish War (1787–92) the Austrian armies fared badly against the Turks, and Joseph II failed to gain any territory in the Balkans. Russia, on the other hand, took full advantage of the diversion offered by Austria in South-East Europe and proceeded to consolidate her hold on the Black Sea coastline. Catherine was unable to carry out the ultimate purpose of the Greek Project – the dismemberment of the Ottoman Empire – because Joseph II's successor, Leopold II, pulled Austria out of the war in 1790. Nevertheless, by the Treaty of Jassy between Russia and Turkey (1792) Russia gained the coastline between the Rivers Dniester and Bug, and her hold on the Crimean Peninsula was fully recognized. Austria had, therefore, been successfully exploited and, unlike Prussia, had not made counter-demands.

At the same time that she was involved in drawing up plans for the future partition of South-East Europe, Catherine faced a problem of a different kind: how was Russia to regard the events occurring in France after 1789? Catherine's reaction to the French Revolution showed a mixture of ideology and pragmatism. Although she professed to be influenced by some of the progressive ideas of the Enlightenment, she was utterly repelled by the internal changes in France, sensing the fundamental threats which they posed to the security of absolutism in the states of the *ancien régime*.

Yet Russia took no military action against France during Catherine's reign. Catherine encouraged Prussia and Austria to issue the Declaration of Pillnitz against the French revolutionaries in 1791 and welcomed the news that Prussia and Austria were at war with France in 1792. But her own policy was largely opportunist, and she observed in a frank moment: 'I rack my brains to engage the courts of Vienna and Berlin in the affairs of France in order to keep my hands free.'[4] Among the advantages gained by Russia during this period was the acquisition of most of Poland in the Second Partition (1793) and the Third Partition (1795); Prussia and Austria were too preoccupied to challenge Russia's claim to the major share of the spoils.

When Catherine died in 1796 Russia was still at peace, but only just. The Empress who for so long been had the principal spokesman for autocracy in Europe, was now forced to reconsider her objections to using force. Prussia and Austria had both done badly against France, and Catherine hoped to redress the balance by sending Russian troops to Italy. Her death, however, postponed Russian intervention until 1798, when her successor, Paul, took Russia into the First Coalition against France. It also marked an important transition; originality and finesse went out of Russian foreign policy, to be replaced by a grim struggle for survival.

30

Austria Under Maria Theresa

Austria was the only European country in the eighteenth century fortunate enough to be ruled by three monarchs who considered reform an absolute priority. Joseph II and Leopold II were both theorists, but Maria Theresa regarded reform as a practical necessity. For her the catalyst of innovation was Austria's poor performance against Prussia in the First and Second Silesian Wars (1740–2 and 1744–5). In her *Political Testament*, written between 1749 and 1750, Maria Theresa made it quite clear that it was the humiliation of losing Silesia to Frederick the Great which produced the decision to reform: 'And when I saw that I must put my hand to the Peace of Dresden, my state of mind suddenly changed, and I directed my whole attention to internal problems and to devising how the German Hereditary Lands could still be preserved and protected.' The need for substantial change was evident, for 'Divine Providence had shown me clearly that the measures essential for the preservation of the monarchy could not be combined with these old institutions, nor put into effect while they existed.' She was advised by her leading ministers that any chance of Austria's regaining Silesia would depend on the maintenance of an army of 110,000 men, together with the necessary reform of the central and local government institutions. Hence Maria Theresa did not hesitate and was prepared 'to alter the whole rotten constitution, central and provincial'.[1]

This was an essentially pragmatic response and it would be difficult to claim that the determination to reform was conditioned by any theoretical or philosophical considerations. Nevertheless, the eighteenth-century Enlightenment did, in certain circumstances, exert some influence, although usually indirectly. Maria Theresa herself was not connected with the mainstream of European intellectual development, unlike Frederick the Great, Catherine the Great and Joseph II; indeed, she was intensely suspicious of the French and German philosophers of the period. She was, however, served by ministers like Haugwitz and Kaunitz who were openly sympathetic to the Enlightenment. Although these adopted a practical approach to institutional reform, their ideas reflected current theories and doubtless derived some inspiration from them. Some advisers, including van Swieten, Müller, von Sperghes and von Sonnenfels, had a direct impact on the Church and education. Their enthusiasm for the Enlightenment, however, was never allowed to get out of hand. Maria Theresa gave them only a certain amount of leeway before seeking to reimpose the clamps of conservatism. Here ministers normally accepted the limits she imposed, but there were occasions on which they clearly regarded her as obstructive and joined with her son and co-regent, Joseph II, in defying her. Maria Theresa became increasingly worried about the radical views of Joseph after 1765, with the result that the second half of her reign was concerned with maintaining the status quo.

The changes made during the reign will be dealt with in three sections: constitutional and judicial, economic and social, and religious.

In her *Political Testament* Maria Theresa considered that the basic problem which confronted her in the administration of the Habsburg Empire was the excessive independence of the provincial estates in Austria and Bohemia from the central government in Vienna. Another issue, with which the *Political Testament* seems to have been much less concerned, was the absence of any common institutions for the Habsburg Empire as a whole: Austria and Bohemia, Hungary, the Netherlands and Milan, all had different forms of government. But Maria Theresa was more immediately concerned with establishing her authority in the Austro-Bohemian Lands than with setting up a new structure which would also incorporate Hungary and Belgium. This decision was the result of a careful appraisal of the political situation. Recentralization at the expense of the Austrian and Bohemian estates seemed a much more realistic proposition than a large-scale attack on Hungarian and Belgian separatism. The former had been identified, with ministerial advice, as a limited objective which could be achieved by careful reform. The latter was little more than a remote ideal and could well precipitate revolution.

The reform of central government in the Austro-Bohemian Lands was to be carried out in two main phases, in direct response to Austria's military failures against Prussia in the Silesian Wars and the Seven Years' War. During the first phase the central departments of the administration were restructured for greater efficiency and were given specialized functions.* As yet, however, there was no really effective co-ordinating body. This was provided during the second phase and took the form of the State Council, which now supervised the activities of those bodies concerned with finance, commerce, justice, internal affairs and foreign affairs. On the whole, the system was more complex than that of Prussia, from which it derived much of its inspiration. This meant that there was less scope for effective royal control at all levels, and that Maria Theresa's bureaucracy was therefore more dependent on the initiative of ministers than Frederick the Great's.

Local government changes were introduced mainly because the inadequate revenues provided by the Provincial Estates made the maintenance of a large army in wartime virtually impossible. In Maria Theresa's words, 'The Crown's resources began to dry up.'[1] Haugwitz, therefore, substituted the annual payment of contributions by the Estates for a ten-year grant, and proceeded to under-

---

* The first reforms occurred during the 1740s and early 1750s. They included the reorganization of the *Hofkriegsrat* (War Council) and the establishment of the *Staatskanzlei* (for foreign affairs), the *Oberste Justizstelle* (Supreme Court), and the *Directorium in Publicis et Cameralibus*. The *Directorium* was in charge of internal affairs and also supervised the *Hofkammer* (Treasury), the *Kommerzdirektorium* (Directory of Commerce) and the *Hofrechnungskammer* (Accounting Office). At first it was assumed that the *Directorium* would be able to co-ordinate the activities of the various bodies; the Seven Years' War, however, soon revealed that it was unequal to the task, and that Austria needed an overall supervisory institution. This was provided in 1760. Consisting of a core of influential ministers and advisers, the new *Staatsrat* (State Council) directed the activities of all other chancelleries and directories. In 1761 the *Directorium in Publicis et Cameralibus* was replaced by the United Austrian and Bohemian Chancellery, which had special responsibility for local government, but no longer for finance.

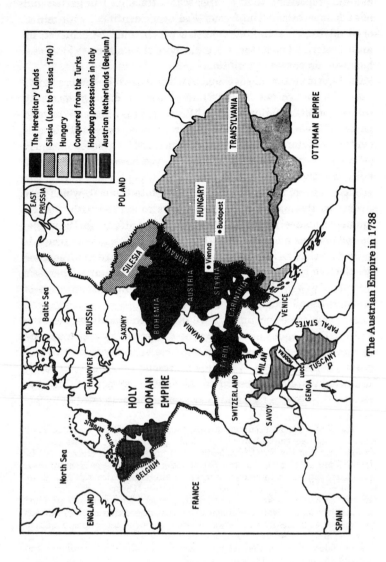

The Austrian Empire in 1738

mine provincial autonomy by extending the scope of central government intervention. Each province within the Hereditary Lands was placed under the control of royal officials, although this replacement of local aristocratic powers by a new bureaucracy met some resistance. The results were not quite as extensive as Maria Theresa had hoped. Nevertheless, there was a steady increase in revenue, that of Bohemia being 25 per cent higher in 1763 than it had been in 1739.*

In 1751 Haugwitz suggested the application of these central and provincial reforms to Hungary. Maria Theresa, however, refused, showing a pronounced degree of cautious conservatism. She was not prepared to risk internal chaos for the sake of establishing the principle of uniformity, even though it was quite clear that uniformity was what her ministers, and later Joseph II, wanted. In 1741 she had agreed with the Hungarian Diet that fundamental Hungarian liberties should be maintained in return for military contributions, and she realized that a frontal assault of the type later attempted by Joseph would certainly be resisted. Consequently, she adopted piecemeal measures, restraining her ministers from producing systematic plans. These measures included enticing the magnates of Hungary into imperial service by granting special honours and privileges, which met with relative success during her reign. From 1765, however, Joseph II made no secret of his reservations; and his eventual solution, direct rule, was the exact opposite of Maria Theresa's. Once the latter's restraining hand had been removed, Joseph threw caution to the winds. He observed, in words which would have made his mother shudder, 'I have tried to grasp the nettle by the root. Should this prove ineffectual, the die has been cast for rebellion.'[2]

The influence of the Enlightenment was directly apparent in the changes made in central and local government in the area concerning the judiciary and the law, particularly in the establishment of an independent Supreme Court. The principle of the separation of powers, especially judicial and executive, was characteristic of the philosophy of the Enlightenment and was best expressed in Montesquieu's *L'Esprit des Lois*. Maria Theresa tolerated a far greater degree of judicial independence than did Frederick the Great, who

* The basic territorial unit of local government was the province. Each province was brought under the control of a *Repräsentation und Kammer* (Representation and Treasury) or, to use a term which came into use later, a *Gubernium*. The *Gubernia* were subdivided into *Kreise* (circles), each of which was under the authority of a *Kreishauptman* (district official).

put a stop to attempts to apply the principle in practice in Prussia. The reason for the acceptance of the separation of powers in Austria was probably that the country's archaic judicial structure needed extensive rationalization, and that this theory seemed to provide a workable basis for a simple and effective solution. The question of codification, however, presented problems: the conservative *Codex Theresiana* (1766) and *Nemesis Theresiana* (1770) were both criticized by ministers like Kaunitz and by intellectuals like Martini and Sonnenfels, all supported by Joseph II. Their complaint was that the Codes contained many anachronisms and that they compromised too heavily with tradition at the expense of improvement. Typically, the result was a long period of stalemate, as Maria Theresa shelved the issue rather than adopt measures she considered innovatory.

The loss of Silesia and, with it, 25 per cent of the Habsburgs' potential revenue, acted as a strong inducement for Maria Theresa's government to stimulate economic growth. The measures taken were not at first influenced directly by the Enlightenment (or, in this instance, by the *Physiocrats*). They tended, at least until the Co-Regency, to conform to mercantilist tradition which had been practised in many European countries in the seventeenth and early eighteenth centuries, including France and Brandenburg-Prussia. The importance of direct government interference was acknowledged and this was achieved through various commissions. The main effects were the gradual industrialization of Bohemia, extensive improvements in transport, and the encouragement of exports by government subsidies. On the other hand, the reforms had an unfinished quality which was recognized by Joseph II. Although not always in agreement with Physiocratic theories, Joseph did agree with Turgot's attack on guild privileges, and he favoured a system which encouraged greater competition. He observed, for example: 'Nothing is more necessary than liberty for commerce and industry; nothing is more harmful than exclusive rights and monopolies.'[3] Less cautious than Maria Theresa, Joseph recommended changes which were not actually introduced until he became sole ruler from 1780. A major example of his more radical approach was his belief that the internal free trade within the Habsburg lands should include Hungary as well as Austria and Bohemia. Maria Theresa had excluded Hungary because of its political separatism and the consequent difficulty of establishing a uniform fiscal and economic structure. Joseph adopted a more theoretical solution to both problems.

The issue of serfdom was directly related to Austria's need to make maximum use of her resources. The institution was therefore attacked mainly on fiscal grounds: that the *Robot* (labour dues) and other forms of subjection to the nobility usually reduced the capacity of the peasantry to contribute to the state revenues. This was an argument which the Enlightenment frequently advanced. Quesnay, for example, wrote: 'Poor peasant, poor kingdom; poor kingdom, poor king.'[4] Maria Theresa's attitude was influenced less by theoretical considerations than by financial need and her own personal aversion to some of the worst excesses of serfdom. More radical by far was the opinion of Sonnenfels, who reflected the general philosophical view of the eighteenth century: 'Despotism of oppressive princes over people is a horror. Yet the most obnoxious, the most intolerable despotism is the one which citizens exercise over their fellow citizens.'[5] Similar views came from Joseph II, who repeatedly reproached the Estates in Austria and Bohemia for their unwillingness to alleviate the burdens of the serfs voluntarily. Yet this more radical approach failed to make much impact while Maria Theresa lived. Some specific concessions, it is true, were granted. These included the right of serfs to marry freely (1753), the fixing of *Robot* dues to a total of three days per week in Silesia in 1771 and two days per week in Lower Austria in 1772, and the introduction of the *Robot* Patent (1775). These, however, were inadequate, especially since they were accompanied by an Edict in 1772 which provided for heavy punishment for intransigent behaviour by the peasantry, and therefore confirmed the nobility's dominance. Slow and limited measures were not to Joseph's taste, and he issued a series of patents emancipating the serfs within one year of Maria Theresa's death.

According to Voltaire, 'The law of intolerance is absurd and barbaric: it is the law of tigers.'[6] The one thing which all the philosophers had in common was a desire for universal religious freedom. Several rulers were affected by the same belief, particularly Frederick the Great and Catherine the Great. Maria Theresa, however, was not among them. She remained staunchly Catholic, and at times appeared rigidly repressive. She told Joseph II in 1777: 'Toleration, indifference are precisely the true means of undermining everything, taking away every foundation.'[7] Her attitude to the Jews was especially violent: 'I know no worse public plague than this people, with their swindling, usury and money making . . . they are therefore to be kept away from here and avoided as far as possible.'[7] Her bigotry was thoroughly unacceptable to her ministers and advisers and Joseph II came into conflict with her more than once. He observed, for example, in 1777: 'In politics, difference of religions in a state is an evil in so far as there exist fanaticism, disunity and party spirit.'[7] As for the Jews, Joseph indicated clearly that he was in favour of their emancipation.

Maria Theresa may have possessed strong prejudices as a side-effect of sincere religious belief. But she did not necessarily equate her convictions with maintaining the power and structure of the Church in its existing form. Again, she showed a pragmatic approach in allowing her ministers to progress so far in the direction of anticlericalism before calling a halt. In 1766, a Decree was issued enforcing a tax on all lands acquired by the Church since 1716. In 1769 the United Bohemian and Austrian Chancellery was given a subcommittee called the *Concessus in Publico Ecclesiasticis*, which proceeded to take a series of actions against monasteries. Furthermore, although Maria Theresa expressed dismay about the suppression of the Society of Jesus in Austria in 1773, she took no direct action to prevent it. It seems possible that she reluctantly sanctioned the efforts of Kaunitz and Sonnenfels to reduce the power of the Church because she felt that this could only lead to the strengthening of monarchical power; she probably regarded it as a struggle against Ultramontanism and papal pretensions. When she felt that the basic tenets of religion were threatened, however, she proved implacable. Kaunitz, Sonnenfels and Joseph II could not budge her from her decision to maintain a rigid censorship and she pointedly told Joseph: 'He is no friend of humanity . . . who allows everyone his own thoughts.'[7] Toleration for the Protestants and Jews therefore had to wait until the end of the co-regency.

The reign of Maria Theresa was essentially a link between the old, archaic Austria which had been struggling to find a new role after the end of the Counter Reformation, and the new experimental period introduced by Joseph II after 1780. Like Frederick William I of Prussia, she presided over extensive institutional changes and, according to Frederick the Great, 'she put her finances into an order

unknown to her ancestors'.[8] Yet she was always conscious of the pull
of tradition and she constantly feared the implications of new ideas.
'I am too old to accommodate myself to such ideas, and pray to God
that my successor will never try them.'[9]

31

Austria Under Joseph II

Turgot, influential *Physiocrat* and Director General of the French finances between 1774 and 1776, once observed that, given five years of despotism, he could make France free. This paradox expressed the disillusionment of eighteenth-century philosophers with any regime neither bold nor powerful enough to impose sweeping reforms from above. The best prospect of success seemed to be offered by those rulers who associated themselves closely with the Enlightenment while retaining their powers intact. This did not really apply to France, but in Austria in the 1780s there was a chance to prove the validity of Turgot's statement. Joseph II, after the removal of his mother's restraining hand in 1780, ruled as an absolute monarch for ten years and introduced a series of radical changes.

Joseph II's enlightened despotism contained two basic elements. First, his politicies and intentions usually had a theoretical foundation. He said, for example: 'Since I have ascended the throne and wear the first diadem in the world, I have made philosophy the legislator of my Empire.'[1] Second, the application of these policies depended on their unquestioning acceptance by his subordinates. 'I insist most forcibly that the principles and orders which I issue are followed and carried out without exception.'[2] He believed, therefore, that enlightenment could be achieved only by absolute rule.

Unfortunately, Joseph II ultimately failed to live up to the reputation of model ruler which he possessed at the beginning of his reign. The reason is often sought in his ideas; but these were fundamentally sound and need not necessarily have been impossible to implement. A more convincing interpretation would blame his methods and the actual use of his autocratic powers. Frederick the Great, who commented freely on most of his contemporaries, believed that Joseph II, in everything he attempted, committed the blunder of taking the second step before the first. Certainly Joseph seemed to move too quickly and impatiently, without adequate preparation or consolidation. The result was twofold. His haste to introduce changes sometimes led him to take short cuts and to endanger some of the very principles which he claimed to uphold. At times, therefore, he came perilously close to crossing over from enlightened despotism to unqualified tyranny. Moreover, sound and urgently needed institutional changes confused and infuriated the people on whom they were imposed, largely because of the lack of any preliminary information, consultation or compromise. Ironically, the most progressive and enlightened of all the Habsburgs became one of the most unpopular, and his own disillusionment was inevitable. Joseph remarked towards the end of his reign that 'almost no-one is animated by zeal for the good of the fatherland; there is no-one to carry out my ideas'.[3] In 1788 and 1789 there was a rapid slide into a reactionary policy, based on extensive police powers, until the whole experiment was abandoned in 1790.

These general comments will be developed in a more detailed examination of Joseph II's administrative and judicial, social and economic, and religious and intellectual changes.

Joseph II was more aware than any of his predecessors of the lack of administrative cohesion within the Habsburg dominions. He accepted and developed the previous measures of centralization initiated during the reign of Maria Theresa, but he was, at the same time, impatient to complete the process. The growth of the bureaucracy had, before 1780, been confined to the Hereditary Lands of Austria and Bohemia. Joseph now intended to spread this from the core of the Habsburg dominions to the peripheral areas, including Hungary, Belgium and Milan. He believed that 'all the provinces of the Monarchy constitute one whole and therefore can have only one aim'.[2] As an overall policy this was clearly desirable; only too often Maria Theresa had shelved the problems of the non-German lands, and in Hungary had maintained harmony only by negative measures.

Aspects of European History 1494-1789

The changes in the administration within the Habsburg lands were conducted strictly according to Joseph's principle of uniformity. The bureaucracy in Austria and Bohemia was not altered fundamentally; the emphasis was on streamlining the departments at the centre and reducing the number of *Gubernia* at local level. The real alterations came to Hungary, who lost her autonomy and was now ruled by the Hungarian and Transylvanian Chancellery. Hungary became a single *Gubernium* and was divided into provinces ruled by *Commissars*. These provinces were further divided into *Comitati* (counties), which were administered by *Vizegespane*. A similar model was applied to Belgium, consisting of a General Council which was served at regional level by *intendants*, the lowest divisions being localities, governed by Commissars. Milan's structure included the new *Consiglio di Governo*, which operated through eight provinces.[4] Joseph's intention was to implement some of the political ideals of the Enlightenment, by establishing administrative harmony, eliminating wasteful regional antipathies, and providing the basis for a common judicial structure and economic policy. In practice, however, the whole system collapsed. His efforts at recentralization misfired and provoked the worst outbreak of regionalism experienced by the Habsburgs in the eighteenth century.

The main reason for this was the method by which the reforms were introduced. Joseph decided from the beginning to deal summarily with any opposition or hesitation, with any vested interest or regional liberty. He tried to achieve within a few years the type of homogeneous empire which had eluded his predecessors for centuries, without taking the essential first step of seeking the confidence of his subjects. For example, he antagonized the Magyars at the beginning of his reign by refusing to be crowned King of Hungary and by withdrawing the concessions which Maria Theresa had made to the nobility. Worse followed when, in 1784, he decreed that German should be the sole official language. This applied to Hungary as well as to Austria and Bohemia, and was an obvious attempt to cement the main parts of the Habsburg dominions together by attacking the basis of their heterogeneity – linguistic and cultural differences. But such precipitate policies were less likely to succeed in establishing uniformity than were carefully planned and phased measures. Joseph II was attempting to solve an historic problem in a single edict. In his haste he overlooked the powerful traditions of the Magyar nobility and managed only to accentuate their dislike of too close a connection with the German core of the Habsburg Empire.

Joseph had the advantage of a corps of officials who had already experienced administrative changes in Austria and Bohemia during the reign of Maria Theresa. Yet he failed to take advantage of their knowledge and, at times, treated them badly. He prevented the formation of a cabinet of ministers, fearing, like Frederick the Great, that it would undermine royal autocracy. He frequently upset his officials by ignoring their advice, and Kaunitz reproached him for this on many occasions. He regarded officials as having a purely executive function, and during his reign the conditions of service deteriorated rapidly, as he demanded that 'they must never flag, physically or mentally'.[3] He bombarded them with abuse and instituted a system of secret police and private dossiers just as extensive as that employed in Prussia. The result was growing resentment and a gradual decline of initiative. Joseph became increasingly impatient with what he saw as deliberate obstruction, laziness and unwillingness to carry out policies. By 1790 the secret police had been extensively reorganized under Pergen and was obvious proof of reaction. Joseph had succumbed to the use of measures which were no more progressive than those of Frederick the Great or Catherine the Great.

Maria Theresa had dabbled with judicial reform but had shown an innate caution which Joseph had found oppressive. The changes after 1780 in the judicial structure and the legal codes of the Habsburg lands were among the most radical in the eighteenth century, and were clearly influenced by the Enlightenment, particularly by Beccaria, Sonnenfels and Martini. Joseph confirmed the principle of the separation of executive and judicial powers and concentrated also on the centralization of the whole system, particularly in Hungary, Belgium and Milan. The overall pattern, introduced from 1781, was of a series of courts of first instance at local and central level, side by side with courts of appeal. Belgium, for example, now possessed sixty-four courts of first instance, two courts of appeal and a Supreme Court of Revision. Criminal law was extensively re-examined by the Penal Code of 1781, which was followed by the Code of Criminal Procedure (1788). The results were remarkable. Where else among the major powers of Europe was the principle of equality before the law fully recognized? What other country had abolished the death sentence? Compared with Prussia, Russia or France, eighteenth-century Austria appears eminently civilized. Yet, even here, Joseph's methods invited opposition. Judicial changes were connected too obviously with administrative centralization, the intention being to undermine simultaneously the political and judicial powers of the nobility. Once again regionalism resisted the new structure, especially in Belgium. Moreover, Joseph himself tended to circumvent some of the basic principles of justice by resorting to undercover methods of dealing with political opposition.

In his consideration of the role of the peasantry in society, Joseph was basically in harmony with the views of the *Physiocrats*. Serfdom was considered objectionable on two grounds. It was morally indefensible, an inhumane anachronism in an era of progress; and it was economically inefficient: the peasantry could not be a fully productive part of the economy, or contribute effectively to the state revenues, while being bound by heavy feudal obligations. Joseph's measures were the most extensive undertaken by any government of a major continental power before the French Revolution. The *Leibeigenschaftspatent* (1781) conferred a considerable degree of personal freedom on the serfs, enabling them, among other things, to marry without the consent of their lords. The *Grundeinkaufungspatent* (1781) enabled the peasantry to buy their strips of land, while the *Untertanspatent* (1781) gave them access to a system of appeals against their landlords at the very time when similar appeals were criminal offences in Russia and Prussia. Finally, the *Strafpatent* (1781) greatly weakened the jurisdiction of the noble courts and clearly defined the punishments which they could and could not impose.[5] Again, this was in marked contrast with the situation in Russia and Prussia, where the judicial powers of the nobility were being confirmed rather than weakened.

Radical theory and progressive legislation were not, however, followed by their successful application. The opposition of the nobility was a foregone conclusion, particularly in Hungary. Yet Joseph made no attempt to soften the blow of a fundamental social upheaval. In fact, he openly expressed his dislike of class distinctions, and was prepared to put aristocratic titles up for sale. Joseph had not been careful to isolate the issue of serfdom and to win acceptance for a specific measure and as a result the nobility felt that their whole status was threatened. Alexander II of Russia managed to avoid the same mistake; after issuing his Edict of Emancipation in 1861, he was prepared to confer certain political powers on the nobility in his local government reforms three years later. What was more surprising was that Joseph did not win the overwhelming support and gratitude of the peasantry. Although little memorials were erected to him in villages after 1790, he aroused some resentment and hostility during his lifetime by several measures which were less radical than a sign of ill-considered opportunism. For example, in 1786 he decreed that peasant holdings should be indivisible, the motive being to ensure the continuing value of the land for the purpose of tax assessment, with much consequent hardship for large families. Furthermore, the peasantry were subject to a harsh system of military recruitment, and most of the reforms generally stopped short of complete emancipation in practice. Smouldering resentment was further aggravated by Joseph's religious changes, which will be examined in the next section.

In his economic policy Joseph tended to combine the latest Physiocratic theories with traditional mercantilism. His intention was clearly to promote economic growth within his dominions, and reference to a few statistics shows that this was not without success. The number of workers employed in the woollen industry in Bohemia and Moravia grew from 80,000 in 1775 to 152,000 in 1789, while the number of factories in Bohemia increased from 24 in 1780 to 86 in 1788.[6] Government revenues advanced from 53·8 m. florins in 1777 to 92·5 m. in 1787. But there is always the feeling that economic growth was less than it could have been and that fundamentally sound policies were weakened by being arbitrarily applied or were undermined by the interference of other motives. Two examples can be used to illustrate this, the land tax and the use of tariffs.

Joseph's proposed land tax was intended to raise a uniform levy of 12·22 per cent of the yield of agricultural land throughout the Habsburg dominions. It was heavily influenced by the *Physiocrats*, who argued that the *impôt unique* was the most effective and the fairest form of raising revenue, reducing the powers of the local Estates to negotiate their fiscal contributions and, at the same time, spreading the load more evenly. According to Chapter II of the 1789 Patent introducing the tax, the objective was 'to establish equality through a proportionate allocation of land taxes, and thus enable the owners of land to carry out their civic duties without hardship'.[7] Certainly, a system which guaranteed that the peasantry would now lose no more than 30 per cent of their total earnings in dues to the state and the nobility would have been regarded with envy by oppressed peoples all over Europe. Yet the scheme was unsuccessful because the opposition to it was too intense to resist. The nobility resented the methods used by the land commissioners in their preliminary survey of land ownership. This was especially noticeable in Hungary, where the nobility regarded the whole scheme as further evidence of heavy-handed bureaucratic encroachment. Even the peasantry found grievances, for they were given no details about the scheme. Those included in the scheme were thoroughly apprehensive about the prospect of making monetary payments to the state, while those who were excluded resented having to continue paying dues (although greatly reduced) to their lords. The last two years of Joseph's reign saw a series of revolts by the peasantry, most of them directed against the nobility. Eventually Joseph had to shelve a promising scheme which had never been properly presented or explained.

Joseph pursued a dual policy over tariffs. Within the monarchy he removed internal customs duties, creating a large free trade area. At the same time, imports from outside the monarchy were curtailed. This policy was sound enough in principle but erratic in application, and was sometimes carried to extremes, arousing extensive opposition from all sections of the community. The abolition of internal tolls was a device which placed Hungary under a great deal of pressure, since it was unevenly enforced. From 1786 Austrian goods could enter Hungary without restriction; but the reverse did not apply. The Magyars rightly deduced that Joseph was using this one way trade to squeeze Hungary for the financial contributions which they were resisting in taxation. The tariff wall round the monarchy was fiercely resisted by a substantial part of the middle class, who considered that it would restrict the flow of trade with other countries. Such fears proved justified; Turkey, Prussia and Saxony all reduced the number of imports from the Habsburg dominions and Joseph was faced with the problem of finding alternative external markets.

Although his economic policies were progressive and adventurous, Joseph tied his own hands as the reign progressed by pursuing an active but unsuccessful foreign policy. His war against the

Austria Under Joseph II

Ottoman Empire as an ally of Russia was a disastrous drain on the finances of his dominions and caused him to adopt any expedients to extract further revenues from his subjects at the very time that the original policies needed explaining. Kaunitz, less bold but also less impulsive, seemed to realize that the population needed to be reassured, and he proposed that the more equal distribution of taxation and the use of tariffs should be allowed to stimulate greater wealth and improved living standards rather than subsidize adventures abroad. On this, as on many other issues, Kaunitz and Joseph II disagreed profoundly.

At one level, Joseph's personal interference in the lives of his subjects was desirable and productive. At another, it was counterproductive and greatly resented. Both were apparent in his approach to religious issues.

At his best, Joseph possessed all the most advanced attitudes of the eighteenth century, as his views on toleration suggest. 'Toleration is the effect of the propagation of the Enlightenment which has now spread through all Europe. It is based on philosophy and on the great men who have established it.'[8] He publicized his contempt for bigotry and persecution and seemed to live up to his pronouncements in his Toleration Patent of 1781 and a series of Jewish Patents in 1781, 1782 and 1789, all of which removed many instances of state persecution and granted a number of defined and circumscribed civil rights. His attitude to the Church as an institution was also influenced by the Enlightenment. He believed, for example, that the power of the Church should be carefully limited by the State. This policy was not uncommon among eighteenth-century monarchs, and there was no reason why Joseph should necessarily encounter any major opposition in its application.

Unless, of course, his methods were too heavy handed. Joseph managed to provoke a quite unnecessary and rather artificial alliance between the Church and the various sections of society, particulary the nobility in Belgium and the peasantry in the Hereditary Lands. His greatest mistakes were to proceed too rapidly with the secularization of monastic lands from 1781, which instantly placed the papacy on the offensive, and, unwittingly, to provide the papacy with considerable public support. In 1782 Pope Pius VI visited Vienna to try to persuade Joseph to reconsider some of his measures. He warned Joseph that 'the hand of the Lord will fall heavily upon you; it will check you in the course of your career, it will dig under you an abyss where you will be engulfed in the flower of your life'.[8] Joseph was not particularly impressed by these threats but he was clearly concerned about the massive demonstrations of popular loyalty for the Pope in the city. The reason for this and future support was intense opposition to Joseph's attempts to alter the liturgy, define the length of Church services, influence the type of religious music and, most important of all, remove the element of superstition in the religion of the peasantry. As an idealist himself, Joseph could have anticipated that interference in the details of religious observance would be more likely than any institutional changes to provoke violent opposition.

During the co-regency Joseph had always maintained the importance of freedom of expression. Shortly after becoming sole ruler he withdrew most forms of censorship (1781) and actually encouraged each section of society to articulate its views. The results clearly showed that the change had been too sudden and that there had been inadequate preparation. It has been argued that the sudden removal of censorship resulted in a flood of criticisms by the Fourth Estate against the nobility and the Church which rapidly exceeded Joseph's expectations. Confronted by a public which had come to demand measures more radical than could be accommodated by enlightened despotism, Joseph was forced to retreat. He reimposed censorship and relied increasingly on spies and secret agents to identify opposition to his policies and regime.[9] Psychologically this was a disastrous move. The withdrawal of concessions because of implied abuse always causes more resentment than the initial reluctance to grant them. By 1790 Joseph's dominions were seething with dissent. Belgium and Hungary were in open revolt against his religious and administrative policies and Austria and Bohemia experienced violence in the rural areas. Even his final act, revoking his constitutions for Hungary and Belgium, failed to restore order. Kaunitz, on being informed of his death, observed that it was not before time, and advised Leopold II to avoid Joseph's main characteristics, 'harshness, exaggerated severity, over hasty decisions, despotic behaviour, obsession with innovations'.[10]

Time, however, has been more favourable to Joseph II than to most other rulers. His shortcomings as an autocrat, more obvious than anything else in 1790, were later considered redeemed by the quality of his intentions. Whatever his personal failings, he was the most radical monarch of pre-revolutionary Europe. His reforms, however, were saluted not by his subjects, who also experienced his methods, but by the revolutionaries of 1848 who had lived through a period of despotism unrelieved by enlightenment.

32
The Age of Reason

The Age of Reason existed between the second half of the seventeenth century and the end of the eighteenth century, between what could be described as the Age of Faith and the Age of Ideologies. It was a period in which beliefs were not accompanied by the urge to convert; it did not, therefore, contain the more aggressive tendencies of the Reformation and Counter Reformation before 1648 or of the series of 'isms' spawned in the nineteenth and twentieth centuries. An integral part of the new mentality was the Enlightenment of the eighteenth century, the philosophers of which entirely abandoned the previous assumption that human nature *per se* was imperfect and therefore in need of divine direction. Instead, the emphasis was placed on deducing from Nature certain precepts which would make possible a new advance towards perfection in human institutions. The basic requirement for this progression was not divine revelation but human Reason.

The Age of Reason grew from seventeenth-century roots, reaching its peak early in the second half of the eighteenth century. By this stage, however, it was already being eroded by philosophers who no longer saw Reason as the universal remedy for all problems, but as an instrument for specific courses of action, incapable of achieving perfection in any form. A new and more profound influence eventually emerged in the form of Romanticism, and Reason was increasingly subordinated to the role of service to the senses rather than mastery over them.

*

The Age of Reason

The Age of Reason originated in a period when the religious and metaphysical approach to philosophy was being abandoned. A new and secular form of philosophy developed, the synthesis of three important changes.

The first was largely a new method of reasoning which made it possible to reject many assumptions which had previously been considered above criticism. Largely responsible for this were Descartes (1596–1650) and Bacon (1561–1626). Descartes subjected the search for truth to the most rigorous logic, based on four principles enumerated in his *Discourse on Method* (1641). Among these was his determination 'never to accept anything for true which I clearly did not know to be such; that is to say, carefully to avoid precipitancy and prejudice'. His method sought to 'divide each of the difficulties under examination into as many parts as possible' and then 'to conduct my thoughts in such order that by beginning with objects the simplest . . . to . . . ascend little by little . . . to the knowledge of the more complex'. The end of the process was 'to make enumerations so complete, and reviews so general, that I might be assured that nothing was omitted'.[1] This produced the most effective means yet devised for the operation of human reason.

The second was the belief that if this rational approach were applied to an examination of Man and Nature, certain principles for future human conduct and progress would emerge, in the form of fundamental laws. This assumption was greatly influenced by the success of Newton (1642–1727), who had deduced the most extensive and far-reaching physical laws then known. His impact on the contemporary imagination was considerable, as is indicated by Pope's epitaph:

> Nature and Nature's laws lay hid in night;
> God said, Let Newton be! and all was light.

There was every expectation that philosophy could be served in the same way as science; that laws for progress and happiness were as deducible as those for dynamics and gravitation.

The third was the existence of certain assumptions which were used as starting points for the elucidation of such laws by Reason. Most of these ideas were provided by Spinoza (1634–1677), Bayle (1647–1706) and, above all, Locke (1632–1704). Locke, for example, made an open plea for religious toleration in his *Epistola de Toleran-tia*. So evident was the connection between toleration and rational

251

behaviour 'that it seems monstrous for men to be blind in so clear a light'.[2] His logical and far-reaching conclusion was that 'The care . . . of every man's soul belongs to himself, and is to be left to him.'[3] He also provided, in his *Second Treatise on Civil Government*, a theoretical structure for representative institutions and, above all, greatly weakened the notion of original sin. For Locke the human mind was initially an empty vessel, gradually filled with impressions and influences from the environment. This sociological approach meant that humanity could be seen as infinitely adaptable and capable of being remoulded in accordance with those basic laws deduced by reason.

The eighteenth century saw the climax of the Age of Reason in the Enlightenment, the undisputed centre of which was France. The Huguenots, in their attack on the establishment after 1685, had created an environment in which the authority of the Church was no longer accepted without criticism, and in which it had become fashionable to examine new ideas on constitutional development. The actual spread of the Enlightenment within France was made possible by a particularly receptive élite which eagerly promoted discussion within the numerous salons. France was also affected by early influences emanating from England. After 1700 Locke's works were published in France; Voltaire visited England in 1726; and the famous *Encyclopédie* grew out of an original intention to produce a French edition of Chambers' Encyclopedia.

Once established in France, the Enlightenment synthesized the influences of Descartes, Newton and Locke, elevating Reason to the highest pinnacle it has ever attained in human history. The common theme was that Man's happiness was the main consideration of philosophy. The potential for this was contained within his nature and could be brought out by the use of Reason. Hence, as Burlamaqui observed, '. . . reason is the only means by which men can seek happiness'.[4] Indeed, Diderot (1713–84) went so far as to claim: 'Reason is for the philosopher what Grace is for the Christian.'[5] Reason could be applied in two ways; it could deduce and analyse the basic traits of human nature and then, step by step, construct the perfect society. By this means, according to Turgot, 'the total mass of the human race . . . marches always, although slowly, towards still higher perfection'.[6] This progress had an absolute aim, for Turgot could envisage the stage where 'humanity perfects itself'. This view

The Age of Reason

was echoed by Condorcet: 'The time will come when the sun will shine only upon free men, who know no other master but their reason.'[7]

What were the implications of this attitude for religion, politics and the economy? The general aim of the philosophers was not to abolish religion but, in Diderot's words, to 'Enlarge and liberate God'.[8] Divinity was seen as the driving spirit of Nature, and was therefore contained within it rather than having a separate existence above it. God, therefore, became more rational and less vengeful, no longer prepared to abandon a large proportion of His creatures. Thus the philosophers demolished the concepts of hell and predestination along with that of original sin. 'Man', according to Voltaire (1694–1778), 'is not born wicked; he becomes wicked, as he falls ill.'[9] The upholder of the traditional concept of God was the Church, which the philosophers wished to see greatly weakened.

Under the influence of Locke's theories, some writers concentrated on examining political institutions. Turgot believed that 'The Science of government will ... become easy, and will cease to be beyond the reach of men endowed with only ordinary good sense.'[6] Montesquieu (1689–1755), basing his analysis of institutions on careful observation, proceeded to generalize about different influences and conditions, and then constructed his ideal, the best known element of which was the separation of the legislative, executive and judicial powers. His whole approach was based on Reason. 'There is, then, a prime reason; and laws are the relations subsisting between it and different beings, and the relations of these to one another.'[10] Economic theories, particularly those of the *Physiocrats*, followed the general dictum 'Let Nature rule.' This came to be closely connected with the policy of free trade and with minimum state interference (*laissez-faire*). At the same time, the chaos of internal customs barriers, unevenly distributed taxation and oppressive guild regulations, had to be dealt with by a carefully planned policy if the government was not to abdicate its responsibilities. Reason again showed the way to a common land tax (*impôt unique*) and the liberation of all serfs. Diderot, d'Alembert (1717–83), Quesnay and Le Mercier all assumed that once the ideal economic environment had been provided, both population and wealth would continue to grow indefinitely. This form of progress would combine with social harmony and new political institutions to bring about the type of optimism about the future which is certainly absent in the twentieth-century predictions of Huxley's *Brave New World* and Orwell's *Nineteen Eighty Four*!

The practical effects of the French Enlightenment are examined in Chapters 28, 29, 30, 31 and 33. The impact was geographically extensive, affecting most countries in Europe and linking up with regional variations like the German and Austrian Enlightenment. Quantitatively, however, it was rather restricted. The vast majority of the population was entirely excluded, for, according to Voltaire, the supremacy of Reason influenced only 'the thinking portion of the human race, i.e. the hundred thousandth part'. This narrow base was the Enlightenment's greatest weakness, for it could not gain the mass appeal of Christianity or of later ideologies. Moreover, since it was monopolized by the wealthy and educated sectors of society, the ideas of the Enlightenment were frequently distorted, either in the form of enlightened despotism (see Chapters 28 and 32) or as the justification for retaining traditional privileges (see Chapters 35 and 37). Any philosophy based on Reason therefore suffered from inherent disadvantages when compared with one based on faith or feeling.

No eighteenth-century philosopher ever launched a direct attack on Reason itself. At times, however, Reason was made the object of satire; Voltaire's *Candide* and Swift's *Gulliver's Travels* both provide examples of this. More fundamentally, the Enlightenment did have a strand of thought which questioned the prevailing view that Reason was a means of achieving perfection. This was particularly apparent in Britain, largely because the British Enlightenment had evolved out of its idealistic phase by the second quarter of the eighteenth century. The struggle between Parliament and the Stuarts, which had made the works of Locke so popular, had long been replaced by a limited monarchy which was acceptable to a larger cross-section of the population. Religious tolerance, although far from complete, was more advanced than in France, and Britain was the one state in Europe where the economic policy of *laissez-faire* was partially working. Most British writers regarded Britain's concrete achievements as a satisfactory compromise and therefore saw little need to pursue an elusive perfection.

Such an environment inevitably reduced the role of Reason. The most articulate and influential writer of the later British Enlightenment was David Hume (1711–76), who observed that Reason was no

The Age of Reason

more than an instrument capable of serving good and evil designs equally since it was 'morally neutral'.[11] He placed far more emphasis than his predecessors on experience and the passions in human development: 'It is certain that the most ignorant and stupid peasants, nay infants, nay even brute beasts, improve by experience and learn the qualities of natural objects by observing the effects which result from them.'[12] Reason is an integral part of the human faculties, but 'is, and ought only to be, the slave of the passions';[13] it is, in other words, merely the means of achieving a specific objective.

The impact of this approach was considerable. Such views were not unique to Hume or to Britain, for there were waverers in France who felt that Reason had its limitations. But the lucid arguments and acid phrases of Hume's *Treatise of Human Nature* (1739) and his *Enquiry Concerning Human Understanding* (1749) did much, during the next few decades, to erode the thesis that Reason provided the means for progress, leading to perfection. He also prepared the way for a continental re-examination of Reason later in the century, particularly by Kant (1724–1804), and left room for a new line of philosophical argument.

The search for a new spirit as an alternative to the mastery of Reason could have led back to the Age of Faith; certainly there were religious revivals towards the end of the eighteenth century. The replacement, however, usually took the form of Romanticism. This emphasized traditions and feelings, thus opening up further areas of expression and making possible a new degree of intensity in the works of Rousseau (1712–78) and Burke (1729–97). Both, it should be emphasized, constructed their arguments by rational methods, but neither accepted the view that pure Reason could show the way to improvement and progress. Rousseau placed his confidence in Nature, and Burke in the accumulated wisdom of a nation's traditions.

Philosophers like Locke and Voltaire had denied that Man is naturally evil. Rousseau now carried this to its extreme conclusion and claimed that 'Man is naturally good'.[14] Rousseau claimed that Man has unfortunately been affected by a combination of irrelevant ideas and vicious social institutions. The former 'sap the foundations of our faith, and destroy virtue'.[14] The latter produced the famous paradox at the beginning of the *Social Contract*: 'Man is born free, and everywhere he is in chains.'[15] The solution, Rousseau believed, is to return to Nature and to the very simplest forms of democratic government. Only in this way will the natural goodness of Man be able to reassert itself, quite independently of Reason. Rousseau seemed to have an aversion to material progress, referring to cities, for example, as 'the sink of the human species'.[16] Since he was challenging one of the most important beliefs of the Enlightenment, he found himself the butt of considerable scorn. Voltaire wrote, in a letter to Rousseau: '. . . one is seized with a desire to walk on four paws. However, as it is more than sixty years since I lost that habit, I feel, unfortunately, that it is impossible for me to recover it.'[14] Voltaire clearly thought that Rousseau's search for natural goodness through simplicity was thoroughly facile, but Rousseau was, in fact, trying to break away from what he considered to be the stultifying tyranny of Reason. 'What can be proved by reason to the majority of men is only the interested calculation of personal benefit.'[14]

Burke emphasized natural goodness less than natural wisdom, believing that 'Man is by nature reasonable'.[17] It was not, however, the type of reason which could be used to construct perfect institutions; it was an accumulation of the wisdom of the past: 'We are afraid to put men to live and trade each on his own private stock of reason: because we suspect that the stock in each man is small, and that the individuals would do better to avail themselves of the general bank and capital of nations, and of ages.'[18] Why, therefore, search for perfection? This can only be based on theories, and theories in themselves, are to be mistrusted. Indeed, 'There is, by the essential fundamental constitution of things, a radical infirmity in all human contrivances; and the weakness is often so attached to the very perfection of our political mechanism, that some defect in it . . . becomes a necessary corrective to the evils that the theoretic perfection would produce.'[19] Progress was possible only in an organic sense. Societies, Burke maintained, are not constructed on principles; they evolve. Any attempts to change the direction of this evolution by imposing different theories can result only in permanent damage and distortion.

Romanticism was capable of providing an enormous variety of views, and it brought extremes to replace the tones of the rule of Reason. Rousseau and Burke were both Romantics, but they stood further apart than had any two philosophers in the Age of Reason. Rousseau condemned most forms of existing society; Burke upheld

The Age of Reason

existing societies because they were the result of organic growth. Rousseau advocated a return to Nature; Burke urged states to hold to an evolutionary course. The greatest difference was apparent in their attitude to political authority. Rousseau had such faith in the innate goodness of the majority that he was prepared to see the dissident minority conform to the 'General Will' in the belief that they were being forced to regain their freedom. Burke regarded such theorizing as futile and dangerous, and upheld the concrete base of parliamentary sovereignty, with all its inherent defects.

Such a capacity for divergent thought meant that Romanticism could flow into many channels, altering its shape in the process. Sometimes this resulted in distortion; Rousseau's ideas, for example, were used by Robespierre between 1792 and 1794 to justify the Reign of Terror. Sometimes, too, Romanticism in political thought was used to glorify the power of the state and to tighten the control of the government over the masses. The one common factor, however, was that Romanticism, in all its forms, affected the majority of the population: either through the arts or through the development in the nineteenth century of modern political ideologies.

33
Enlightened Despotism:
A General Survey

The term 'enlightened despotism' was probably coined by the *Physiocrats* and is known to have been used by Diderot in the 1760s. It implies a connection between the type of autocracy practised in certain parts of Europe in the eighteenth century and some of the ideas of the philosophers of the French and German Enlightenment. This was largely a marriage of convenience. On one side, French writers like Voltaire, the *Encyclopédistes* and the *Physiocrats*, found themselves out of favour with the establishment in France. They turned, therefore, to the rulers of Eastern and Central Europe, from whom they received greater sympathy. Voltaire observed to Diderot: 'What a time we live in! France persecutes philosophers, while the Scythians protect them.'[1] Some writers, however, had reservations about this association; d'Alembert, for example, considered that 'they fawned with Lucifer to rid themselves of Beelzebub'. On the other side, Prussian, Russian and Austrian rulers found the Enlightenment a useful source of ideas for three main aspects of their policies: method, content and justification. They used a more logical and rational approach to identify their priorities, borrowed some of the philosophers' ideas in drawing up their reforms, and liberally quoted Montesquieu and others, sometimes out of context, to justify their actions.

If this connection between kings and philosophers is taken as the basic requirement of enlightened despotism, identification is fairly simple. Peter the Great (1682–1725) and Frederick William I (1713–40) can be excluded; although they were reformers, they had

258

Enlightened Despotism: A General Survey

no contacts with the Enlightenment in any of its forms. By contrast, Frederick the Great (1740–86), Catherine the Great (1762–96) and Joseph II (1780–90) had direct links with both the French and German channels. Other rulers deserving the title are Leopold of Tuscany (who became Emperor Leopold II in 1790) and Margrave Charles Frederick of Baden. Two countries came under the influence of the Enlightenment through ministers rather than rulers: Denmark under Struensee and Portugal under Pombal. Two rulers can be regarded as borderline cases: Maria Theresa (1740–80), who was advised by ministers directly associated with the Enlightenment but who distrusted new ideas herself, and Charles III of Spain (1759–88), who was influenced by the *Physiocrats* but remained too closely connected with the Church to allow this to have much effect.

This chapter will examine the three main exponents of enlightened despotism, Frederick the Great, Catherine the Great and Joseph II, in the light of their theoretical justification of power, their administrative and judicial reform, their economic policies, and their attitudes to religion and culture. Where possible, comparisons will be drawn between these rulers and their predecessors, Frederick William I, Peter the Great and Maria Theresa. The third section will consider whether or not the Enlightenment had any real impact on the diplomacy of the enlightened despots.

Voltaire claimed that 'The happiest thing that can happen to Man is for the prince to be a philosopher.'[2] The connection of the three leading enlightened despots with philosophy was quite explicit. Frederick the Great, in fact, described himself as 'philosophe par inclination, politique par devoir',[3] and believed that 'A well conducted government must have a system as coherent as a system of philosophy.'[4] Catherine the Great professed to be governed by 'my heart and reason', and Voltaire enthused: 'Every writer in Europe ought to be at your feet.'[5] Joseph II commented that he had made philosophy the law-giver of his empire.[6]

Their predecessors' concept of kingship had been fundamentally different. Frederick William I combined a fervent Calvinism with an open assertion of autocracy which bordered on the irresponsible: 'We are Lord and Master and can do what we like.'[7] His contacts with the Enlightenment were negligible, and he even expelled the leading German philosopher, Wolffe, from Prussia. Peter the Great had an almost obsessive zeal for modernization, but this was in a utilitarian and technical sense; beneath the surface he remained a traditional autocrat, his power based on Divine Right, whatever his contempt for religion or the established institutions of the Church. Maria Theresa was greatly influenced by Austrian theorists like Sonnenfels, but feared direct contact with French ideas. She went along with certain reforms but refused to abandon religion as the basis of her power.

The new rationalism in autocracy was apparent in the ruler's willingness to justify his authority. He no longer sheltered behind the term 'Divine Right' or quoted the old maxim *'a deo rex, a rege lex'* ('From God, the King; from the King, the law'). Instead, he placed more emphasis on the monarch as a servant of the state. Only by total dedication could he hope to rule effectively and justify the absolute power which he had inherited. Hence Frederick the Great frequently referred to himself as Prussia's *premier domestique*. It followed that policies should be based on what seemed most 'reasonable'. The best means of deciding this was for the ruler to acquaint himself with the works of the *philosophes* and *Physiocrats* so that he could acquire a more balanced picture of the needs of his subjects and the capacity to deduce the course of action needed. Frederick the Great, for example, believed: 'My principal occupation is to combat ignorance and prejudice . . . to enlighten minds, to refine manners, to make people as happy as human nature and my means allow.'[8]

At no stage, however, was the rational examination of the purpose of autocracy intended as a criticism of autocracy itself. Frederick, Catherine and Joseph were all influenced, to some extent, by the concept that their power was based on a theoretical contract with their subjects, enlightened rule from above depending on total obedience from below. But there was no advance towards the theory of replacing one contract by another, or of safeguarding against inefficiency and tyranny. There could be no possibility of introducing representative institutions, and any intellectual challenge to the basis of autocracy was dealt with by the full arsenal of traditional powers. Catherine the Great, for example, overreacted wildly to the criticisms of Radishchev in 1790, and Joseph II developed a ruthless secret police force.

The enlightened despots emphasized the importance of efficient and rational administration, although their methods varied. Austria and Prussia possessed expanding bureaucracies, to which

Enlightened Despotism: A General Survey

the enlightened despots added distinctive features, while keeping the base which had been constructed in previous reigns. Frederick the Great, for example, inherited the General Directory and the local government institutions known as the *Kriegs-und-Domänen-Kammern*. He refrained from abolishing any of his father's creations, although he added his own superstructure to form a new departmental system which increased his own personal authority. Joseph II streamlined Maria Theresa's bureaucracy for the Hereditary Lands but concentrated his attention on those areas which Maria Theresa had avoided – Hungary, Belgium and Milan. Catherine the Great, by contrast, gradually conceded that the maintenance of her authority was best served by minimal bureaucratic changes and a measured degree of decentralization in favour of the nobility. This, in effect, continued the winding down of Peter the Great's collegiate system which had started after his death in 1725.

The Enlightenment intruded more obviously into the development of judiciaries and the codification of law. The three major enlightened despots all expressed considerable personal interest in legal projects which their predecessors had either ignored or shelved. Frederick the Great, for example, encouraged the development of Prussia's first legal code by Cocceji, although the final results were not fully effective until after his death. Joseph II introduced the most advanced criminal and civil codes in Europe, and Austria was the only state on the Continent where the concept of equality before the law, fundamental to the aspirations of the *philosophes*, could be seen in practice. Catherine the Great made a great many more public statements about her desire to reform Russia's legal system along the lines mapped out by the Enlightenment, but she found that the forces of tradition in Russia were too powerful to allow anything radical to come out of the 1767 Commission. Each ruler, therefore, made an individual adjustment to the Enlightenment. Frederick presided over gradual infiltration of ideas in the construction of a legal code which was carefully controlled and circumscribed by the monarch. Joseph II acted more quickly, ignoring opposition and depending on his own judgement. Catherine's association was largely verbal and her plagiarism of Montesquieu in her *Instructions* had few practical results.

According to Le Mercier, government policy should aim at 'the greatest possible increase of production and population and assure the greatest possible happiness to those living in society'.[9] The *Physiocrats* were convinced that these ends could be achieved by reducing restrictions on economic activity, encouraging free trade, emancipating the serfs, and introducing a common land tax (*impôt unique*) to spread the burden of taxation more evenly. The enlightened despots were conscious of these broad principles, although each adapted them to the conditions of their states and usually fell far short of total implementation. Joseh II went furthest; he abolished serfdom in 1781 and made preparations to introduce a land tax. Such reforms were subsequently imitated by several lesser rulers within the Holy Roman Empire. Frederick the Great adopted a more systematic approach to economic planning than that of Frederick William I, and no longer regarded Crown land merely as the personal property of the Hohenzollerns. Catherine the Great included a substantial section on the economy in her *Instructions*, much of it influenced directly by the *Physiocrats*. In the long term, however, the pull of the past was decisive, and experimentation with the ideas of the Enlightenment was considerably diluted in two ways. First, all three rulers continued to pursue traditional mercantilist policies which, at times, degenerated into heavy-handed state interference. Second, social changes were inevitably restricted by the power of the nobility. Frederick the Great realized from the start that he could not deprive the Prussian Junkers of their serf-owning rights if he hoped to keep them as one of the props of Hohenzollern absolutism. Catherine the Great was, at first, favourable to emancipating the serfs, but came round to the view that the hostility of the Russian *Dvorianstvo* would be so intense that she would run the risk of being deposed. Only Joseph II attempted radical social change. His edict of emancipation, however, was never successfully enforced and, under pressure of the nobility, was eventually repealed after his death.

Voltaire maintained: 'We ought to bless a crowned head who makes religious toleration universal throughout 135 degrees of longitude.'[10] He was referring to Catherine the Great's more lenient attitude towards Protestants and Catholics, which was fully in accord with the spirit of the Enlightenment. Frederick the Great held that each of his subjects should 'get to heaven in his own way' and Joseph II expressed open contempt for divisions based on religion. Frederick was an agnostic, Catherine a practising Russian Orthodox and Joseph a devout Catholic. Yet they had a common

Enlightened Despotism: A General Survey

awareness that the foundation of the monarchy must be fully secular and that state control over the Church should be extended.

The enlightened despots were culturally far in advance of their predecessors. Frederick William I, the 'drill sergeant' of Prussia, was surpassed in philistinism only by Peter the Great, who was sometimes referred to as 'the barbarian who civilized Russia'. Maria Theresa, although far less uncouth than the other two, had one eye permanently fixed on the political implications of all literature and even banned the use of English in Austria. Vienna during her reign was a cultural backwater of Europe. By contrast, Frederick the Great created in Berlin a late eighteenth-century rival to Paris as a literary centre. Joseph II removed the stifling censorship of Maria Theresa and made possible a flood of French literature into Austria. Catherine the Great brought the Russian mind into contact with the West for the first time. There were, however, notable anomalies and shortcomings in this hectic activity. Frederick the Great, referring to German as 'that uncouth speech', became an ardent Francophile, thus laying himself open to Goethe's charge that he was 'bound in intellectual vassalage to Voltaire'. Catherine became increasingly aware of the political side-effects of literature emanating from France, and concentrated all western influences on developing a politically stable élite, imbued with a politically neutralized form of French culture. Joseph II discovered, to his horror, that Austria was open to extensive radical influences and felt obliged to restore heavy censorship towards the end of his reign. On the whole, however, there was less distortion of the Enlightenment in Austria than in Russia and Prussia, where it changed shape as it was absorbed into the system, adapted to the different social environment and, in some cases, trivialized.

It would be difficult to establish any direct connection between the Enlightenment and the aims of any of the eighteenth-century monarchs in diplomacy and warfare. All of the philosophers condemned warfare, regarding it as the ultimate form of irrational behaviour in a world which they believed could be ruled by reason. But none of the monarchs, whether clients of the Enlightenment or not, paid the slightest heed to pacific principles. Indeed, the most aggressive of all the eighteenth-century statesmen were precisely those rulers who claimed to be philosophers themselves, or those ministers, like Kaunitz, who had close connections with the Enlightenment. Frederick the Great set the tone by attacking Silesia in 1740. He subsequently invaded Saxony in 1756 and brought about the First Partition of Poland in 1772. Catherine the Great acquired huge areas of Poland in three Partitions and tried to dismember the Ottoman Empire as well. Even Joseph II became involved in this search for territory, committing Austria to the side of Russia against Turkey. There was no difference between the policies of the enlightened despots and their contemporaries; all pursued territorial expansion through dynastic claims. Their ambitions were often quite explicitly stated. Frederick the Great observed: 'Of all states, from the smallest to the biggest, one can safely say that the fundamental rule of government is the principle of extending their territories.'[11] Catherine the Great believed that 'he who gains nothing loses'.[11]

Nevertheless, the Enlightenment did have some influence over the diplomatic methods used by Frederick the Great, Catherine the Great, Joseph II and Maria Theresa's foreign minister, Kaunitz, who all showed a new assurance and self-confidence in handling foreign affairs. This came from a belief that diplomacy had a form of inherent logic which could be deduced by a mind in tune with the rationalist approach encouraged by the Enlightenment and accustomed to subjecting any problem to penetrating analysis. By contrast, Frederick William I had been far more cautious, wanting, in the words of Peter the Great, to fish without wetting his feet; Peter himself had led a massive struggle against Sweden, but encountered little success in his experiments with diplomacy. Louis XIV had acted on impulse as much as on consideration, and Charles XII of Sweden had shown no diplomatic finesse whatsoever.

What gave added scope for the intrigues of the enlightened despots was the unstable diplomatic scene in eighteenth-century Europe. This instability was due mainly to the absence of ideology in warfare. Ideological differences intensify divisions between states and create a degree of permanence in their conflict with each other. Before 1648 the main ideological influence had been religion, and there had been very little room for side-changing in, for example, the Thirty Years' War. A similar form of 'stability' in conflict occurred when French revolutionary ideas spread through Europe after 1792, and the countries of the *ancien régime* combined in an attempt to stamp them out. But in the eighteenth century alliances could be made and broken without any consideration of underlying

Enlightened Despotism: A General Survey

enmities or commitments. Catherine the Great, for example, signed an alliance with Prussia in 1764 but resumed an older contact with Austria in 1781. Between 1755 and 1757 Kaunitz played the game of the enlightened despots with consummate skill. He managed, in the Diplomatic Revolution, to bring about a complete reversal of the alliances of the War of the Austrian Succession, enticing former opponents into supporting Austria as part of a general strategy to build up a huge coalition against Prussia. A fluctuating diplomatic scene was essential for his success, and he welcomed a state of chaos from which he could reconstruct, to carefully devised plans, for Austria's benefit.

Such designs always presupposed a close connection between diplomacy and warfare; these were in greater harmony in the eighteenth century than at any other time in history. The purpose of diplomacy was to accumulate allies and military resources so as to apply pressure on a point which was likely to yield territorial concessions. Hence the normal pattern was the formation of the military alliance by diplomacy, followed by a round of warfare and the adjustment of territory by peace treaty. If the peace treaty proved unsatisfactory it might be necessary to change the alliance so as to be in a better position for the next round of warfare. The eighteenth century was, therefore, a period in which shifting relationships between states could be used empirically and with almost brutal calculation. It is ironical that the Enlightenment, opposed to war as the antithesis of Reason, should have provided rulers and statesmen with a means of deducing, by use of Reason, the most successful tactics of aggression.

The end of enlightened despotism came in the 1790s, when the continental autocracies were threatened by a rejuvenated and republican France. Confronted with the sweeping ideology of Jacobinism, the uneasy co-operation between autocracy and the earlier elements of the French Enlightenment finally collapsed. It had always been an artificial alliance; absolutism had reached that point in its history where it had abandoned its traditional justification by Divine Right, and had experimented with theories which owed their origin not to the feudal state but to the growing self-awareness of the middle class. As the eighteenth century drew to a close a direct clash occurred in France between the older forms of autocracy and the most revolutionary elements of the middle class.

'Enlightened' rulers, now embarrassed by their former association
with the leading spokesmen of the bourgeoisie and its culture,
hastened to confirm their support for tradition in a manner which
was aggressively dogmatic, both in the elimination of internal
dissent and in its prosecution of the war with France from 1792.

34
France Under the Regency and Cardinal Fleury 1715–1743

Louis XV did not assert his full authority until 1743. Before this France was governed, during the king's minority, by the Regency of Orleans (1715–23) and then, as the king accustomed himself to his role, by Cardinal Fleury (1726–43).

This interim was of the utmost importance for the development of the French monarchy in the eighteenth century and had far-reaching results. The Regency was a period of experimentation, an attempt to draw away from Louis XIV's system. But attempts at constitutional progress were overshadowed by aristocratic reaction, while the Regency's economic experiments ended in failure and precipitated revulsion against any further changes. By the 1720s the power of absolute monarchy had been greatly undermined and the future was uncertain. At this point France's third great Cardinal took the helm and, after 1726, introduced a period of retrenchment and consolidation which restored political and economic stability. He did not, however, deal with some of the more crucial issues raised by the failures of the Regency; too often he sidestepped the major constitutional problems and left them to work themselves out in the future.

The death of Louis XIV in 1715 left the anticipated power vacuum which had to be filled by yet another Regency. How would this temporary regime respond? The Duc d'Orleans was a known moderate in politics (if not in his private life), ordering the release of many political prisoners and suspending the use of *lettres de cachet*. He was also sympathetic towards the English parliamentary system. This was not, however, to be the direction in which he steered France. He succumbed instead to safer and more reactionary counsels, typified by Dubois's words: 'Let your wisdom avert from France the dangerous project of making the French a free people.'[1] His experiments were conducted in favour of the aristocracy, who gained ground temporarily in the conciliar system and permanently in the Paris *Parlement*.

The major institutional change brought about by the Regency was the alteration of Louis XIV's structure of Councils, which had been dominated by Secretaries of State and which had not drawn upon the services of the *noblesse d'épée*. Orleans was persuaded by articulate spokesmen of this section of the nobility to restore their constitutional role. The result was the establishment of the *Polysynodie*, consisting of the Council of Regency and seven subordinate Councils for internal affairs, finance, religion, foreign affairs, war, navy and commerce. The experiment was a miserable failure, as the *noblesse d'épée* proved incapable of responding to the demands of routine and committee work. Saint-Simon, who had been instrumental in establishing the *Polysynodie*, was taken aback by 'l'ignorance, la légèreté, l'inapplication de cette noblesse',[2] while the Duc d'Antin remarked 'that men of this class are not suited to government affairs, they are good only to be killed off in war'.[3] The system was in trouble by 1718 and had collapsed by the end of the Regency. Nevertheless, the *noblesse d'épée* had no intention of being left once more in obscurity. One of the manifestations of their revived self-consciousness was a willingness to sink their differences with the more recent *noblesse de robe* by a process of social integration through intermarriage. The *noblesse de robe*, in turn, upheld the interests of the entire aristocracy, old and new, by means of the Paris *Parlement*.

The Paris *Parlement* underwent its customary revival during a Regency period, although this time, in the absence of a Richelieu or a Mazarin to cut it down to size, it maintained its influence. Ironically, it was Louis XIV, who had formerly written the Letters Patent of 1673 which had weakened the *Parlement*, who provided the occasion. His Political Will stated that Orleans was to possess no more than nominal authority in the form of a casting vote in the Council of Regency. In this way Louis hoped to limit the powers of the *noblesse d'épée* by restricting its leader; he was merely confirming the distrust of the old aristocracy in a political context which he had shown throughout his reign. Orleans found the restriction incompatible with effective government and appealed to the *Parlement*, as the repository and interpreter of the nation's law, to remove it. This was done, on condition that Orleans restored the traditional right of remonstrance against royal edicts. The Regency therefore released the *Parlement* from the restraints of Louis XIV in order to release itself. The result was momentous. Although Orleans emphasized in 1715 that it was to behave 'avec tant de sagesse et de circonspection', the *Parlement* soon increased its claims and attempted to become, according to Saint-Simon, 'le tuteur du roi et le maître du royaume'.[2] The *Parlement* challenged the Regency's financial reforms in 1718 and the prolonged conflict over the issue of Jansenism (including the registration of the Bill *Unigenitus*) resulted in an uneasy compromise. The Regency had clearly revived the most powerful and conservative of all the instruments of the nobility. The full effects of this were not to become apparent until the second half of the century.

The economic situation offered greater scope for innovation, although there was a desperate tone to the reforms introduced. France was on the verge of bankruptcy on the death of Louis XIV; according to Noailles: 'We have found matters in a more terrible state than can be described. Both King and his subjects are ruined.'[4] The overall debt stood at 3,000 m. livres, a testimony to Louis XIV's active foreign policy; and annual expenditure continued to outstrip revenue from taxation. Orleans tried the usual methods of reissuing the coinage and investigating the worst cases of corruption through a *Chambre de Justice*. Eventually, however, he turned away from the economic theories prevalent in the previous reign, and gave John Law the opportunity to introduce radical changes. The first requisite, in Law's words, was to increase the flow of trade, for ultimately 'wealth depends on commerce'. This could best be achieved by ending the mercantilist policies of Colbert, based on the backing of bullion for all transactions. Instead, Law emphasized the importance of free circulation and stressed, therefore, that 'what is needed is credit'.[5] Gradually an enormous new economic structure was built, linking commercial expansion to the state revenues. In 1716 Law formed the *Banque Générale* which was linked to the new Mississippi Company in 1717. By 1719 this had been united with other companies to form the Company of the Indies and, by 1720, it had assumed responsibility for the collection of taxation and the reduction of the national debt. Unfortunately, this remarkable experiment was short-lived, for it left too much to chance and operated with inadequate safeguards, owing to a complete lack of experience with this type of reform. Wild speculation brought about the collapse of the Company and the Bank in 1720, with serious long-term consequences. Distrust of credit and paper issue hampered the flow of trade for the rest of the century, and the Bank of France was not set up until 1800. Law's attempts to alter the tax collection system were also suspended; the 'farming-out' process was restored in full, and any prospect of re-examining the methods by which taxation was apportioned and raised was ended. Reaction was able to justify itself for some time to come on the grounds that reform had failed.

Although Cardinal Fleury (who replaced the incompetent Duc de Bourbon in 1726) was never formally entitled First Minister, he exercised more power than any of the king's servants since Mazarin. He used this authority to make the best of the status quo by following a general policy of retrenchment. According to Voltaire, 'The good of the state was for a long time in accord with his moderation.'[6] At the same time, he made no attempt to introduce fundamental reforms and his ministry had fewer long-term effects than that of Richelieu, which also followed a period of Regency and aristocratic reaction.

Fleury's main constitutional achievement was to re-establish harmony in the conciliar system which had had to be restored after the failure of the Regency's *Polysynodie* by 1718. But this was accompanied at a personal level by effective leadership, rather than by any institutional surgery. To his credit, he brought out the best qualities of Louis XV so that, according to d'Argenson, the King, in 1730, 'works with his ministers, does it admirably, and reaches just decisions'.[7] He also made effective use of the best available personnel in administration: Orry as Controller General, d'Angervilliers as Secretary of State for War, Maurepas and d'Aguesseau. Fleury acted as policy co-ordinator, and knew when to exert pressure or to maintain a low profile. Unfortunately, his talents were less appreciated by the late 1730s. In 1738 d'Argenson observed: 'His credit wanes from day to day . . . the King hopes to drive him to resign by petty slight.'[7] Fleury's influence faded after his death in 1742, and the Councils assumed a noisy and disjointed character – according to d'Argenson 'celestial thunder could not have been heard in them'.[8]

Fleury's handling of the recently liberated Paris *Parlement* was not unlike the method used by Mazarin in the 1640s and 1650s: harsh measures alternating with retreat. The main difference, however, was that the *Parlement* never reached the point of rebellion under Fleury; it backed up its claims with constitutional and legal argument rather than the use of force. This meant that Fleury was in an anomalous position: the aspirations of the *Parlement* needed to be controlled, but the bad old days of the Frondes had to be avoided. Fleury tackled the problem with short-term success but provided no long-term solution. In 1730 the *Parlement* had to be compelled by a *lit de justice* to register an edict enforcing general acceptance of the Bull *Unigenitus* by the clergy. In the ensuing clash over the right of the *Parlement* to hold up royal legislation, the *Parlement* refused to conduct its normal judicial duties. The government, faced with vast numbers of resignations, exiled 139 judges to the provinces. Eventually Fleury recalled the officials; he had shown the weight of royal displeasure and was amenable to a compromise. The powers of the *Parlement* were not, however, curbed, and were to reassert themselves with greater force in the 1750s.

In his economic policy, Fleury was careful to avoid the type of experiment which had failed so disastrously during the Regency period. Unlike Law, he advanced no blueprint for reform, and his whole approach was pragmatic rather than theoretical. His first major act was to stabilize the value of the coinage in 1726, thus reviving confidence in the medium of exchange after the wild fluctuations of the early 1720s. There is no doubt that commerce benefited from this revaluation but the short-term gain was partially offset by the long-term effects of Fleury's return to mercantilist policies. Preferring the methods of Colbert to the theories of Law, Fleury reimposed heavy duties to reduce imports, and re-established many privileged industries with which the *ancien régime* is normally associated. Similarly, the state finances received effective short-term treatment without radical change. The Controller General, Orry (1730–45) produced the only balanced budgets of the century through rigid economy and more systematic accounting. Nevertheless, the traditional methods of tax collection by the *fermiers*, *receveurs des tailles* and *receveurs généraux des finances* were retained; in fact, Orry and Fleury yielded to the 'farming out' system to the extent of allowing the officials to keep between 30 and 50 per cent of the revenue collected. The result was the confirmation of privilege and the inadequate use of France's economic resources. Fleury's conservatism worked well in the 1730s but only because of careful management and the pursuit of a peaceful foreign policy. Active involvement in warfare from 1740 placed an intolerable strain on the whole financial structure, resulting eventually in attempts at more radical reforms by Marchault, Choiseul and Turgot.

It would be difficult to disagree with G. P. Gooch that Fleury presided over 'the happiest phase of an unhappy reign' or to deny the evident capacity of the cardinal to restore order from chaos. But it could be argued that many of his achievements were cosmetic and that his very success created serious delusions about the health of the financial structure until the 1780s.

35
France Under Louis XV and Louis XVI

It is often assumed that France under Louis XV and Louis XVI saw a dearth of reform when compared with those countries in which enlightened despotism became established. This is far from the truth. The theme of this chapter is that reforms were attempted which, in some cases, rivalled those of the enlightened despots. Unfortunately, resistance from the conservative elements of society proved stronger and more stubborn in France than elsewhere, with the result that these innovations were greatly impeded. Finally, the monarchy itself lacked the personal authority to overcome the obstacles; there was a marked contrast between, for example, Louis XVI and Frederick the Great.

On taking over the direction of domestic policy from Cardinal Fleury in 1743, Louis XV possessed no clearly defined attitude towards reform and certainly developed no fundamental plan. Under the pressure of war, however, several of his ministers felt impelled to introduce changes which would have more widespread effects than those of Fleury. After the accession of Louis XVI in 1774 the impetus of reform increased rapidly, as a result partly of the deteriorating financial situation and partly of more direct influences from the Enlightenment.

The economic reforms of the 1740s were precipitated by the War of the Austrian Succession (1740–8), into which France had been dragged despite Fleury's resistance. By 1749 the annual expenditure had regularly exceeded revenue, making a balanced budget impossible without a basic change in the taxation system. A start

273

was made by Marchault, an efficient administrator who had accumulated considerable experience of the nation's fiscal problems while he had served as an *intendant*. As Controller General (1745 –54) he cut back the amounts payable on the *taille* and, in an effort to spread the burden of taxation more evenly, introduced the *vingtième* in 1749. This was a significant attempt to end the exemptions of the clergy and nobility, and it imposed a basic tax of 5 per cent. The subsequent distorted operation of the *vingtième* induced Choiseul (1758–70) to conduct a general land survey in order to overcome the unequal assessment. This process was continued by Terray, who served as Controller General in the Triumvirate (1771–4). Although the *vingtième* never operated as it was intended, it did become the least burdensome of all the taxes in eighteenth-century France and gave a certain amount of social justice, at least whenever it could be enforced.

Louis XVI was served by a succession of Controllers General who advocated more sweeping measures. Turgot (1774–6) was a leading *Physiocrat* and had been closely associated with the *philosophes*. He therefore possessed more radical views, based on the theories which were influencing the enlightened despots. In 1774, for example, he justified his edict to eliminate controls over the price of grain with the consideration that it was necessary 'to remove monopoly . . . in favour of full competition'.[1] His Six Edicts of 1776 were the most complete programme of economic reform that France had yet seen, and included the ending of the compulsory *corvée* (to be superseded by another property tax), and the abolition of the system of restrictive trade guilds in which the majority of the craftsmen 'were reduced to a precarious existence under the sway of the masters, with no choice but to live in penury'.[1] Turgot appealed to the King to make his choice between backing privilege and considering the grievances of the oppressed, adding that 'he must judge in favour of the people, for this class is the most unhappy'.[1] Turgot hoped that the whole system of taxation could be restructured so that, in Voltaire's words, 'chacun donne, non selon sa qualité (ce qui est absurde) mais selon son revenu'.[2] After Turgot's fall, the subsequent Controllers General (excluding Clugny) all began as critics of Turgot but ended by pressing for reforms as the urgency of the situation impressed itself upon them. Necker (1777–81) tried to reduce the extravagance of the court. Calonne (1783–7) switched in midstream from a policy of expenditure (popular with the court) to one of fiscal reform. His main proposal was the introduction of the *subvention territoriale*, a single, universal land tax similar to the *impôt unique* suggested by the *Physiocrats* and currently being drawn up by Joseph II in Austria. Calonne also made a direct appeal for the restructuring of the existing taxes 'which bear heavily upon the most productive and laborious class'.[1] Brienne (1787–8) continued to press for the *subvention territoriale* against heavy resistance from the Assembly of Notables and the Paris *Parlement*, although he was to be no more successful than his predecessors. The whole period between 1774 and 1788 shows an impressive record of attempts at economic reform, with no lack of warning as to what would happen if these were not implemented.

Proposals for institutional reform were confined largely to the period 1770–89. Although they were not consistent in their application, they were all based on a desire to facilitate economic reform. The major change of Louis XV's reign was the abolition of the Paris *Parlement* by Maupeou in 1771 and its replacement by a Supreme Tribunal, the purpose being to end the constant opposition of the *noblesse de robe* to the financial and religious policies of the administration. The provincial *Parlements* were also dealt with, being replaced by *Conseils Supérieurs*. The policy as a whole was similar to the reduction of the role of the aristocratic assemblies and estates in Austria and Prussia. Whether this would have eased the passage of reforming legislation must remain a matter for speculation, for Louis XVI restored the *Parlements* in 1774 and his ministers focused their attention on another institutional change – the introduction of provincial assemblies. First put forward by Turgot as a scheme to reform local government, this became, under Calonne, an essential part of the scheme to alter the taxation system. The provincial assemblies would replace the 'farming out' methods currently employed and would be responsible for their own tax assessment and collection in their own area. These plans, however, were never implemented, and the period 1787–9 saw a constitutional crisis in which the Crown resorted to the use of historic expedients like the Assembly of Notables and the Estates General.

This was done more under pressure of those who resisted the reforming proposals of the ministers than in the name of reform itself. Such resistance was more firmly entrenched in France than in any of the states governed by enlightened despotism. It was made possible by the survival of traditional forces not fully dealt with by Louis XIV, and given new freedom during the period 1715-43. It manifested itself in three ways, leading to the gradual disillusionment of the enlightened element which the King's government undoubtedly possessed.

It appeared, first of all, in the administration itself. The centralizing policies of Richelieu and Louis XIV had aimed at reducing the influence of the *noblesse d'épée*, identified as the main obstacle to royal power. A counter-balance had therefore been established, and all the key administrative positions under Louis XIV were filled by recently ennobled members of the bourgeoisie, who were dependent of royal favour. Little attempt was made, however, to set up a structured bureaucracy, and many of the offices connected with the 'farming out' method of tax collection remained untouched. Furthermore, Louis XIV failed to control the number of offices for sale in both central and local administration, not wanting to cut off a valuable source of revenue. By the first half of the eighteenth century the administration was in a grave state. The new nobility had established a monopoly on all the lucrative posts and had merged socially with the *noblesse d'épée*, creating the very aristocratic stranglehold on government which Louis XIV had feared. Even the office of *Intendant* became a semi-autonomous aristocratic preserve. Assuming, therefore, that the impetus of reform had to come from the top, how could it be sustained below ministerial level?

Social privilege was jealously guarded throughout the two reigns and both sections of the nobility resisted any attempt to redistribute the burden of taxation. They opposed the introduction of the *vingtième* in 1749, the Six Edicts of 1776, the proposals for the *subvention territoriale* and the abolition of sinecures. They were given the lead by the Court at Versailles, which was instrumental in the dismissal of all of Louis XVI's most able ministers. Joseph II referred in 1777 to 'the aristocratic despotism'[3] of this court, even though his sister, Marie Antoinette, was one of its most irresponsible members. Joseph was also surprised by the intensity of the struggle put up by the Church against reform proposals and took measures to weaken the political influence of the Church in Austria. The higher clergy of France were drawn exclusively from the nobility and expressed their determination to uphold the privileges of the Church in matters of taxation through their main mouthpiece, the Assembly of Clergy. In 1749, for example, they fought Marchault's proposal to make the First Estate subject to the *vingtième* and declared in 1750 that the Church would not be forced to give up its traditional exemptions; any contributions would continue to be made 'volontairement et par don gratuit'.[4] The Church refused to countenance any of the proposed reforms of Turgot and his successors and the Assembly of Clergy in 1788 actually reduced its *don gratuit* to 25 per cent of the expected amount. Altogether, the contributions made by this method were insignificant, amounting to a total of only 3·5 m. livres between 1715 and 1788.

Reaction was most effectively displayed in the Paris *Parlement*, of which there was no equivalent in Prussia or Austria. Here the *noblesse de robe* represented all the privileged interests of the First and Second Estates and displayed its new solidarity with the *noblesse d'épée*. By using its right of remonstrance (restored by the Regency in 1715) the Paris *Parlement* resisted virtually every economic edict brought before it for registration, with the result that the King either had to resort to a series of *lits de justice* to force the measure through or abandon it altogether. To give only a few examples, the *Parlement* fought edicts concerning taxation in 1749, 1756, 1763, 1768, 1769, 1776 and 1787, and a constitutional edict for the establishment of provincial assemblies in 1780. In 1788 it resisted the King's *lits de justice* to force through Brienne's land tax and placed pressure on bankers to withdraw loan facilities essential for the conduct of the administration.

What made the *Parlement* a particularly formidable opponent to the reforming ministers was its discovery of an effective method of protecting privilege. In addition to its appeal to its historic rights and powers, it claimed in the eighteenth century to represent the freedoms of the nation and to be the one major guarantee against despotism. In 1755, for example, it claimed to be 'la vraie cour de France', its purpose being 'tempérer le pouvoir absolu de la souveraineté'.[4] It even made use of the theories of limited sovereignty and the balance of power advanced by Montesquieu, and acquired some sympathy from the *philosophes* (except for Voltaire) during the period of its abolition (1771–4). By the late 1780s the Paris *Parlement* was projecting itself as the only defence against encroaching royal powers, and it attracted considerable popular support. Eventually the *Parlement* advanced its arguments to their logical conclusion and insisted that the reform proposals of the administration needed the consent of a fully assembled Estates

Aspects of European History 1494–1789

General. After Louis XVI agreed to summon the first meeting of this body since 1614, the *Parlement* demanded that the voting procedure should be conducted by Estate rather than '*par tête*', thus ensuring a veto on any proposals put forward by the Third Estate. In so doing, it revealed itself as the bastion of privilege and the main obstacle to reform.

The role of the king himself was inevitably impeded by such reactionary moves. Much therefore depended on the extent to which he was able to exercise his authority. France needed an active monarch more desperately in the eighteenth century than ever before, and it was her misfortune that Louis XV and Louis XVI were less capable of dealing with entrenched opposition than their own predecessors or their contemporaries in Austria, Russia and Prussia.

Much has been made of the deficiencies of Louis XV, especially by d'Argenson, who developed a strong aversion to his king after being dismissed in 1747. But, even allowing for exaggeration, it cannot be denied that Louis XV was a pale imitation of Louis XIV. He lacked his great-grandfather's sense of dedication and, as Voltaire told Frederick the Great, 'was indifferent to his post'.[5] Choiseul echoed this view: 'He displays the most repulsive indifference to every sort of business and all kinds of people.'[3] He therefore found difficulty in maintaining his absolute power; as Sorel states: 'There was the most intolerable incoherence in despotism, irresolution in omnipotence, anarchy in centralization.'[6] On the whole, he resorted to the line of least resistance. Although he was prepared, on occasions, to assert that 'it is in my person that the sovereign power resides',[7] he rarely backed this up by a consistent course of action. When Marchault introduced his *vingtième* in 1749, Louis gave way to the demands of the *Parlement* and the Assembly of Clergy that the traditional exemptions should be continued. Marchault became so much of an embarrassment that he was eventually dismissed in 1754. Choiseul's attempt to establish the *vingtième* more evenly gained slightly more support, and Louis XV held *lits de justice* in 1759 and 1761 to force the *Parlement* to consent to a land survey. Further resistance followed, as the provincial *Parlements* raised their objections, and Louis once again dropped the issue. His firmest decisions came in 1771, when he supported Maupeou's abolition of the Paris *Parlement*. But this was not followed by an extensive reform programme, and there is no reason to suppose that

France Under Louis XV and Louis XVI

Louis XV had undergone any basic change of attitude or character.

Louis XVI showed a more highly developed sense of royal responsibility and a more definite commitment to reform. The jibe of the Count of Provence that he was as indecisive 'as balls of ivory that you try in vain to hold together'[6] can be discounted as inaccurate, particularly in view of the eminent opinions pointing in the opposite direction. Joseph II observed: 'Il a des notions, il a du jugement.'[8] Prince Henry of Prussia appeared to confirm this: 'He had sound ideas in politics'.[1] Goethe added that he 'evinced the best intentions',[1] while Frederick the Great simply told d'Alembert: 'You have a very good King.'[1]

His main problem was that he lacked staying power, the capacity to hold out against prolonged resistance. In this respect he differed from Joseph II, who showed a remarkable degree of perseverance, or Frederick the Great, so ruthless in eliminating dissent. Prince Henry believed that the reason for Louis XVI's reticence was that 'he distrusted himself too much'.[1] Although he was sincere in his intentions to reform, he lacked the enlightened despot's characteristic ruthlessness in pushing it through. The growing constitutional crisis of his reign resulted partly from his failure to support his ministers beyond a certain point. When five of Turgot's Six Edicts were rejected by the Paris *Parlement* in 1776, Louis XVI observed: 'I see well that there is no-one here but M. Turgot and myself who love the people.'[1] He then proceeded to hold a *lit de justice*. But, as the opposition to Turgot mounted in the administration and the court, the King yielded and dismissed his minister. When Necker sought greater authority and was opposed by the other officials, Louis responded in the same manner. Calonne and Brienne also became victims of Louis's desire to escape a final confrontation with the combined forces of the opposition.

It would probably have been unwise for Louis XVI to resist the demand of the Paris *Parlement* for the convocation of the Estates General. But during the course of 1789 he committed his most serious mistake, one which may well have cost the King his life and France her monarchy. Against all his reforming instincts he agreed that the Estates should convene and vote separately, thus aligning himself with privilege and reaction. In so doing he seemed to identify himself with the famous paradox of Marie Antoinette: 'The nobility will destroy us, but it seems to me that we cannot save ourselves without it.'[3]

36
French Foreign Policy in the Eighteenth Century

France reached the first peak of her military power and diplomatic prestige under Louis XIV, the second under Napoleon I. Between the two reigns French foreign policy was no less active but a great deal less successful.

In retrospect, it seems that a realistic course could have been followed in the eighteenth century, based on two underlying principles. The first would have been the establishment of a period of peace and the avoidance of any commitment involving military intervention. This was necessary to enable France to recover internally from the economic problems induced by Louis XIV's designs. The second principle would have been an extension of the first. On recovering her internal equilibrium, France could have concentrated on maintaining the status quo in Europe by upholding the balance of power and avoiding a continental war. Instead, an active foreign policy could have been directed towards building up France's imperial and maritime power, and could have been instrumental in undermining France's greatest threat, Britain.

The Regency of the Duc d'Orleans (1715–23) and the administration of Cardinal Fleury (1726–43) fulfilled the general requirements of the first principle by concentrating on a pacific foreign policy. After 1740, however, the growing personal influence of Louis XV (1715–74) in French politics and diplomacy reversed this trend and introduced a period of intensive continental warfare. He made the disastrous mistake of giving priority to the struggles of the War of the Austrian Succession (1740–8) and the Seven Years' War

French Foreign Policy 1700–1800

(1756–63). Meanwhile, during these wars, Britain attacked French commercial and imperial interests. The result of this was a serious decline in French power by the middle of the eighteenth century. France began to emerge from this between 1763 and 1774, due to the success of Choiseul, who laid the foundations for the policies of Louis XVI (1774–92). Louis XVI and Vergennes changed Louis XV's continental emphasis and fulfilled the general requirements of the second principle. France remained at peace on the Continent and concentrated instead on undermining British maritime strength by supporting the American cause in the War of American Independence (1777–83). France was well under way to recovering some of her military and naval power when the accumulated strains of the wars of the eighteenth century caused the collapse of the French finances and administration in 1789.

The Regency of Orleans (1715–23) was dedicated to reconstructing France after the hectic foreign policy of Louis XIV. Orleans was prepared to experiment with new ideas in diplomacy, although most of the details were carried out by Dubois, Secretary of State for Foreign Affairs from 1718.

Orleans and Dubois dealt successfully with what could have been a period of crisis in international relations and what Louis XIV would probably have transformed into a major war. The main threat to the peace of Western Europe came from Philip V. The Treaty of Utrecht (1713) had recognized this Bourbon candidate as King of Spain, provided that he renounce any future claim to the French throne. Philip's wife, Elizabeth Farnese, and his Foreign Minister, Alberoni, aimed at reviving his candidature when the health of the young French king, Louis XV, was very much in doubt. Many statesmen began to wonder whether the War of the Spanish Succession (1702–13) would now be followed by a War of the French Succession.

The answer of the Regency was unusual and subtle – to form an alliance system which would protect France by bringing all the major powers of Western Europe to her side and to pressurize any potential rivals into joining. No state would be the target of this alliance because the underlying diplomacy lacked aggression and emphasized only peace and consolidation. Short conflicts might prove necessary but long wars were to be avoided at all costs; reconciliation and diplomatic contacts with France's opponents, rather than their defeat and humiliation, were seen as the most durable basis of peace. In 1716 the Anglo-French Alliance was drawn up, England also being anxious for a period of peace to enable her to resolve her own succession problem by overcoming Jacobite threats to the new Hanoverian dynasty. In 1717 the Netherlands joined, thus forming the Triple Alliance. This grew into the Quadruple Alliance as the Emperor came into the system in 1718. A short war followed, in which Britain and France felt obliged to frustrate Spain's expansionist policies in Italy. By the Treaty of London (1720) Philip V renounced his candidature to the French throne and brought Spain into the Alliance system. By patient diplomacy, therefore, the Regency overcame a major threat to the stability of France from Spain and, at the same time, secured a much needed *rapprochement* with Britain.

The policy of Orleans and Dubois was maintained for a time by Cardinal Fleury, who directed the French administration, finances and diplomacy from 1726 to 1743. He realized that a major war would cripple France, and that he needed to be able to concentrate on internal consolidation after the relatively unsuccessful domestic policies of the Regency. His main priorities were, therefore, to prevent the isolation of France in Europe, and to convince the more belligerent statesmen in France that the successful conduct of war required a full treasury and a just cause, neither of which were apparent at the time. His pacific aims were shared by his English counterpart, Sir Robert Walpole (Prime Minister from 1721 to 1742), who had similar difficulties in restraining a vociferous war faction. Fleury was so convinced that the interests of France were best served by peace that, when war did break out, he did his best to shorten it, even at the expense of French military prestige. The War of the Polish Succession (1733–5) was a case in point. The more militant politicians in France forced Fleury to advance the candidature of Louis XV's father-in-law, Stanislaus Leszczynski, to the Polish throne, which became vacant in 1733. France was supported by Spain and Sardinia, but was opposed by Austria and Russia, who backed the claim of Augustus III. Fleury refused to commit all of France's resources to the struggle and devoted his efforts not to winning the war, but to extracting France from the prospect of a more general European conflict like the War of the Spanish Succession. Above all, he avoided antagonizing Britain. He even kept French troops away from the Austrian Netherlands, thus foregoing the prospect of conquest, in case Britain should join the other side to protect what she regarded as a vital strategic area. It is hardly surprising, therefore, that the next King of Poland was Augustus III, not Stanislaus Leszczynski, and that Fleury was virulently attacked by the war party in France.

The last few years of Fleury's administration saw the final failure of his pacific policies; by the time of his death in 1743 he was already discredited and France was deeply involved in the War of the Austrian Succession, the first major conflict in western and central Europe since 1713.

Louis XV (1715–74) had decided by 1740 that the period of influential ministers should end and that he should assume far greater personal responsibility. This proved to be detrimental in two ways. First, he was determined that any policy should be an active one, that France should become fully involved again in continental affairs. This decision put a severe strain upon France's military capacity, since she also had to deal with the growing threat of Britain. Second, he failed to pursue any consistent overall aim in his continental policy; he alternated between secret diplomacy, of which his ministers were frequently unaware, and open decisions hastily arrived at.

His desire for action was not without support. Many of the King's ministers became increasingly scornful of Fleury's methods after 1733. They backed any policy which would lead to an increase in French military involvement, with the prospect of acquiring territory in the Rhineland and the Austrian Netherlands. This would inevitably mean an anti-Austrian alliance. Other ministers, however, were thoroughly opposed to this trend. They feared a revival of the ambitious foreign policy of Louis XIV at a time when France was not as strong as she had been in the seventeenth century in relation to the other major powers. They therefore urged the King to concentrate on commercial and maritime consolidation, to prepare France for the conflict which was likely to occur with Britain sometime in the future, and to avoid military commitments on the Continent.

The policy pursued by Louis XV satisfied no-one and ultimately proved very unsuccessful. Under the influence of the war party he allied with Prussia in 1741, thus involving France in the War of the Austrian Succession (1740–8). Ranged against France and Prussia were Austria, Britain and Russia, and it soon became clear that there were no quick conquests or acquisitions to be won. In fact, France was seriously embarrassed in two ways. Firstly, she was duped by Frederick the Great of Prussia, who proved a treacherous ally. He deserted France in 1742, making peace with Austria by the Treaty of Berlin, re-entered the war in 1744 and withdrew unilaterally in 1745 by the Treaty of Dresden. While Prussia acquired Silesia from the war, France, who had maintained the struggle over a longer period, gained nothing. Secondly, Britain threatened French colonies and commercial interests. The French fleet was unable to protect these as it was defeated in 1747 by Anson off Cape Finisterre and by Hawke at Belle Isle. By the time that the Treaty of Aix-la-Chapelle was drawn up in 1748 to end the War of the Austrian Succession, France was nearing the point of exhaustion.

Louis XV's reaction to France's predicament in the war had a glimmering of perception but proved to be totally incoherent. For example, he secretly aimed, from 1745 onwards, to strengthen French links with Northern and Eastern Europe, particularly with Poland, Turkey, Sweden and Prussia. The intentions were to reduce Russian influence in Poland and to break the alliance between Russia and Austria, thus isolating the latter. Yet, in 1756, his official policy proved to be completely different. Frederick the Great, relying on continuing his friendship with France, formed the Convention of Westminster with Britain, thereby unintentionally precipitating the Diplomatic Revolution. Louis XV reacted to this Machiavellian diplomacy with fury and made a fundamental miscalculation in his desire to express his feelings about Prussia's treachery. He formed a very unpopular alliance with Austria by the Treaties of Versailles (1756 and 1757) on the mistaken assumption that the collapse of one alliance should always be followed by the formation of another. A more appropriate line of action would have been to maintain French neutrality in Europe and to concentrate French resources against Britain. France possessed sufficient military strength to deter either Prussia or Austria from considering unprovoked aggression against her, and Louis XV could have made the formation of non-aggression treaties the basis of his diplomacy, instead of alliances which led to military obligations. Besides, Prussia's main enemies were Austria and Russia, while Austria aimed primarily at regaining Silesia from Prussia. France was therefore, ideally placed to encourage continental conflicts between the other powers, while keeping out of them herself.

French Foreign Policy 1700–1800

The alliance with Austria involved France in the Seven Years' War (1756–63). This struggle was disastrous to France; it brought no permanent success on the Continent, and open failure at sea and in the colonies. Austria was of no practical use to France, and it was ironical that France was now committing her resources to helping Austria regain Silesia from Prussia, after having assisted Prussia in the previous war to steal it from Austria. The futility of this policy was seen by contemporaries, even those in office. In 1758, for example, Bernis observed to Choiseul that French policy had been absurd and shameful. Anti-Austrian feeling ran high in France and never really subsided.

While France was heavily committed to a continental war, Britain was concentrating all her resources on attacking French shipping and colonies. William Pitt (the Elder) organized raids on the French coast, naval blockades and expeditions to capture French colonies like Goree, Quebec, Montreal, Martinique and the West African fortresses. British foreign policy was carefully planned and took full advantage of the miscalculations of Louis XV. Pitt ensured that Prussia was given adequate subsidies to enable her to continue the war against France and to distract the attention of the French government from the substantial losses which France was incurring overseas.

The Seven Years' War was ended in 1763 by two treaties, both of which were humiliating to France. The continental war was concluded by the Treaty of Hubertusberg, which acknowledged Prussian possession of Silesia but gave France no territorial compensation for her efforts. The maritime and colonial war was settled by the Treaty of Paris. By this, French losses to Britain included Canada, West Indian islands like Guadeloupe and Martinique, and several Indian possessions. France paid a heavier price than any other participant in the Seven Years' War. But then she had also been more extensively involved. Britain had conducted a naval and imperial war; Russia, Prussia and Austria had fought an exclusively continental struggle. France had fallen between two stools and had been the only combatant to be involved in both spheres.

The last ten years of the reign of Louis XV and the short reign of Louis XVI saw the gradual revival of France as a major power and the pursuit of a more purposeful and successful policy against Britain. The precedent was established by Choiseul, who worked to achieve French stability in Europe and power at sea in order to switch the aggressive capacity of France from the Continent to the Atlantic. Of particular importance was his revival of French naval power, which he effectively doubled between 1763 and 1775. The process was continued by Louis XVI. The new king had a far greater interest than his late grandfather in foreign policy, and his ability has been generally underrated. He displayed greater perception and followed a more meaningful strategy for France, assisted by Vergennes, who had been heavily influenced by Choiseul. The basis of French foreign policy was now to shake off the Austrian alliance, maintain peace with other continental countries and undermine the strength of Britain, now, at last, identified as France's natural enemy.

Between 1740 and 1774 France had been duped by the other powers. Now it was Austria's turn. Joseph II, although a reformer of real ability in the domestic field, made some monumental blunders in his foreign policy after 1775, which worked in France's favour. In 1778, for example, he claimed the Bavarian throne, anticipating French support against the hostile reactions of Prussia; he discovered instead that France was now prepared to ditch the Austrian connection. Vergennes now aimed at maintaining the balance of power in Europe so that he could withdraw France from military commitments. The result of France's change of policy was a hectic round of alliance-making and breaking in Central and Eastern Europe which kept Russia, Prussia and Austria preoccupied and left France free to concentrate on Britain.

Vergennes' main priority was to rebuild French naval power and to reverse the British advantage gained in the Treaty of Paris in 1763. The ideal opportunity arose with the War of American Independence (1777–83). In 1778 France assisted the American colonists and, in 1779, formed an alliance with Spain. Britain, meanwhile, was isolated, committed to fighting a war in North America while, at the same time, struggling to maintain her naval power. France, by contrast, had withdrawn from complications in Europe and was leaving the main burden of the fighting in America to the rebels. She also had the support of a neighbouring power (Spain) with maritime resources and no continental ties. It appeared that Vergennes had turned the tables and proved that, given the right strategy, French success against Britain was still possible.

Unfortunately for France, this policy was not quite as effective as

French Foreign Policy 1700–1800

it might have been. Although Britain experienced defeats in America itself, for example at Yorktown in 1781, she was able to cling on to her naval power, and it was this which prevented the French from regaining by the Treaty of Versailles (1783) the colonies which had been lost in the Seven Years' War. It seemed, therefore, that the sad neglect of maritime, naval and imperial interests by Louis XV had given Britain a head start over France which Louis XVI found impossible to make up fully. Moreover, the situation was now complicated by impending financial collapse within France. The French economy had been seriously weakened by decades of warfare. Most of the damage had been done by Louis XV, but the War of American Independence had the most spectacular results as a series of Controllers General tried to grapple with the threat of bankruptcy. It was ironical that the War of American Independence was, for France, the right struggle pursued at the wrong time, and that the most successful period of French foreign policy between 1713 and 1789 coincided with the worst internal crises.

37

The Origins of the French Revolution

The purpose of this concluding chapter is to provide a synthesis of some of the more important interpretations of the outbreak of the French Revolution.

The 1770s and 1780s brought with them a serious economic depression. This seemed the worse because it followed a long period of mounting prosperity and it caused a sense of resentment and bitterness as all classes faced a decline in their status. The fabric of society was now threatened with rupture by the exertion of two internal forces. These had existed for much of the century but were now greatly accentuated by the economic crisis. The first force was the hostility between the Second Estate (aristocracy) and the Third Estate (bourgeoisie, peasantry and urban proletariat) as they pulled further apart from each other. The second force was the simultaneous attempt of both Estates to pull away from the policies of the monarchy and the implications of absolutism. For a while the Estates formed an unnatural alliance against the central power of the monarchy, and so the second force was the stronger. The king, finding himself in serious difficulties, yielded to the combined demands of the different classes, and agreed to summon the Estates General. Now that the central authority seemed to have collapsed, the original antagonism between the Estates reasserted itself so violently that this first force tore through the fabric of the *ancien régime*. The influence of the nobility was now overwhelmed by successive waves from the Third Estate as the bourgeoisie,

The Origins of the French Revolution

peasantry and urban proletariat each pressed for the achievement of their aspirations.

It is a common assumption that revolution is caused by misery; Marx certainly believed that worsening conditions create a situation favourable to revolution. In the mid-nineteenth century, however, Alexis de Tocqueville advanced the theory that the French Revolution broke out when conditions were improving. He observed: 'It is not always by going from bad to worse that a country falls into a revolution.' Moreover, 'the state of things destroyed by a revolution is almost always somewhat better than that which immediately precedes it'.[1] In 1962 J. C. Davies used a slightly different approach, but covered some of de Tocqueville's ground. He suggested that 'revolutions are most likely to occur when a prolonged period of objective economic and social development is followed by a short period of sharp reversal'.[2] This seems to be borne out by the general economic trends of the eighteenth century.

Between 1741 and 1776 France experienced a high overall economic growth rate. Large sections of the bourgeoisie benefited from the threefold increase of trade and the fivefold increase of overseas trade, together with the revived prosperity of ports like Dunkirk, Le Havre, La Rochelle, Bordeaux, Nantes and Marseilles. The increase in prices (estimated at 65 per cent between 1741 and 1765) drove up the value of farm produce and greatly improved the living conditions of the tenant farmers. Although famines did occur, for example in 1725, 1740, 1759 and 1766–8, there was nothing in the 1780s to compare with the catastrophic levels of starvation during the years 1693–4 and 1709–10. In the general upsurge of prosperity the French bourgeoisie and peasantry seemed distinctly better off than their counterparts in Central and Eastern Europe.

When it came, during the 1770s and 1780s, the slump had a profound effect. France experienced a recession similar to that suffered by other countries; this was probably no more than a temporary dip in a lengthy economic cycle, possibly precipitated by a shortage of bullion from the New World. French industry and commerce were, however, badly affected because of the inadequate nature of French credit facilities. Production therefore declined, unemployment increased and the recession soon communicated itself to the agricultural sector. To make matters worse, there was a severe drought in 1785, and in the following years the peasants were

289

unable to afford the usual quantity of seed, the inevitable result being short yields. The 1788 harvest was ruined by an abnormally wet summer and the position was even worse in 1789. The degree of starvation was lower than it had been at various stages during the reign of Louis XIV; but the sudden decline in the fortunes of each class in the 1770s and 1780s had a far more dangerous psychological impact. The bourgeoisie and peasantry, in particular, saw the gap between their aspirations and their achievements growing ever wider, while the nobility struggled desperately to hold what they had. The result was deep resentment and growing bitterness, both of them more inflammable revolutionary material than suffering by itself. The social classes looked with increasing suspicion at each other and at the regime itself, trying desperately to recapture their former share of the national wealth and to continue their previous quest for material advancement.

The eighteenth century saw a gradual deterioration in relations between the Second and Third Estates. Each had improved its position economically compared to its own past; but each came to regard the other as a serious threat to its security and well-being. The resentment greatly increased after 1776.

The nobility had managed to reassert its influence over the administration and local government by the alliance between the *nobless d'épée* and the *noblesse de robe*, while the highest positions of authority within the Church had, in the words of Talleyrand, become the preserve 'presque exclusif de la classe noble'.[3] On the other hand, the nobility feared the ambitions of the wealthy sections of the bourgeoisie and resisted fiercely any attempts by the latter to break the monopoly of the *noblesse de robe* over the administrative offices and the *Parlements*. The bourgeoisie regarded their ultimate aim as passage into the First Estate by the traditional method of ennoblement. Increasingly, however, this form of upward mobility was blocked and with it any chance of gaining political power. Two revolutionary leaders showed the effects that disillusionment with this state of affairs could produce. Carnot's radical views followed his unsuccessful attempts to gain ennoblement, while Danton believed that 'The Old Régime drove us to it [revolution] by giving us a good education, without opening any opportunity for our talents.'[4] The peasantry, although lacking the education and economic power of the bourgeoisie, had their own aspirations which were challenged

The Origins of the French Revolution

by the rural nobility. Seigneurial rights and dues were extracted to the full, and the peasantry had to suffer the inconveniences and hardships produced by the *banalité du moulin, banalité du four, banalité du pressoir, droit de chasse* and *droit de bauvin*. And, according to one of the *cahiers* of the peasantry in 1789, 'the contempt of the nobility for the commonality is beyond belief'.[5] The nobility therefore came to be regarded as a parasitic element, enjoying seigneurial privileges without carrying out the functions which had once accompanied them.

The rift between the Second and Third Estates widened during the 1770s and 1780s. Under the impact of the recession the peasantry found the seigneurial dues particularly onerous, while the nobility increasingly tightened up their exactions in order to solve their own difficulties. The burden of the depression was therefore passed downwards, to the section of society least able to bear it. The bourgeois complaint about the nobility was more indirect, but, nevertheless, significant for the future. They accused the nobility of resisting any rationalization of the economic and financial structure and of perpetuating anachronistic institutions at a time when reform was most urgently needed.

Yet tensions between the social classes did not result in immediate conflict. For a while they were partially restrained by a temporary and basically artificial coalition against a common target, the absolute power of the monarch.

The motives of each class in establishing this common front against the central government differed widely, but each had a fixed idea that the regime in its present form could no longer serve its interests or guarantee it from exploitation. The government had, therefore, to be modified. Precisely how remained a matter of vague speculation until the monarchy actually collapsed under the combined pressure.

The nobility feared absolutism more profoundly in the 1770s and 1780s than ever before. The banning of the *Parlements* in 1771 seemed to be an attack on the most cherished power of the nobility, gained after a long struggle since 1715, namely, the questioning of royal legislation. When the *Parlements* were restored in 1774 the nobility returned to the offensive, only to be confronted by the appalling spectre of a reforming monarch, who, to make matters worse, was served by ministers who openly expressed reservations about the existing fiscal system and the exemptions from taxation.

Aspects of European History 1494–1789

Louis XVI seemed a greater menace than Louis XIV because he appeared to be willing to embark upon an extensive remodelling programme which would reduce the social status of the nobility in a way never even considered in the seventeenth century. The nobility therefore used every device available; they fought the reform programme in the *Parlements,* in the court and in the Assembly of Notables. As the financial crisis worsened after 1787 they demanded the convocation of the Estates General. This was merely an appeal to an early precedent, one which the nobility knew the monarch could not ignore. The Estates General would naturally confirm the powers of the nobility, since the First and Second Estates would outnumber the Third Estate on the traditional voting method.

The bourgeoisie saw matters differently but went along with the tactics of the nobility. To them the Estates General offered the prospect of fundamental constitutional reform, which would enable the bourgeoisie to exert more control over the political institutions and to redesign the economic structure. The latter had become increasingly burdensome. After the brief experiments of the Regency with *laissez-faire,* France had seen the return of the mercantilist policies of Colbert from 1726 onwards, and the continuation of the oppressive guild system and internal customs barriers. Then, during the reign of Louis XVI, government policy seemed to lose all sense of overall direction. At the very depth of the economic depression the government seemed prepared to unleash the market forces of Great Britain; by the free trade treaty of 1786 it exposed the declining French industries to *laissez-faire* at the very time that protection was most needed. If the chaotic economic and fiscal system were to be reorganized, the bourgeoisie would have to play an active role. This could no longer be done by relying on a special relationship with the monarchy; the nobility had already blocked the access to political positions. The solution, therefore, had to be found in representative institutions – in a parliamentary monarchy. Much as the bourgeoisie resented the nobility, they therefore supported the demands for the convocation of the Estates General.

The peasantry also regarded the meeting of the Estates General as a panacea. It would be the instrument whereby the unequal distribution of taxation would be remedied. The *taille, capitation, vingtième, gabelle* and *aides* would be reassessed or possibly replaced by a graduated land, or income, tax. The institution of monarchy still commanded respect, but it was felt increasingly that

The Origins of the French Revolution

its powers should be limited. The peasantry suspected that the government had been making profits from fluctuations in the price of grain; this and other grievances could now be articulated openly, with greater hope of redress.

In expressing its opposition to the policies of the regime each class made use of the ideas of the leading French *philosophes*. It is often assumed that Montesquieu, Voltaire and Rousseau exerted a direct influence on the growth of revolutionary feeling and thereby precipitated the events of 1789. In reality, the growth of dissent was not actually stimulated by the *philosophes*; dissent, however, was frequently expressed with the help of quotations taken liberally from their writings. The Paris *Parlement*, for example, made frequent use of Montesquieu's theories of the balance of power. Sometimes the phrases used to support claims bore a close resemblance to the American constitution which, in turn, borrowed from the *philosophes*. The *Parlement* of Rennes, for example, declared in 1788: 'That man is born free, that originally men are equal, these are truths that have no need of proof',[6] an obvious mixture of Jefferson and Rousseau. The *cahiers* of each social group in 1789 contained examples of an unusually lucid statement of general grievances. It appears, therefore, that Montesquieu and Rousseau had more influence on the expression of opposition than on its actual formation.

Such a distinction would have offered little comfort to Louis XVI. During his reign monarchy not only reached its lowest ebb for two centuries; it eventually proved incapable of presiding over the normal process of government. The main problem was that the monarchy could no longer maintain a careful balance between the divergent social forces, for the simple reason that it had no consistent basis of support. Louis XIV had promoted the image of absolutism by elevating the monarchy into a lofty position of isolation. But he had taken care to maintain the support of the bourgeoisie to balance the alienated *noblesse d'épée*. After 1851 Napoleon III was to depend on the backing of the peasantry to counterbalance the opposition of the workers. The French monarchy could survive only if it was able to rely upon a politically significant section of the population or to pursue the more difficult policy of 'divide and rule'.

The vulnerability of Louis XVI was all the greater because of the financial crisis which lasted throughout his reign, and which proved that he could not maintain his authority without the goodwill, or at least, indifference, of his subjects. Intolerable strains had been imposed on the financial structure by the Seven Years' War and the War of American Independence, and he was forced to consider changes in the methods and assessment of taxation. This situation was not without precedent; Louis XIV had had to agree to the introduction of the *dixième* and *capitation* during the War of the League of Augsburg and the War of the Spanish Succession. But Louis XIV had to deal only with a relatively docile nobility and with an impoverished and not yet articulate peasantry. Louis XVI encountered much more widespread opposition, and in particular a concerted demand, from 1787, for the convocation of the Estates General. In finally giving way, in 1788, he acknowledged the collapse of absolutism and the existence of a political vacuum at the centre.

Freed from the necessity of having to co-operate against the regime, the Second and Third Estates now expressed their fears of each other more openly, and crisis became revolution.

The nobility showed their determination to maintain the traditional voting procedures once the Estates General had convened. This brought out into the open their differences with the Third Estate, which proceeded to reconstitute itself as the National Assembly. This was the first sign of institutional revolution, as it was an open defiance of the authority and procedure of a traditional body. From this stage onwards, as G. Lefebvre argues, the momentum was increased by the participation of each element of the Third Estate. The bourgeoisie appeared to have accepted the new political situation of July 1789 as permanent. The peasantry, however, hastened the destruction of feudal and seigneurial rights in August by a series of riots in the provinces. The artisans and proletariat of Paris pushed the Revolution into the more violent phase of 1791–3, providing solid support for the sweeping changes made by the National Convention under the direction of the Jacobins.

It is often stated that the Revolution broke out in 1787 as a result of the pressure exerted by the Paris *Parlement*. It is possible, however, to put this a different way. For a revolution to begin a certain momentum is needed. In the nineteenth century France possessed a large repository of revolutionary experience which exerted the vital push on several occasions (1830, 1848, 1871). During the 1780s there was no such knowledge or leadership; but the

The Origins of the French Revolution

nobility, from their position of strength, delivered the first blow to the monarchy as part of their reactionary stance. The momentum of this act of political defiance was enough to encourage the different sections of the Third Estate to bring about the destruction of the *ancien régime* and, with it, the Second Estate. This seems to confirm the view put forward by Montaigne as far back as 1580 that 'Those who give the first shock to a state are the first overwhelmed in its ruin.'

Recent research, particularly by R. R. Palmer and J. Godechot, has placed France in a more general context of revolutionary change which also affected Geneva (1768 and 1792), Ireland (1778 and 1798), and Netherlands (1784–7), Poland (1788–92), the Austrian Netherlands (1787–90) and Hungary (1790), as well as the North American colonies (from 1775). There certainly appear to have been major common problems affecting Europe as a whole. One was a rapid growth in population (100 m. to 200 m. between 1700 and 1800). Another was a sharp depression in the 1770s and 1780s, following a long period of economic growth. The overall result was increased competition for existing land resources, a huge rise in unemployment and serious financial problems, which confronted virtually every government in Europe, and forced a re-examination of the traditional forms of revenue extraction. Given the inability of most governments to deal with a major recession, it is hardly surprising that unrest should have been so widespread.

The majority of the revolutions, however, ended in failure. Palmer emphasizes the importance of a strong bourgeoisie (lacking in Poland and Hungary) and of close co-operation between the different social classes. In Poland and Hungary the huge peasantry remained largely indifferent, while in the Netherlands they backed the forces of counter-revolution. Ultimately the country which possessed the largest bourgeoisie and the most extensive dissatisfaction within each class was the most likely to experience fundamental change. This is why, despite the widespread incidence of unrest in the late eighteenth century, it was France which experienced the most violent upheaval and the most advanced political, social and economic reforms.

Notes

CHAPTER 1

1   Oration of Celtis in L. W. SPITZ (ed.): *The Northern Renaissance.*
2   K. H. DANNENFELDT (ed.):*Problems in European Civilisation: The Renaissance,* p. vii.
3   W. DURANT:*The Story of Civilisation: The Renaissance,* Ch. XVII, Part III.
4   E. F. RICE: *The Foundations of Early Modern Europe 1460–1559,* Ch. 3.
5   ERASMUS:*Praise of Folly,* trans. B. Radice (Penguin edition), p. 153.
6   LEONARDO DA VINCI:*Treatise on Painting,* trans. A. P. McMahon, Part II, Section 248.
7   N. PEVSNER:*An Outline of European Architecture,* Ch. 5.
8   MACHIAVELLI: *The Prince,* trans. G. Bull (Penguin edition), XIV.
9   MACHIAVELLI: *The Discourses,* trans. B. Crick (Penguin edition), II, 2.
10 Ibid., I, 9.
11 *The Prince,* Letter to Lorenzo de' Medici.
12 Ibid., XXI.
13 Ibid., XXVI.

CHAPTER 2

1   W. DURANT: *The Story of Civilisation: The Reformation,* Ch. XIV.
2   G. R. ELTON:*Reformation Europe,* Ch. VII.
3   P. JANELLE: in W. STANFORD REID (ed.): *The Reformation.*
4   G. STRAUSS:*Manifestations of Discontent in Germany on the Eve of the Reformation,* extracts from Martin Mair's letter.
5   R. H. BAINTON:*Here I Stand,* Ch. 4.

CHAPTER 3

1   LUTHER: *Friendly Admonition to Peace Concerning the Twelve Articles of the Swabian Peasants,* in H. H. HILLERBRAND (ed.): *The Protestant Reformation: Selected Documents.*

Notes

2   w. durant: *The Story of Civilisation: The Reformation*, Ch. XX.
3   e. f. rice: *The Foundations of Early Modern Europe*, Ch. 6.
4   g. rupp: 'Luther and Government', in h. g. koenigsberger (ed.): *Luther: A Profile*.
5   h. holborn: *A History of Modern Germany*, Vol. 1, *The Reformation*, Ch. 9.
6   a. j. grant: *A History of Europe 1494–1610*, Ch. IV.

chapter 4

1   h. j. hillerbrand (ed.): *The Protestant Reformation*; from calvin: *Institutes of the Christian Religion*.
2   r. w. green (ed.): *Problems in European Civilisation: Protestantism and Capitalism*, p. 30.
3   l. w. spitz (ed.): *Problems in European Civilisation: The Reformation*, p. 31.

chapter 5

1   h. j. hillerbrand (ed.): *The Protestant Reformation*; from Calvin's reply to Sadoleto.
2   e. m. burns: *The Counter Reformation*; from Loyola: *Spiritual Exercises*.
3   h. j. hillerbrand (ed.): op. cit.; from Calvin: *Institutes of the Christian Religion*.
4   w. durant: *The Story of Civilisation: The Reformation*, Ch. XXXVIII.

chapter 6

1   e. m. burns: *The Counter Reformation*; from *The Propositions of Wycliffe*.
2   w. durant: *The Story of Civilisation: the Reformation*, Ch. XXVIII.
3   e. m. burns: op. cit.; from *Decree Frequens* (1417).
4   Ibid.; from: *Council of Constance* (1415).
5   Ibid.; from: *Bull Execrabilis*.
6   w. durant: op. cit., Ch. XXXIX.
7   e. f. rice: *The Foundations of Early Modern Europe 1460–1559*, Ch. 1.

chapter 7

1   a. j. grant: *A History of Europe 1494–1610*, Ch. 1.
2   j. h. elliott: *Imperial Spain 1469–1716*, Ch. 3.
3   *New Cambridge Modern History*, Vol. I, p. 332.
4   w. c. atkinson: *A History of Spain and Portugal*, Ch. 7.
5   j. h. elliott: op. cit., Ch. 5.

chapter 8

1   guicciardini: *The History of Italy* (1561), Book I, Prologue.
2   machiavelli: *The Prince*, XXVI.

Notes

CHAPTER 9

1 J. C. RULE and J. J. TE PASKE (eds): *Problems in European Civilisation: the Character of Philip II*; 'Apologia'.
2 J. LYNCH: *Spain under the Habsburgs*, p. 216.
3 J. LYNCH: op. cit., p. 271.
4 P. PIERSON: *Philip II of Spain*, p. 167.
5 C. PETRIE: *Philip II of Spain*, p. 195.
6 J. LYNCH: op. cit., p. 322.

CHAPTER 11

1 W. YALE: *The Near East: A Modern History*, p. 23.
2 D. W. MILLER and C. D. MOORE (eds): *The Middle East Yesterday and Today*, Part III.
3 W. YALE: op. cit., p. 24.

CHAPTER 12

1 W. H. MCNEILL: *Plagues and Peoples*, Ch. 4.
2 *Cambridge Economic History of Europe*, Vol. IV, Ch. 1, Part II.
3 Ibid., Ch. 1, Part III.
4 C. M. CIPOLLA (ed.): *The Fontana History of Europe*, Vol. 2, *The Sixteenth and Seventeenth Centuries*, Ch. 1.
5 H. G. KOENIGSBERGER and G. L. MOSSE: *Europe in the Sixteenth Century*, Ch. III.
6 *Cambridge Economic History of Europe*, Vol. IV, Ch. 1, Part IV.
7 W. DURANT: *The Story of Civilisation: The Age of Reason Begins*, Ch. XXI.
8 *Cambridge Economic History of Europe*, Vol. IV, tables (pp. 63–7).
9 Ibid., Ch. 1, Part VI.
10 M. S. ANDERSON: *Europe in the Eighteenth Century*, Ch. IV.
11 J. GODECHOT: *France and the Atlantic Revolution of the Eighteenth Century*, Ch. 1.
12 *New Cambridge Modern History*, Vol. III, Ch. 1, table on p. 19.
13 D. OGG: *Europe in the Seventeenth Century*, Ch. XI.
14 W. H. MCNEILL: op. cit., Ch. V.
15 J. D. FAGE: *An Introduction to the History of West Africa*, Ch. V.

CHAPTER 13

1 H. HOLBORN: *A History of Modern Germany: The Reformation*, Ch. 3.

CHAPTER 14

1 C. V. WEDGWOOD: *Richelieu and the French Monarchy*, Ch. 5.
2 L. BATTIFOL in T. K. RABB (ed.): *Problems in European Civilisation: The Thirty Years' War*.
3 Ibid.; from Statements of Intent by Gustavus Adolphus and Axel Oxenstierna.

Notes

4   D. OGG: *Europe in the Seventeenth Century*, Ch. IV.
5   C. J. FRIEDRICH: *The Age of the Baroque 1610–1660*.

CHAPTER 15

1   T. K. RABB (ed.): *Problems in European Civilisation: The Thirty Years' War*, extract by G. Freytag.
2   S. H. STEINBERG in *History*, Vol. XXXII, 1947.
3   W. DURANT: *The Story of Civilisation: The Age of Reason Begins*, Ch. XXI.
4   C. V. WEDGWOOD: *The Thirty Years' War*, Ch. 12.
5   Ibid., Ch. 8.
6   *New Cambridge Modern History*, Vol. V, Ch. XVIII.
7   D. OGG: *Europe in the Seventeenth Century*, Ch. IV.

CHAPTER 16

1   H. HOLBORN: *A History of Modern Germany*, Vol. 1, Ch. 14.
2   C. V. WEDGWOOD: *The Thirty Years' War*, Ch. 12.
3   G. PAGES: *The Thirty Years' War 1618–1648*, Ch. I.

CHAPTER 17

1   H. G. KOENIGSBERGER and G. L. MOSSE: *Europe in the Sixteenth Century*, Ch. IX.

CHAPTER 18

1   J. H. PARRY: *The Spanish Seaborne Empire*, Ch. 12.
2   J. H. ELLIOTT: *Imperial Spain 1469–1716*, Ch. 5.
3   C. M. CIPOLLA (ed.): *The Fontana Economic History of Europe*, Vol. 2, Ch. 5.
4   V. H. H. GREEN: *Renaissance and Reformation*, Ch. XIII.
5   L. W. COWIE: *Seventeenth Century Europe*, Ch. IX.
6   H. G. KOENIGSBERGER and G. L. MOSSE: *Europe in the Sixteenth Century*, Ch. III.
7   L. W. COWIE: op. cit., Ch. IX.

CHAPTER 19

1   M. ROBERTS: *Sweden as a Great Power 1611–1697*, Document XVII.
2   *Cambridge Economic History of Europe*, Vol. IV, tables (pp. 63–7).
3   M. ROBERTS: op. cit., Document XXIX.
4   Ibid., Document XXXIX.

CHAPTER 20

1   E. N. WILLIAMS: *The Ancien Régime in Europe*, Ch. 2.
2   H. H. ROWEN (ed.): *The Low Countries in Early Modern Times*, Document 32.
3   C. WILSON: *The Dutch Republic*, Ch. 1.
4   H. H. ROWEN: op. cit., Document 16.

Notes

5 Ibid., Document 46.
6 Ibid., Document 40.

CHAPTER 21

1 W. F. CHURCH: *Richelieu and Reason of State*, p. 26.
2 C. V. WEDGWOOD: *Richelieu and the French Monarchy*, Ch. 3.
3 M. PRESTWICH: The Making of Absolute Monarchy (1559–1683), in J. M. WALLACE HADRILL and J. MCMANNERS: *France: Government and Society*.
4 W. E. BROWN: *The First Bourbon Century in France*, Part II.
5 W. F. CHURCH: op. cit., p. 189.
6 Ibid., p. 487.
7 W. F. CHURCH: *Richelieu and Reason of State*, p. 178.
8 C. V. WEDGWOOD: op. cit., Ch. 8.
9 W. F. CHURCH: *Richelieu and Reason of State*, p. 339.

CHAPTER 22

1 W. F. CHURCH (ed.): *Problems in European Civilisation: The Greatness of Louis XIV*, from Bossuet.
2 J. B. WOLF: 'Formation of a King', in J. B. WOLF: *Louis XIV: a Profile*.
3 LOUIS XIV: *Mémoires*, 1661.
4 W. E. BROWN: *The First Bourbon Century in France*, Part IV.
5 W. F. CHURCH (ed.): *Problems in European Civilisation: The Greatness of Louis XIV*, from Voltaire.
6 F. NUSSBAUM: *The Triumph of Science and Reason 1660–1685*, Ch. 3.
7 *New Cambridge Modern History*, Vol. V, Ch. 10.
8 G. N. CLARK: *The Seventeenth Century*, Ch. V.

CHAPTER 23

1 C. V. WEDGWOOD: *Richelieu and the French Monarchy*, Ch. 5.
2 L. BATIFFOL in T. K. RABB (ed.): *Problems in European Civilisation: The Thirty Years' War*.
3 LOUIS XIV: *Mémoires*.
4 G. R. R. TREASURE: *Seventeenth Century France*, Ch. 16.
5 VOLTAIRE: *Age of Louis XIV*, Ch. XXVIII.
6 G. R. R. TREASURE: op. cit., Ch. 22.
7 Ibid., Ch. 27.

CHAPTER 24

1 Much of the information in this chapter is derived from the works of F. L. CARSTEN, listed in the Bibliography.
2 C. A. MACARTNEY (ed.): *The Habsburg and Hohenzollern Dynasties*, Part II, Document 3, 'The Brandenburg Recess'.

Notes

CHAPTER 25

1 E. N. WILLIAMS: *The Ancien Régime in Europe*, Ch. 14.
2 P. GAXOTTE: *Frederick the Great*, Ch. XI.
3 W. HUBATSCH: *Frederick the Great: Absolutism and Administration*, Ch. V.
4 H. C. JOHNSON: *Frederick the Great and His Officials*, Ch. II.
5 W. HUBATSCH: op. cit., Ch. II.
6 W. L. DORN in P. PARET (ed.): *Frederick the Great: A Profile*, p. 69.
7 W. HUBATSCH: op. cit., Ch. VI.

CHAPTER 26

1 J. MARRIOTT and C. G. ROBERTSON: *The Evolution of Prussia*, Ch. III.
2 G. A. MACARTNEY (ed.): *The Habsburg and Hohenzollern Dynasties*, Part II, Document 18, 'Political Testament (1752)'.
3 G. P. GOOCH: *Frederick the Great*, Ch. XIII.
4 Ibid., Ch. I.
5 Ibid., Ch. II.
6 P. GAXOTTE: *Frederick the Great*, Ch. X.
7 E. J. FEUCHTWANGER: *Prussia: Myth and Reality*, Ch. III.
8 W. DURANT: *The Story of Civilisation: Rousseau and Revolution*, Ch. II.

CHAPTER 27

1 N. BERDYAEV: *The Origin of Russian Communism*, Introduction.
2 M. RAEFF (ed.): *Problems of European Civilisation: Peter the Great*, from Soloviev.
3 Ibid., p. xvii.
4 POBEDONOSTSEV: in *Problems in European Civilisation: Imperial Russia after 1861*.

CHAPTER 28

1 Extract from Herzen in JAY OLIVA (ed.): *Catherine the Great: Great Lives Observed*.
2 E. N. WILLIAMS: *The Ancien Régime in Europe*, Ch. 10.
3 Extracts from the *Nakaz* of Catherine II in B. DMYTRYSHYN (ed.): *Imperial Russia: A Source Book 1700–1917*, Document 10.
4 Interview with Diderot; extract in JAY OLIVA: op. cit.
5 B. DMYTRYSHYN: op. cit., Document 14.
6 G. P. GOOCH: *Catherine the Great*, Ch. VII.
7 A. RADISHCHEV: *Journey from St. Petersburg to Moscow*, trans. Leo Werner. Empress Catherine's notes.

CHAPTER 29

1 D. OGG: *Europe in the Seventeenth Century*, Ch. XI.
2 A. LENTIN: *Russia in the Eighteenth Century*, Ch. I.

Notes

3   S. V. BAKRUSHIN and S. D. SKAZKIN: 'Diplomacy' in M. RAEFF: *Catherine the Great: A Profile*, Part III.
4   G. P. GOOCH: *Catherine the Great*, Ch. VII.

CHAPTER 30

1   C. A. MACARTNEY (ed.): *The Habsburg and Hohenzollern Dynasties*, Part I, Document 12.
2   Ibid., Document 13B.
3   L. GERSHOY: *From Despotism to Revolution*, Ch. IV.
4   E. N. WILLIAMS; op. cit., Ch. 18.
5   T. C. W. BLANNING: *Joseph II and Enlightened Despotism*, Ch. 2.
6   Ibid., Document 1.
7   C. A. MACARTNEY: op. cit., Document 14.
8   K. ROIDER: *Maria Theresa*, p. 115.
9   W. DURANT: *The Story of Civilisation: Rousseau and Revolution*, Ch. XIII.

CHAPTER 31

1   R. W. HARRIS: *Absolutism and Enlightenment*, Ch. 8.
2   T. C. W. BLANNING: *Joseph II and Enlightened Despotism*, Document 7.
3   Ibid., Ch. 5.
4   Ibid. Ch. 3.; E. N. WILLIAMS: *The Ancien Régime in Europe*, Ch. 19.
5   C. A. MACARTNEY: *The Habsburg Empire 1790–1918*, p. 127; E. N. WILLIAMS: op. cit., Ch. 5.
6   T. C. W. BLANNING: op. cit., Ch. 3.
7   C. A. MACARTNEY: *The Habsburg and Hohenzollern Dynasties*, Part I, Document 15B.
8   W. DURANT: *The Story of Civilisation: Rousseau and Revolution*, Ch. XIII.
9   E. WANGERMANN: *From Joseph II to the Jacobin Trials*.
10 T. C. W. BLANNING: op. cit., Document 17.

CHAPTER 32

1   R. DESCARTES: in A. D. LINDSAY (ed.), *Discourse on Method*, Part II.
2   J. LOCKE: in R. K. LIBANSKY (ed.), *Epistola de Tolerantia*, p. 65.
3   Ibid., p. 91.
4   D. OGG: *Europe of the Ancien Régime 1715–1783*, Ch. XII.
5   W. DURANT: *The Story of Civilisation: The Age of Voltaire*, Ch. XXI.
6   S. POLLARD: *The Idea of Progress*, Ch. 3.
7   W. DURANT: *The Story of Civilisation: Rousseau and Revolution*, Ch. XXXV.
8   W. DURANT: *The Age of Voltaire*, Ch. XIX.
9   VOLTAIRE: *Philosophical Dictionary*.
10 MONTESQUIEU: *The Spirit of the Laws*, trans. T. Nugent; Ch. I, Part i.
11 J. BOWLE: *Western Political Thought*, Ch. VIII.

Notes

12 D. HUME: *On Human Nature and Understanding*, ed. A. FLEW; 'An Essay Concerning Human Understanding', Section 4.

13 HUME: *Treatise of Human Nature*, ed. L. A. SELBY BIGGS, Book II, Part III, Section III.

14 W. DURANT: *Rousseau and Revolution*, Ch. I.

15 J. J. ROUSSEAU: *The Social Contract*, ed. E. BARKER, Ch. I.

16 J. J. ROUSSEAU: *Emile*, Book I, Ch. VII.

17 C. PARKIN: *The Moral Basis of Burke's Political Thought*, Ch. II.

18 Ibid., Ch. VI.

19 Ibid., Ch. V.

CHAPTER 33

1 M. RAEFF (ed.): *Catherine the Great: A Profile*, from Miliukov.

2 R. WINES (ed.): *Problems in European Civilisation: Enlightened Despotism*, from Voltaire.

3 G. P. GOOCH: *Frederick the Great*, Ch. VII.

4 C. A. MACARTNEY (ed.): *The Habsburg and Hohenzollern Dynasties*, Part II, Document 18, 'Political Testament' (1752).

5 G. P. GOOCH: *Catherine the Great*, Ch. 7.

6 W. DURANT: *The Story of Civilisation: Rousseau and Revolution*, Ch. XIII.

7 T. C. W. BLANNING: *Joseph II and Enlightened Despotism*, Ch. 6.

8 G. P. GOOCH: *Frederick the Great*, Ch. 8.

9 L. GERSHOY: *From Despotism to Revolution*.

10 W. DURANT: op. cit., Ch. XVIII.

11 L. KRIEGER: *Kings and Philosophers*, Ch. 9.

CHAPTER 34

1 J. B. PERKINS: *France Under the Regency*, Ch. XVI.

2 J. LOUGH: *An Introduction to Eighteenth Century France*, Ch. IV.

3 P. ROBERTS: *The Quest for Security 1715–1740*, Ch. III.

4 J. B. PERKINS: op. cit., Ch. X.

5 Ibid., Ch. XIII.

6 P. ROBERTS: op. cit., Ch. VIII.

7 G. P. GOOCH: *Louis XV*, Ch. 3.

8 A. SOREL: *Europe and the French Revolution*, Book II, Ch. 1.

CHAPTER 35

1 W. DURANT: *The Story of Civilisation: Rousseau and Revolution*, Ch. XXXIV.

2 J. LOUGH: *An Introduction to Eighteenth-Century France*, Ch. I.

3 E. N. WILLIAMS: *The Ancien Régime in Europe*, Ch. 8.

4 J. LOUGH: op. cit., Ch. V.

5 G. P. GOOCH: *Louis XV*, Ch. 12.

6 A. SOREL: *Europe and the French Revolution*, trans. in G. P. GOOCH: *Louis XV*, Ch. 4.

Notes

7   G. P. GOOCH: op. cit., Ch. 11.
8   J. LOUGH: op. cit., Ch. VI.

CHAPTER 37

1   A. DE TOCQUEVILLE: *The Ancien Régime.*
2   J. C. DAVIES: 'Toward a Theory of Revolution', in J. C. DAVIES (ed.), *When Men Revolt and Why.*
3   J. LOUGH: *An Introduction to Eighteenth-Century France*, Ch. III.
4   E. N. WILLIAMS: *The Ancien Régime in Europe*, Ch. 8.
5   P. GOUBERT: *The Ancien Régime*, Ch. I, Part 2.
6   K. KUMAR: *Revolution*, Introduction, Part 6.

Bibliography

The reading material in this Bibliography covers the range of topics outlined in the table of contents.

GENERAL

W. DURANT: *The Story of Civilisation* (New York):
   The Renaissance (1953)
   The Reformation (1957)
   The Age of Reason Begins (1961)
   The Age of Louis XIV (1963)
   The Age of Voltaire (1965)
   Rousseau and Revolution (1967)
New Cambridge Modern History (Cambridge):
   I *The Renaissance 1493–1520* (1957)
   II *The Reformation 1520–59* (1958)
   III *The Counter Reformation and the Price Revolution 1559–1610* (1968)
   IV *The Decline of Spain and the Thirty Years' War 1609–48/59* (1970)
   V *The Ascendancy of France 1648–88* (1961)
   VI *The Rise of Great Britain and Russia 1688–1725* (1970)
   VII *The Old Regime 1713–63* (1957)
   VIII *The American and French Revolutions 1763–93* (1965)
J. PIRENNE: *The Tides of History*, Vol. II (London, 1963).
J. M. THOMPSON: *Lectures on Foreign History 1494–1789*, 2nd Edition (Oxford, 1956).
J. H. SHENNAN: *The Origins of the Modern European State 1450–1725* (London, 1974).
A. J. GRANT: *A History of Europe 1494–1610* (London, 1931).
Problems in European Civilisation (Boston):
   K. H. DANNENFELDT (ed.): *The Renaissance* (1959)
   L. W. SPITZ (ed.): *The Reformation* (1962)
   R. W. GREEN (ed.): *Protestantism and Capitalism* (1959)
   T. K. RABB (ed.): *The Thirty Years' War* (1964)

Bibliography

J. C. RULE and J. J. TE PASKE (eds): *The Character of Philip II* (1963)

W. F. CHURCH (ed.): *The Greatness of Louis XIV* (1959)

M. RAEFF (ed.): *Peter the Great* (1963)

R. WINES (ed.): *Enlightened Despotism* (1967)

R. W. GREENLAW (ed.): *The Economic Origins of the French Revolution* (1958).

M. P. GILMORE: *The World of Humanism 1453–1517* (New York, 1952).

V. H. H. GREEN: *Renaissance and Reformation* (London, 1952).

G. R. ELTON: *Reformation Europe 1517–1559* (London, 1963).

L. W. COWIE: *Sixteenth-Century Europe* (London, 1977).

R. LOCKYER: *Habsburg and Bourbon Europe 1470–1770* (London, 1974).

H. G. KOENIGSBERGER and G. L. MOSSE: *Europe in the Sixteenth Century* (London and New York, 1968).

E. F. RICE: *The Foundations of Early Modern Europe 1460–1559* (London, 1970).

D. HAY: *The Italian Renaissance in its Historical Background* (Cambridge, 1961).

J. BURCKHARDT: *The Civilisation of the Renaissance in Italy* (New York, 1928–9).

V. GRONIN: *The Flowering of the Renaissance* (London, 1969).

E. F. JACOB: *Italian Renaissance Studies* (London, 1940).

E. R. CHAMBERLIN: *The World of the Italian Renaissance* (London, 1982).

J. R. HALE: *Machiavelli and Renaissance Italy* (London, 1961).

J. R. HALE (ed.): *A Concise Encyclopaedia of the Italian Renaissance* (London, 1981).

G. MATTINGLY: *Renaissance Diplomacy* (London, 1955).

L. W. SPITZ (ed.): *The Northern Renaissance* (Englewood Cliffs, N.J., 1972).

PRESERVED SMITH: *The Social Background of the Reformation* (Collier Books ed., West Drayton, Middx, 1962).

A. G. DICKENS: *Reformation and Society in Sixteenth Century Europe* (London, 1966).

R. H. BAINTON: *The Reformation of the Sixteenth Century* (Boston, 1952).

R. H. BAINTON: *Here I Stand: A Life of Martin Luther* (New York, 1950).

V. H. H. GREEN: *Martin Luther* (London, 1964).

H. G. KOENIGSBERGER (ed.): *Luther: A Profile* (London and New York, 1973).

R. H. TAWNEY: *Religion and the Rise of Capitalism* (London, 1926).

M. WEBER: *The Protestant Ethic and the Spirit of Capitalism* (London, 1930).

W. SOMBART: *The Quintessence of Capitalism* (New York, 1915).

E. M. BURNS: *The Counter Reformation* (Princeton, N.J., 1964).

R. S. DUNN: *The Age of Religious Wars 1559–1689* (London, 1970).

K. LEACH: *Documents and Debates. Sixteenth Century Europe* (London, 1980).

G. M. BEST: *Documents and Debates. Seventeenth Century Europe* (London, 1982).

D. OGG: *Europe in the Seventeenth Century* (London, 1925).

G. PARKER: *Europe in Crisis 1598–1648* (London, 1979).

G. PARKER and L. M. SMITH (eds): *The General Crisis of the Seventeenth Century* (London, 1978).

Bibliography

C. EMSLEY (ed.): *Conflict and Stability in Europe* (London, 1979).

C. V. WEDGWOOD: *The Thirty Years' War* (London, 1938).

G. PAGES: *The Thirty Years' War 1618–1648* (London, 1971).

S. H. STEINBERG: *The Thirty Years' War* (London, 1966).

V. POLISENSKY: *The Thirty Years' War* (London, 1970).

H. LANGER: *The Thirty Years' War* (Poole, Dorset, 1980).

D. MALAND: *Europe at War 1600–1650* (London, 1980).

J. V. POLISENSKY: *War and Society in Europe 1618–1648* (Cambridge, 1978).

L. W. COWIE: *Seventeenth-Century Europe* (London, 1960).

G. N. CLARK: *The Seventeenth Century* (Oxford, 1929).

R. W. HARRIS: *Absolutism and Enlightenment 1660–1789* (London, 1964).

C. J. FRIEDRICH: *The Age of the Baroque 1610–1660* (New York, 1952).

F. L. NUSSBAUM: *The Triumph of Science and Reason 1660–1685* (New York, 1953).

W. DOYLE: *The Old European Order 1660–1800* (Oxford, 1978).

D. MCKAY: *The Rise of the Great Powers 1648–1815* (Harlow, Essex, 1983).

J. B. WOLF: *The Emergence of the Great Powers 1685–1715* (New York, 1951).

PENFIELD ROBERTS: *The Quest for Security 1715–1740* (New York, 1947).

W. L. DORN: *The Competition for Empire 1740–1763* (New York, 1940).

L. GERSHOY: *From Despotism to Revolution 1763–1789* (New York, 1944).

E. N. WILLIAMS: *The Ancien Régime in Europe 1648–1789* (London, 1970).

M. S. ANDERSON: *Europe in the Eighteenth Century 1713–1783* (London, 1961).

D. OGG: *Europe of the Ancien Régime 1715–1783* (London, 1965).

L. W. COWIE: *Eighteenth-Century Europe* (London, 1966).

O. F. HUFTON: *Europe: Privilege and Protest 1730–1789* (London, 1980).

A. H. JOHNSON: *The Age of Enlightened Despotism 1660–1789* (London, 1921).

J. GAGLIARDO: *Enlightened Despotism* (London, 1968).

F. HARTUNG: *Enlightened Despotism* (Historical Association Pamphlet G. 36).

G. RUDÉ: *Revolutionary Europe 1783–1815* (London, 1964).

A. GOODWIN (ed.): *The European Nobility in the Eighteenth Century* (London, 1953).

G. H. SABINE: *A History of Political Theory* (London, 1937).

J. BOWLE: *Western Political Thought* (London, 1947).

J. W. ALLEN: *A History of Political Thought in the Sixteenth Century* (London, 1928).

B. H. KINGSLEY MARTIN: *French Liberal Thought in the Eighteenth Century* (London, 1929).

C. BECKER: *The Heavenly City of the Eighteenth-Century Philosophers* (New Haven, Conn., 1932).

P. HAZARD: *The Crisis of the European Mind 1680–1715* (Penguin ed., Harmondsworth, Middx, 1964).

P. HAZARD: *European Thought in the Eighteenth Century* (Penguin ed., Harmondsworth, Middx, 1965).

J. LIVELY: *The Enlightenment* (London, 1966).

Bibliography

SPAIN

w. c. ATKINSON: *A History of Spain and Portugal* (London, 1960).
H. LIVERMORE: *A History of Spain* (London, 1958).
s. c. PAYNE: *A History of Spain and Portugal* (Madison, Wis., 1973).
J. H. ELLIOTT: *Imperial Spain* (London, 1963).
J. LYNCH: *Spain Under the Habsburgs*, Vol. I (Oxford, 1964).
R. B. MERRIMAN: *Rise of the Spanish Empire*, Vols II–IV (New York, 1918–34).
R. TREVOR DAVIES: *The Golden Century of Spain 1501–1621* (London, 1937).
R. TREVOR DAVIES: *Spain in Decline 1621–1700* (London, 1957).
P. PIERSON: *Philip II of Spain* (London, 1975).
c. PETRIE: *Philip II of Spain* (London, 1963).
G. PARKER: *Philip II* (London, 1979).

SPANISH AND PORTUGUESE EMPIRES

J. H. PARRY: *Europe and a Wider World 1415–1715* (London, 1966).
J. H. PARRY: *The Age of Reconaissance* (London, 1963).
B. DIAZ: *The Conquest of New Spain* (Penguin ed., Harmondsworth, Middx, 1963).
w. PRESCOTT: *History of the Conquest of Peru* (New York, 1847).
w. PRESCOTT: *History of the Conquest of Mexico* (New York, 1843).
J. H. PARRY: *The Spanish Seaborne Empire* (London, 1966).
H. HERRING: *A History of Latin America* (London, 1955).
s. DE MADARIAGA: *The Fall of the Spanish American Empire* (London, 1947).
c. R. BOXER: *The Portuguese Seaborne Empire 1415–1825* (London, 1969).
M. MURIAS: *Short History of Portuguese Colonisation* (Lisbon, 1940).
J. DUFFY: *Portugal in Africa* (London, 1962).

GERMANY AND PRUSSIA

H. HOLBORN: *A History of Modern Germany*, Vols I and II (London, 1959).
A. J. P. TAYLOR: *The Course of German History* (London, 1945).
E. J. FEUCHTWANGER: *Prussia: Myth and Reality* (London, 1970).
H. w. KOCH: *A History of Prussia* (Harlow, Essex, 1978).
s. B. FAY: *The Rise of Brandenburg-Prussia to 1786* (New York and London, 1964).
J. A. R. MARRIOTT and c. G. ROBERTSON: *The Evolution of Prussia* (Oxford, 1937).
F. L. CARSTEN: *The Origins of Prussia* (Oxford, 1954).
F. L. CARSTEN: 'The Great Elector and the Foundation of Hohenzollern Despotism', *English Historical Review*, Vol. 65 (1950).
F. L. CARSTEN: 'The Resistance of Cleves and Mark to the Despotic Policy of the Great Elector', *English Historical Review*, Vol. 66 (1951).
F. L. CARSTEN: *Princes and Parliaments in Germany* (Oxford, 1959).
G. P. GOOCH: *Frederick the Great* (London, 1947).
P. GAXOTTE: *Frederick the Great* (London, 1941).
E. SIMON: *The Making of Frederick the Great* (London, 1963).
P. PARET (ed.): *Frederick the Great: A Profile* (New York, 1972).

Bibliography

H. C. JOHNSON: *Frederick the Great and His Officials* (New Haven and London, 1975).

W. HUBATSCH: *Frederick the Great: Absolutism and Administration* (London, 1973).

W. H. BRUFORD: *Germany in the Eighteenth Century* (Cambridge, 1939).

AUSTRIA AND THE HABSBURGS

R. A. KANN: *A History of the Habsburg Empire 1526–1918* (Berkeley, Calif., 1974).

K. BRANDI: *The Emperor Charles V* (London, 1939).

M. F. ALVAREZ: *Charles V: Elected Emperor and Hereditary Ruler* (London, 1975).

G. MANN: *Wallenstein* (English trans., London, 1976).

G. P. GOOCH: *Maria Theresa* (London, 1947).

K. A. ROIDER (ed.): *Maria Theresa* (Englewood Cliffs, N.J., 1973).

T. C. W. BLANNING: *Joseph II and Enlightened Despotism* (London, 1970).

E. WANGERMANN: *From Joseph II to the Jacobin Trials* (Oxford, 1969).

R. A. KANN: *A Study in Austrian Intellectual History* (London, 1960).

C. A. MACARTNEY: *The Habsburg and Hohenzollern Dynasties* (New York, 1970).

RUSSIA

R. A. CHARQUES: *A Short History of Russia* (London, 1956).

L. KOCHAN: *The Making of Modern Russia* (London, 1962).

M. T. FLORINSKY: *Russia: A History and an Interpretation* (New York, 1947).

B. PARES: *A History of Russia* (London, 1955).

B. H. SUMNER: *Survey of Russian History* (London, 1944).

G. VERNADSKY: *A History of Russia* (New Haven, Conn., 1929).

L. JAY OLIVA (ed.): *Peter the Great* (Englewood Cliffs, N.J., 1970).

B. H. SUMNER: *Peter the Great and the Emergence of Russia* (London, 1950).

V. O. KLYUCHEVSKY: *Peter the Great* (English ed., London, 1958).

I. GREY: *Peter the Great* (London, 1962).

R. K. MASSIE: *Peter the Great, His Life and Work* (London, 1981).

I. GREY: *Catherine the Great* (London, 1961).

M. RAEFF (ed.): *Catherine the Great: A Profile* (New York, 1972).

G. SCOTT THOMPSON: *Catherine the Great and the Expansion of Russia* (London, 1947).

G. P. GOOCH: *Catherine the Great* (London, 1954).

L. JAY OLIVA: *Catherine the Great* (Englewood Cliffs, N.J., 1971).

P. DUKES: *Catherine the Great and the Russian Nobility* (Cambridge, 1967).

I. DE MADARIAGA: *Russia in the Age of Catherine the Great* (London, 1981).

A. LENTIN: *Russia in the Eighteenth Century* (London, 1973).

B. DMYTRYSHYN: *Imperial Russia: A Source Book 1700–1917* (Hinsdale, Ill., 1974).

Bibliography

FRANCE

J. LOUGH: *An Introduction to Seventeenth Century France* (London, 1954).

J. M. WALLACE-HADRILL and J. MCMANNERS (eds): *France: Government and Society* (London, 1957).

J. HAMPDEN JACKSON (ed.): *A Short History of France* (Cambridge, 1959).

R. METTAM and D. JOHNSON: *French History and Society* (London, 1972).

J. H. SHENNAN: *Government and Society in France 1461–1661* (London, 1969).

R. BRIGGS: *Early Modern France 1560–1715* (Oxford, 1977).

G. R. TREASURE: *Seventeenth Century France* (London, 1966).

W. E. BROWN: *The First Bourbon Century in France* (London, 1971).

C. V. WEDGWOOD: *Richelieu and the French Monarchy* (Eng. UP, 1949).

W. F. CHURCH: *Richelieu and Reason of State* (Princeton, 1972.)

D. P. O'CONNELL: *Richelieu* (London, 1968).

G. R. TREASURE: *Cardinal Richelieu and the Development of Absolutism* (London, 1972).

A. D. LUBLINSKAYA: *French Absolutism: The Crucial Phase 1620–1629* (Cambridge, 1968).

O. RANUM: *Richelieu and the Councillors of Louis XIII* (Oxford, 1963).

W. F. CHURCH: *The Impact of Absolutism on France* (New York, 1969).

P. GAXOTTE: *The Age of Louis XIV* (English trans., New York, 1970).

P. ERLANGER: *Louis XIV* (English trans., London, 1970).

M. ASHLEY: *Louis XIV and the Greatness of France* (London, 1946).

D. OGG: *Louis XIV* (Oxford, 1933).

J. B. WOLF (ed.): *Louis XIV: A Profile* (London, 1972).

R. HATTON (ed.): *Louis XIV and Absolutism* (London, 1976).

R. HATTON (ed.): *Louis XIV and Europe* (London, 1976).

LOUIS XIV: *Mémoires for the Instruction of the Dauphin*, trans. P. Sonnino (New York, 1970).

DUC DE SAINT SIMON: *Historical Memoires* (3 Vols) ed. L. NORTON (London, 1967, 1968 and 1972).

J. LOUGH: *An Introduction to Eighteenth-Century France* (London, 1960).

A. COBBAN: *A History of Modern France* (London, 1957).

J. B. PERKINS: *France Under the Regency* (Cambridge, Mass., 1892).

J. H. SHENNAN: *Philippe, Duke of Orleans, Regent of France, 1715–1723* (London, 1979).

G. P. GOOCH: *Louis XV* (London, 1956).

P. GOUBERT: *The Ancien Régime* (English trans., London, 1973).

D. DAKIN: *Turgot and the Ancien Régime in France* (London, 1939).

A. YOUNG: *Travels in France* (Cambridge, 1929).

A. DE TOCQUEVILLE: *The Ancien Régime* (Fontana ed., London, 1966).

A. GOODWIN: *The French Revolution* (London, 1953).

D. JOHNSON (ed.): *French Society and the Revolution* (Cambridge, 1976).

A. COBBAN: *The Social Interpretation of the French Revolution* (Cambridge, 1974).

J. H. SHENNAN: *France Before the Revolution* (London, 1983).

R. D. HARRIS: *Necker, Reform Statesman of the Ancien Régime* (Berkeley, Calif., 1979).

Bibliography

G. LEFEBVRE: *The French Revolution* (London and New York, 1964).

R. BEN JONES: *The French Revolution* (London, 1974).

A. COBBAN: *Aspects of the French Revolution* (London, 1968).

J. KAPLOW (ed.): *France on the Eve of Revolution* (New York, 1971).

J. GODECHOT: *France and the Atlantic Revolution of the Eighteenth Century 1770–1799* (New York and London, 1965).

R. R. PALMER: *The Age of Democratic Revolution* (2 Vols) (Princeton, N.J., 1958 and 1964).

R. R. PALMER: *The World of the French Revolution* (London, 1971).

DUTCH REPUBLIC

P. GEYL: *History of the Low Countries: Episodes and Problems* (London, 1964).

P. GEYL: *The Revolt of the Netherlands 1555–1609* (London, 1932).

P. GEYL: *The Netherlands in the Seventeenth Century: Part I 1609–48* (1961); *Part II 1648–1715* (1964) (London and New York).

G. J. RENIER: *The Dutch Nation* (London, 1944).

G. PARKER: *The Dutch Revolt* (London, 1977).

G. PARKER: *Spain and the Netherlands 1559–1659, Ten Studies* (London, 1979).

E. GRIERSON: *The Fatal Inheritance* (London, 1969).

C. V. WEDGWOOD: *William the Silent* (London, 1944).

J. I. ISRAEL: *The Dutch Republic and the Hispanic World 1606–1661* (Oxford, 1982).

C. WILSON: *The Dutch Republic* (London, 1968).

K. H. D. HALEY: *The Dutch in the Seventeenth Century* (London, 1972).

J. HUIZINGA: *Dutch Civilisation in the Seventeenth Century* (English trans., London, 1968).

J. L. PRICE: *Culture and Society in the Dutch Republic During the Seventeenth Century* (London, 1974).

A. C. CARTER: *Neutrality or Commitment: The Evolution of Dutch Foreign Policy 1667–1795* (London, 1975).

H. H. ROWEN (ed.): *The Low Countries in Early Modern Times: Selected Documents* (London, 1972).

OTTOMAN EMPIRE

S. N. FISHER: *The Middle East: A History* (New York, 1960).

A. D. ANDERSON: *The Eastern Question 1423–1774* (London, 1966).

R. H. DAVISON: *Turkey* (Englewood Cliffs, N.J., 1968).

G. LEWIS: *Turkey* (London, 1955).

S. J. SHAW: *History of the Ottoman Empire and Modern Turkey*, Vol. 1, *Empire of the Gazis* (Cambridge, 1976).

R. B. MERRIMAN: *Suleiman the Magnificent* (Cambridge, Mass., 1944).

J. A. R. MARRIOTT: *The Eastern Question: An Historical Study in European Diplomacy* (Oxford, 1917).

P. COLES: *The Ottoman Impact on Europe* (London, 1968).

Bibliography

SWEDEN

I. ANDERSON: *A History of Sweden* (London, 1956).

S. OAKLEY: *The Story of Sweden* (London, 1966).

M. ROBERTS: *Essays in Swedish History* (London, 1967).

M. ROBERTS: *The Reign of Gustavus Adolphus* (2 Vols) (London, 1953 and 8).

M. ROBERTS (ed.): *Sweden as a Great Power, Documents* (London, 1968).

J. LISK: *The Struggle for Supremacy in the Baltic 1600–1725* (London, 1967).

R. M. HATTON: *Charles XII of Sweden* (London, 1968).

312